POWERS OF THE CROWN

AD 1600-1700

NORTH AMERICA

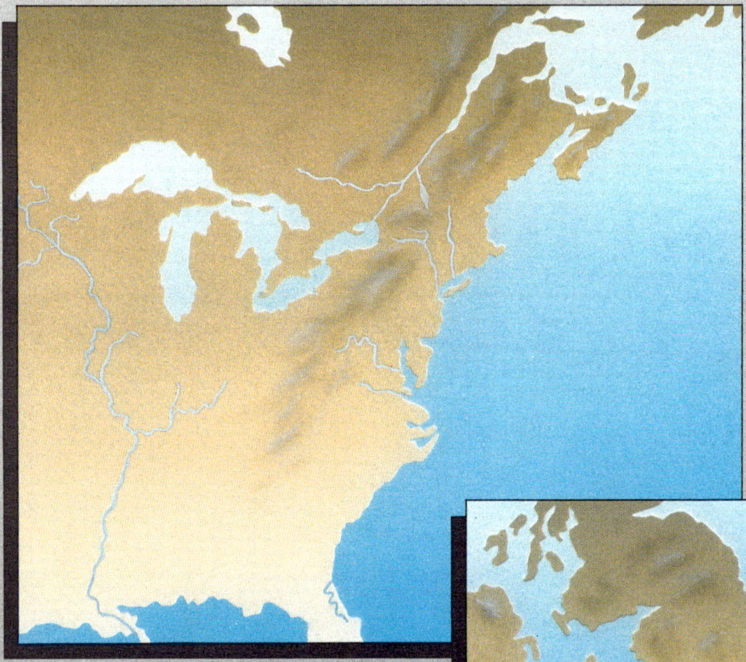

DUTCH REPUBLIC

ENGLAND

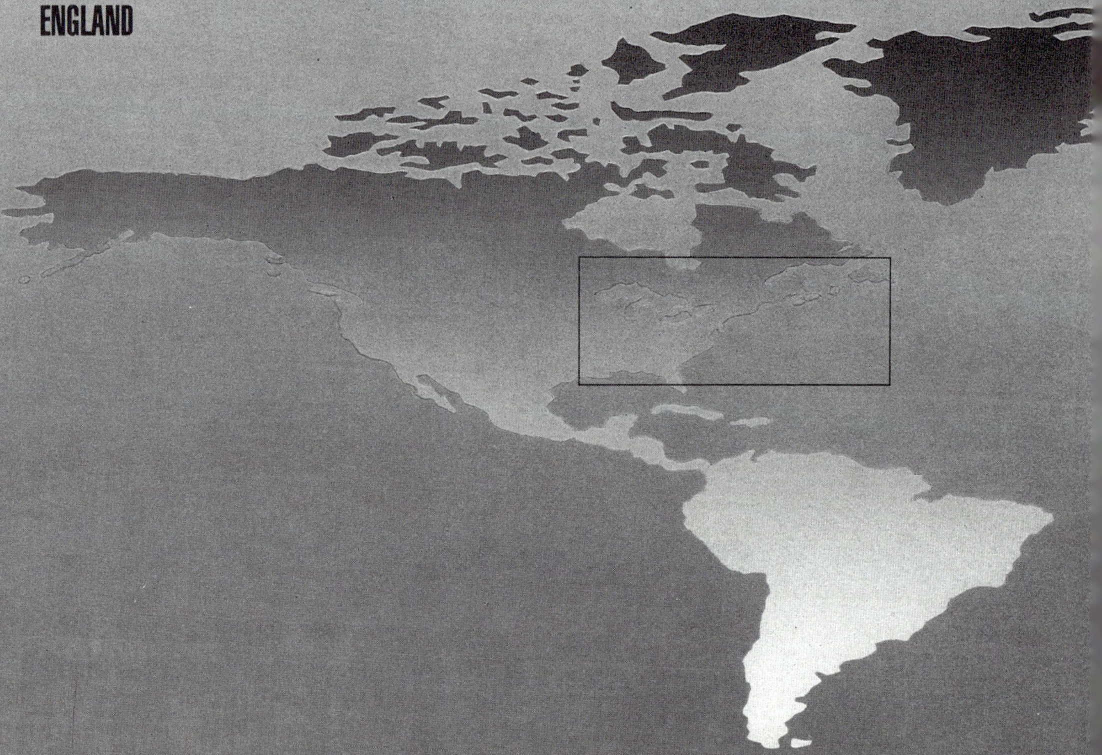

AD 1600-1700

PERSIA

JAPAN

CHINA

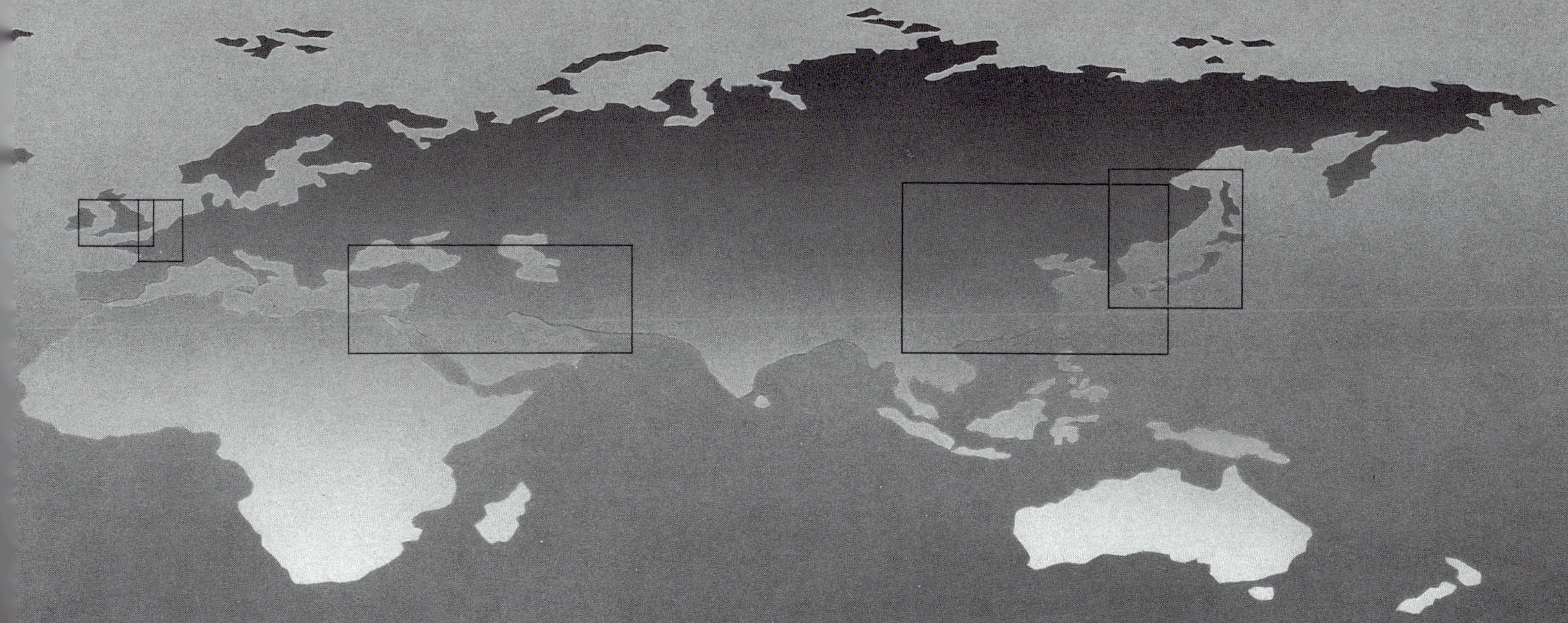

TIME
LIFE
BOOKS

This volume is one in the Time-Life series
HISTORY OF THE WORLD.

POWERS OF THE CROWN

AD 1600-1700

BY THE EDITORS OF TIME-LIFE BOOKS

TIME-LIFE BOOKS, AMSTERDAM

TIME-LIFE BOOKS

European Executive Editor: Gillian Moore
Design Director: Ed Skyner
Assistant Design Director: Mary Staples
Chief of Research: Vanessa Kramer
Chief Sub-Editor: Ilse Gray

TIME-LIFE HISTORY OF THE WORLD

SERIES EDITOR: Tony Allan

Editorial Staff for *Powers of the Crown*
Designer: Mary Staples
Writer: Fergus Fleming
Researchers: Caroline Alcock, Paul Dowswell
Sub-Editor: Christine Noble
Design Assistant: Rachel Gibson
Editorial Assistant: Molly Sutherland

Picture Department
Picture Administrator: Amanda Hindley
Picture Coordinator: Zoë Spencer

Editorial Production
Chief: Samantha Hill
Traffic Controller: Emma Veys
Editorial Department: Theresa John, Debra Lelliott

ISBN 0 7054 0983 X

CONSULTANTS

General:
GEOFFREY PARKER, Professor of History, University of Illinois, Urbana-Champaign, Illinois.

CHRISTOPHER BAYLY, Reader in Modern Indian History, St. Catharine's College, Cambridge University.

Japan:
I.J. McMULLEN, Lecturer in Japanese, Oxford University.

China:
DENIS TWITCHETT, Gorden Wu Professor of Chinese Studies, Princeton University, Princeton, New Jersey.

Persia:
DAVID MORGAN, Reader in the History of the Middle East, School of Oriental and African Studies, University of London.

England:
NICHOLAS TYACKE, Senior Lecturer in History, University College, London.

Dutch Republic:
JONATHAN I. ISRAEL, Professor of Dutch History and Institutions, University College, London.

North America:
G.V. SCAMMELL, Fellow of Pembroke College, Cambridge University.

SPECIAL CONTRIBUTORS: James, Chambers, Stephen Downes, Neil Fairbairn, Ellen Galford, Robert Irwin, David Nicolle (text); Sheila Corr, Timothy Fraser, Barbara Hicks, Caroline Lucas, Jackie Matthews (research).

Correspondents: Elisabeth Kraemer-Singh (Bonn); Christina Lieberman (New York); Maria Vincenza Aloisi (Paris); Ann Natanson (Rome). Valuable assistance was also provided by: Karel Ornstein, Saskia Vanderlinde, Wibo Vanderlinde, Erik Van Zwam (Amsterdam); Yang Jinquan (Beijing); Otto Gobius, Robert Kroon (Geneva); Trini Bandres (Madrid); Elizabeth Brown (New York); Mary Johnson (Stockholm); Dick Berry, Mieko Ikeda (Tokyo); Traudl Lessing (Vienna).

CONTENTS

TOKUGAWA JAPAN

1

For the 8,000 men camped on Matsuo Hill under the command of Kobayagawa Hideaki, the night of October 21, 1600, was an evil time to be abroad. The weather was seasonally foul; a light evening drizzle had developed, as darkness had fallen, into a raking downpour. And their hilltop position above the village of Sekigahara in central Honshu, the main island of Japan, exposed them to the full force of a westerly gale that was howling through the defile that led from Lake Biwa. Nevertheless, they could still consider themselves lucky on two counts: the storm had not deteriorated into one of the *taifu* or "great winds" that frequently devastated Japan in late summer and fall; and at least they were not on the move – unlike their allies in the valley below.

For in the hours after midnight, Sekigahara had witnessed the drenched arrival of some 70,000 men, the combined armies of the warlord Ishida Mitsunari. Almost blinded by the rain and hampered by knee-deep mud, they had struggled 16 kilometres through the night to reach this defensive position. Their journey represented the climax of two months of campaigning, during which Mitsunari had battled with the powerful eastern lord, Tokugawa Ieyasu, for control of Japan. A clash on the previous day had both revealed Ieyasu's strength – approximately equal to that of Mitsunari – and suggested his strategy: to sweep through the pass at Sekigahara and take the ancient capital of Kyoto and the key port of Osaka. Now, at Sekigahara, where the mountains protected his flanks, Mitsunari hoped to draw the pursuing Tokugawa forces into a decisive confrontation.

As dawn came the storm passed on over the country, leaving behind a legacy of drizzle and thick, blanketing fog. Secure on their hilltop, Hideaki's men could hear, through the whiteness, the muffled curses of the last bedraggled units arriving in Sekigahara below them. Visibility was down to no more than a couple of paces, and there was only the noise of the men in front to guide the troops. Accordingly it was some time before anyone realized that the clash and rumble of marching soldiers was coming not from Mitsunari's forces alone: into their ranks had stumbled the vanguard of the Tokugawa army.

For some time complete confusion reigned. The enveloping fog prevented anything other than a muddled withdrawal by both sides. The Tokugawa advance guard, which had already been marching hard for some four hours, took up their positions while the rest of their army arrived. It was a further hour before the mist lifted, rolling away up the slopes of nearby Mount Ibuki to reveal a clear view of Sekigahara. Then battle commenced.

Safe on the hilltop, Hideaki watched for four hours as fighting raged along the line with neither side gaining advantage. According to plan, he was to wait until the Tokugawa army was fully engaged, then swoop down to attack them on their

Shown in a detail from a 17th-century silk scroll painting, an ageing Japanese warrior prepares for battle. The man portrayed, Nabeshima Naoshige, began his career as a minor retainer of a southern warlord, and fought bravely in the civil wars that split the nation during the late 16th century, supporting the victorious military leader Tokugawa Ieyasu, who with his heirs imposed unity on the divided nation. Naoshige died peacefully in 1618 at the age of 80, having lived to savour, as a provincial noble, the first fruits of the long Tokugawa peace.

left flank. By noon, the time was ripe. Some 60,000 of Ieyasu's men were pressing into the valley, and Mitsunari gave the signal for Hideaki to move.

Not a man stirred on Matsuo Hill. For weeks, the 22-year-old Hideaki had been playing a waiting game. Each time he had fought on Mitsunari's side, he had covered himself by making overtures to the enemy. Today was no exception; Ieyasu expected the troops on the hill to play for him the role expected of them by Mitsunari. Initially, he too was disappointed. Hideaki – still undecided as to where his loyalties best lay – failed to respond to his signal also. Only after being prompted by a hail of Tokugawa arrows did he send his troops into action against Mitsunari.

Mitsunari was not entirely unprepared. He had been aware of his young ally's plotting. What the general did not expect, however, was that his leaders on the left flank would take their cue from Hideaki, and also turn against him. Attacked on all sides, his formations disintegrated. Mitsunari himself was killed, and his men fled westwards in disorder through the pass to Lake Biwa. That night Ieyasu's victorious army bivouacked on the battlefield. The road to Osaka was open.

The battle at Sekigahara marked a turning point in the fortunes of Japan. Not only did it give Tokugawa Ieyasu mastery of the nation, but it also heralded an era of

The story of Japan's political reunification in the late 16th and early 17th century is in part a tale of three cities, all of them on the central island of Honshu. The nation's imperial capital was the ancient city of Kyoto, where the emperor – a venerated figure who wielded little real power – presided over a glittering court. The true rulers of the country were a succession of military leaders, the greatest of whom, Toyotomi Hideyoshi, ruled from the port city of Osaka on the Inland Sea, from where he mounted two unsuccessful invasions of Korea. When Tokugawa Ieyasu won power after Hideyoshi's death, he moved the seat of government to the eastern city of Edo – today's Tokyo – which lay at the heart of the rich agricultural region of the Kanto, his power base in the earlier civil wars.

Portrayed in court dress by an anonymous artist, Tokugawa Ieyasu is shown in this posthumous portrait as he appeared shortly before his death in 1616 at the age of 73. By that time all his rivals were dead and he was firmly established as shogun, or military governor of the nation. Ieyasu, who personally fought in more than 50 battles, pursued his objectives with cunning, patience and enormous tenacity; his soldiers called him "the old badger". He built the fortunes of his family, which was to rule Japan for the next 250 years, not just on military supremacy but also on his skill in administering his domains, increasing revenues and dispossessing his enemies – talents which his successors of the Tokugawa dynasty also inherited.

extraordinary isolation and stasis. Under Ieyasu's successors Japan would make the momentous decision to close itself off almost entirely from the outside world.

Japan's choice was the more surprising in that it was made at a time when horizons elsewhere were widening. The 17th century was a period of worldwide change and growing prosperity, as well as of exploration and pioneering settlement typified by the European peopling of North America. Elsewhere the age took its character from a clutch of exceptionally able and long-lived monarchs, who increased their control over their realms with the help of guns, printing and improved communications – all products of relatively recent technological advancement.

In the course of the century Japan's neighbour, China, fell to a new dynasty that produced one of the greatest emperors the nation had known in two millennia of imperial rule. Persia too experienced a revival under Shah Abbas, who fought off enemies to east and west and built the city of Isfahan to reflect his glory. In Europe no monarch ruled more resplendently than France's Sun King, Louis XIV, whose palace of Versailles became a temple to the doctrine of royal absolutism.

Two nations, however, stood as exceptions to the rule: in England two kings were dethroned, one to be beheaded; and the Dutch Republic, newly independent of Spain, chose – to the horror of its royalist neighbours – to opt for a republican form of government. Yet such events meant little to Japan, which by that time had emerged from the trauma of its civil wars to wrap itself in a cocoon of isolationism.

For centuries the mountainous archipelago of Japan had been ruled by a blend of ancient tradition and military pragmatism. The symbolic head of the nation was the emperor, descended, according to Japanese legend, from the sun goddess who had created the islands. Presiding over his court in Kyoto, he conducted sacred rites to ensure Japan's continued prosperity, and was himself worshipped as a semi-divinity. It was by imperial decree that the state was officially governed; and it was to the emperor that all Japanese paid homage.

In terms of real, rather than ceremonial, power, however, the emperor's influence counted for less than that of his mightiest subject, the military dictator known as the shogun. Since the late 12th century, when armed forces had seized control of the country, it had been to the shogun's commands that the emperor assented and to the shogun's administration that imperial approval was given. Resistance to shogunal demands was useless, as the imperial family had soon learnt. For the shogun was not only the nation's commander in chief, he was also its greatest landowner. And power lay in the land, in the myriad tiny thatched villages whose rice crops provided not only the nation's staple but also the medium of exchange by which all wealth was counted.

As well as yielding food, the land provided manpower. The countryside was divided into fiefs, each of which was run by a provincial lord or daimyo. Within his domain, the daimyo maintained order by means of his samurai, armed retainers to whom he allotted small portions of land in return for their continued loyalty. The daimyo himself owed allegiance to the shogun, whether in gratitude for the grant of his land or through fear that it might be taken away from him. These local lords acknowledged the sovereignty of their emperor; but it was to the shogun's banner that they rallied in war.

Just as there was no single ruler of Japan, so there was no one religion to which all Japanese subscribed. The indigenous faith of the islands, Shinto, acknowledged innumerable divine spirits, both animate and inanimate. It was to the Shinto deities that the emperor offered worship; by them, believers thought, all human activities were sustained and were allotted good or ill fortune. From China, during the sixth century AD, the Japanese had acquired Buddhism, by whose tenets the individual could, after undergoing numerous reincarnations, ultimately achieve release from the trials of mortal existence. Coexisting with these two faiths was the philosophy of Confucianism, also derived from China, which placed its emphasis on dutiful subordination, filial loyalty and public service.

Despite this melange of conflicting fealties, the nation had, for a while, achieved a certain degree of stability. By the middle of the 15th century, however, the complex strands of Japanese harmony were beginning to unravel. Part of the trouble was that Kyoto was an unsuitable seat of power. Situated on the main island of Honshu, it lay some 360 kilometres to the west of the Kanto, the richest tract of agricultural land in the entire nation. Too far away to be easily controlled, this fertile plain was, however, near enough to provide a base from which to threaten the capital. More disadvantageously still, the city was 60 kilometres from the Inland Sea which, hemmed in by Honshu, the western island of Kyushu and the southern island of Shikoku, was the true heart of the archipelago. Maritime cities such as Osaka and Sakai in the east or Nagasaki in the west could not easily be

A detail from a screen that formed part of the trousseau of a daughter of Tokugawa Ieyasu shows the general's troops sweeping to victory in the Battle of Sekigahara in 1600. Outmanoeuvred and betrayed by allies who switched their loyalties during the conflict, the army of Ieyasu's rival flees from the blazing remains of their fortified camp; the banners they left behind indicate that many of them were Christians. To the right and on the left, Ieyasu's troops surge forwards under cover of a low cloud that suggests the mist that delayed the start of the combat by more than an hour. The fighting was actually more obstinate, protracted and confused than this picture, commissioned by the victor, would suggest; but afterwards no Japanese lords dared to meet the Tokugawa armies in open warfare again.

dominated from the inland capital. And the whole western coast, which formed Japan's gateway to the outside world, lay beyond Kyoto's vigilance.

The capital's strategic weakness did not in itself matter, so long as the shogun was Japan's undisputed master. But over the years, the daimyo had gradually accreted power to themselves and their families. Local forces became stronger while the shogun's diminished, since the only way he could reward his followers was by granting them estates of their own, thereby diminishing his own land base while increasing that of his subjects. The religious establishment, too, was becoming restive. Many Buddhist monks saw no incongruity in also being warriors, converting their temples into fortresses and acquiring large tracts of land.

The crisis came in 1467, when the shogun found himself unable to make his ruling accepted in a case of disputed inheritance, and the contending parties came to blows in the streets of Kyoto itself. Prolonged fighting within the capital reduced the once-populous and thriving city to a charred wasteland across which armies could manoeuvre as if they were in open country. The imperial lineage was reduced to penury. Central power vanished and civil war spread throughout the land. Here, great lords were overthrown by lesser; there, confederations of samurai asserted their power; elsewhere Buddhist warrior-monks, supported by breakaway bands of peasants, established their dominance. Different daimyo supported rival claimants to the shogunate; during the course of the 16th century only one shogun escaped deposition, and he was murdered.

The interminable wars were not entirely destructive; indeed, the nation's economy flourished. The fighting usually did no more harm to towns and villages than was unavoidable, for no lord wished to devastate lands he might come to own. Successful commanders could establish, for a while at least, unified control across entire provinces, making possible large-scale improvements in irrigation and drainage. Agricultural production grew steadily, and the daimyo were not the only ones to benefit. In the nationwide convulsion, peasants could easily avoid high taxes and repression by fleeing to neighbouring estates, and the more enlightened rulers, therefore, sought to govern by efficient and beneficial methods. Several families set up private codes to regulate their own behaviour, emphasising such virtues as impartial adjudication and honest administration.

Urban dwellers, too, prospered. The incessant campaigns had to be supplied, and towns grew rich by providing munitions. Some cities even took advantage of the precarious balance of power to achieve a moderate degree of independence. In most of the wars, for example, the flourishing port of Sakai remained neutral, and hostile lords visiting the city had to surrender their weapons and keep the peace during their stay within the walls.

The lack of supervision also benefited seafarers, who could do virtually as they pleased. Japanese pirates and slave-raiders were dreaded all along the Chinese coast. More peaceable commerce was conducted as far afield as Indonesia. Japan generally gained from such exchanges: from the 1530s, when skilled Chinese and Korean engineers and metallurgists were imported to work in Japan's mines, silver and gold production soared.

Not long afterwards came the double-edged benefits of Western civilization. In 1542, when Portuguese sailors first reached the southern island of Tanegashima, they astonished the inhabitants by their exotic ways and especially by their

This suit of ceremonial armour was the favourite outfit of Tokugawa Yoshinao, lord of Owari (modern Nagoya) and Ieyasu's third son. Like all the best work of its day, it combines lightness and strength to a remarkable degree. Made primarily of silver or scarlet-lacquered iron, it follows exclusively Japanese traditions in its use of laced plates and strips rather than the solid steelwork that was favoured by Europeans. Even by 1600, however, suits designed for battle use rather than for display often incorporated some European features in an attempt to give increased protection against firearms.

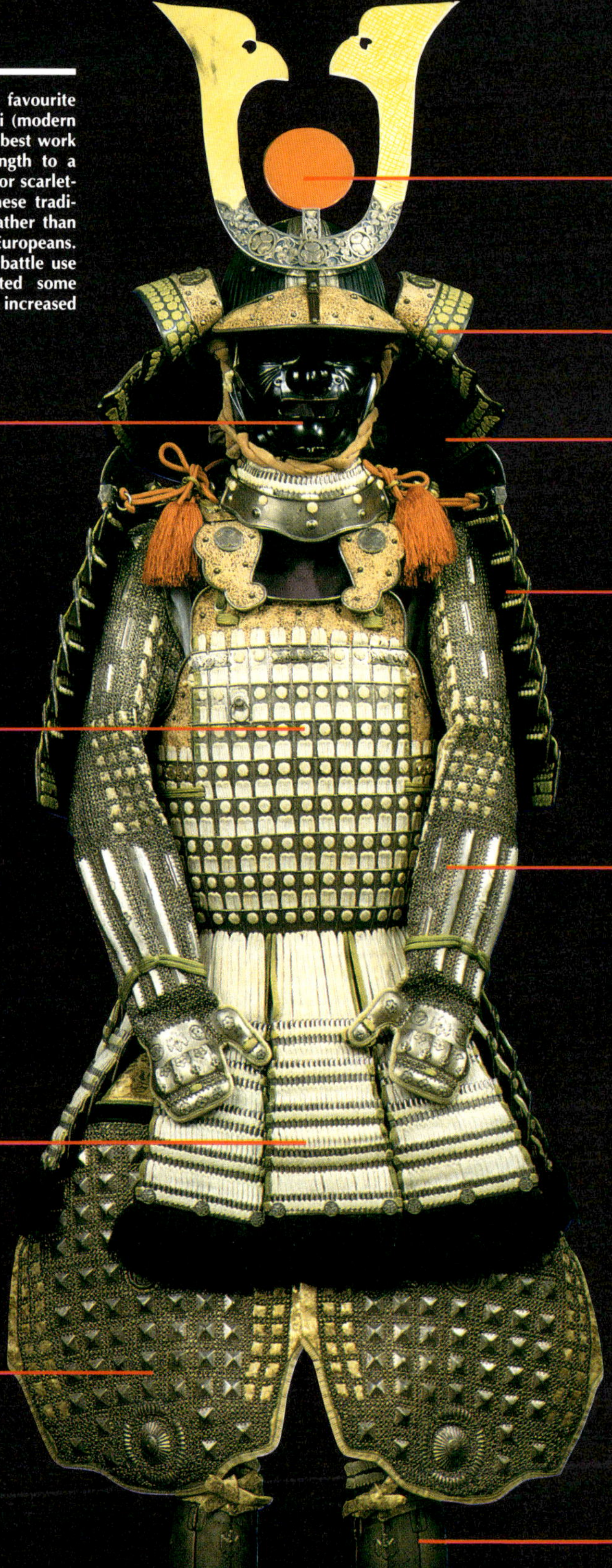

KABUTO
Made of joined iron plates, this crested helmet served to identify its wearer in battle.

FUKIGAESHI
These helmet flaps helped protect against sword cuts.

HO-ATE
The nose and upper lip of this face mask could be removed to permit the wearer to talk and drink. Below hangs a flexible neck protector.

SHIKORŌ
Lacquered iron plates hanging from the helmet guarded the neck and shoulders.

SODE
Oversleeves of loosely laced lacquered plates shielded the upper arms and body from sideways sword thrusts or arrows.

DO
This breastplate was made up of many small, tightly braided plates of lacquered iron. It provided good protection against spears, swords and arrows, but not against musketballs.

KOTE
Chainmail sewn on to a silken base was reinforced with iron strips to protect the forearm and hands.

GESAN
The plates constituting the skirt were larger and looser-laced to give flexibility for riding while protecting the lower body.

HAIDATE
This underskirt of silk sewn with chainmail was studded with iron plates to protect the front of the upper legs.

TSUNE-ATE

firearms. Gunpowder, a Chinese discovery, had been known in Japan for some time; but the European matchlock arquebus, an efficient, portable, armour-piercing weapon, was something new. Within a year the smiths of Tanegashima were turning out imitations of the guns which would do everything except shoot. On a later visit, a Portuguese gunner disclosed (in exchange, it was said, for a Japanese master smith's daughter) the secret of making Western-style gun barrels. Thereafter the "Tanegashima pieces", as they became known, spread through the country. Rare at first, they were increasingly valued, particularly by the Buddhist warrior-monks. Ultimately they would threaten Japan's social order: a humble infantryman armed with such a weapon was a match for even the most skilful samurai.

The Europeans brought other innovations: tobacco, spectacles, new styles of clothing and of cooking, as well as improved armour, made with wrought-iron plates instead of the traditional Japanese lacquered silk and bamboo, which offered some protection against arquebus bullets. They also brought with them Catholic Christianity, whose Jesuit missionaries were potentially even more threatening to the established order than Western firearms: a Japanese Catholic had loyalties that transcended those that he owed to his country and his emperor. Initially, however, the missionaries made few converts. They were nonetheless greatly impressed by the cleanliness and intelligence of the Japanese, while also lamenting their cruelty and the cunning of their merchants, who commonly possessed two sets of scales, an accurate one for weighing what they received and another to mislead their purchasers. They further noted with sadness the fact that such a beautiful land should be overwhelmed by incessant wars.

The spiral of violence seemed set to continue indefinitely when, during the late 16th century, a leader came to prominence who was to set Japan on the path to centuries of peace. In 1568, after eight years of battles, sieges and betrayals, a 35-year-old daimyo named Oda Nobunaga had grown strong enough to march into Kyoto and nominate his own candidate for shogun. In this enterprise he was aided by two outstanding lieutenants: Kinoshita – later known as Toyotomi – Hideyoshi, a small, withered figure of uncertain parentage and deep guile, who had risen from the position of a humble foot soldier (or, according to some, a bandit) to serving as a loyal samurai; and Tokugawa Ieyasu, a young warrior who had originally been opposed to Nobunaga but had later changed allegiance and advanced to become one of his most favoured generals.

In itself, Nobunaga's achievement was not unprecedented. Unlike other successful commanders, however, he was not simply ambitious for himself and his family. Instead, he was inspired by the aim of restoring peace and unity throughout the land. He saw only one way to achieve this goal. His motto, stamped on his official documents, was "Rule the Empire by Armed Force". Father Luis Frois, a Jesuit priest who knew Nobunaga in Kyoto, left a vivid description of him: "extremely warlike . . . despises all other Japanese kings and princes and speaks to them over his shoulder in a loud voice as if they were lowly servants . . . intensely dislikes any delays or long speeches."

An early casualty of Nobunaga's intolerance was the puppet shogun whom he had helped to instal. Their relationship was difficult from the beginning. On assuming office the shogun showed his gratitude by inviting the general to an evening's entertainment – 13 successive pieces of classical drama. Nobunaga's patience snapped after the fifth. By the year 1573, relations had become so bad that Nobunaga deposed his nominee and, without venturing to take any official title, thereafter gave orders in his own name.

Nobunaga reserved a particular hatred for the Buddhist warrior-monks, burning their temples, melting down their statues to cast guns and mercilessly slaughtering their supporters. It was from the unmounted Buddhist warriors, however, that he learnt the importance of infantry. In 1575 his foot soldiers, clad in waterproof straw jackets and toting matchlocks, decimated the armoured cavalry of the Kanto. By 1582, the great monastery of Osaka had been destroyed, its monks burnt alive within it, and the rich port of Sakai had lost all pretensions to independence and submitted to Nobunaga's authority.

Nobunaga now had all of the central region of Honshu under his control. The Buddhist warrior-monks had been crushed, and it remained only to subdue the rest of the daimyo. To this end, Ieyasu's armies advanced eastwards into the Kanto, while the western front was put in the hands of Hideyoshi, who was now a trusted general (though his master still called him "Monkey"). It was while his subordinates were thus occupied that Nobunaga met his death. He was attacked and murdered in Kyoto by one of his own daimyo.

Possibly the treacherous act was carried out at the instigation of Hideyoshi, who lost very little time in taking full advantage of the situation. Within a mere eight days he had returned to Kyoto, where he killed Nobunaga's assassins and seized control of the capital himself. Taken completely unawares by the coup d'état, Tokugawa Ieyasu put up a token show of resistance but ultimately he had little choice other than to submit to Hideyoshi's rule.

The new ruler's first priority was to make himself respected by those lords who still thought of him as a successful peasant who had been nicknamed "Monkey". There was no shogun in office, nor did Hideyoshi aspire to such a position, not being of the expected lineage. Instead, he legitimized his status by taking the aristocratic title of *kanpaku*, or imperial regent, one of the great ceremonial offices of the emperor's court. Armed with this resounding title, he built up his strength until by 1591, through a combination of force and persuasion, he had obtained oaths of loyalty from every daimyo in the country.

The new regent decided to rule from the port of Osaka rather than from Kyoto. There he built a castle that was worthy of his position: the moats were almost a hundred metres across; the walls, lined with dozens of towers, were built of massive masonry, and their gates were reinforced by blocks of stone measuring six by nine metres; and in the centre the great keep, with whitewashed walls and sweeping golden roofs, rose eight stories high. Within, Hideyoshi lived in bejewelled luxury, surrounded by elaborate gilt decorations and whole walls covered with gold. He also kept a palace in Kyoto, where he entertained the emperor with feasts of unexampled magnificence.

Amidst all of this grandeur, Hideyoshi tried to show that he could also appreciate the more austere traditions of Japanese culture. Notable among these was the tea ceremony, which initially had been imported from China but had since been refined by the Japanese into an aesthetic ritual that called for a simplicity of manners and a heightened appreciation of texture and form. Japan's greatest master of the art, Sen Rikyu, did his best to educate the Regent's taste in these matters.

During the civil wars of the 16th century, Japanese society had become unusually fluid. The fortunes of war favoured some upwardly mobile samurai who became known as "sudden lords"; and even a few peasants had a chance to attain the coveted status of warriors. In the 17th century, however, the Tokugawa shoguns enhanced the stability of their regime by imposing a rigid class system that was based on the Confucian principles of loyalty and obedience.

Under Tokugawa legislation, four principal groups were recognized. A warrior elite had the highest status, followed by peasants, artisans and merchants in that order. Class distinctions were regarded as hereditary and unchangeable. Nevertheless, a degree of social mobility survived. Favoured artisans could be rewarded with privileges far above their station; and by the end of the century, many merchants enjoyed wealth and positions of trust that were the envy of their social superiors.

THE FOUR ORDERS OF SOCIETY

Details from contemporary paintings illustrate the four estates of Tokugawa society. A warrior *(top)*, commander's baton in hand, rides a richly caparisoned warhorse. At centre, a peasant hoes a rice paddy. The skilled workers preparing beams for a temple *(bottom left)* were members of the artisan class. Lowest of all in status was the merchant *(bottom right)*, shown toting his wares to market.

Hideyoshi's response was to commission a portable teahouse in which every accessible surface, including the ceiling, was plated with gold.

Such were the trappings of Hideyoshi's power. The reality that underlay them was a complete reform of the system of land tenure, intended to make Japan a stable country in which civil war and rebellion would be as difficult as possible. With this aim in mind, Hideyoshi ordered a survey of land ownership throughout Japan, and used the results to impose a rational and uniform system of taxation. He rewarded those daimyo who had chosen to become his vassals with grants of land that were conditional on his pleasure. His most dangerous rival, Ieyasu, received the governorship of the Kanto, where, from the eastern castle of Edo, he served Hideyoshi loyally. He lacked the opportunity to do otherwise: the lands between the Kanto and the capital that he had formerly held under Nobunaga were given to trusted supporters of Hideyoshi.

Resistance to the new order was widespread. During the long civil wars, many peasants had grown used to a tax-free and unregimented existence. But protest was quite literally disarmed when, in 1588, Hideyoshi ordered the confiscation of all weapons from the peasantry and from those warrior-monks who had survived Nobunaga's massacres. After the Sword Hunt, as it became known, only samurai could bear arms. Hideyoshi consoled his subjects with the promise that the confiscated items would be melted down to construct a great statue of the Buddha, to the spiritual benefit of the unwilling donors.

In the cities, the Regent's control was no less firm. The urban guilds that had established local monopolies were abolished, and trade became free; even foreigners were encouraged. Chinese, Portuguese and Spanish merchants arrived in some numbers, attracted by the new abundance of precious metals. Conversely, Japanese vessels sailed to distant waters: by 1600, a few pirates had established themselves as far away as the Mediterranean port of Tunis.

Continuing contact with Europeans, however, had consequences that Hideyoshi did not entirely welcome. Under Nobunaga's rule, Christianity had become almost fashionable in court circles, and by the 1580s the converts, centred on the western island of Kyushu and especially around the port of Nagasaki, numbered 100,000 or more. Hideyoshi regarded them with suspicion as a possible source of disloyalty, and in 1587 issued an edict expelling all Christian missionaries from Japan. But merchants were still welcome, and the two classes of foreigners were easily confused. Protected by judicious bribery as well as by distance, the Jesuit missions in Kyushu managed to continue their work while Hideyoshi turned to other matters.

He had risen far; now he aspired even higher. Concerned no doubt to keep the battle-hardened samurai occupied with foreign wars, he conceived the ambition of using the armies of his newly reunited country to invade and conquer Korea. In 1592, a force of Japanese soldiers numbering some 160,000 landed in the south of that country and poured up the peninsula. By the winter of 1593, however, they were floundering. The weather was execrable and communications with Japan were precarious. The Korean peasants resisted the invaders with a bitter guerrilla campaign. Worst of all, the Chinese came to the Koreans' aid. By summer, the Japanese had been driven back to the south. Negotiations followed and failed; undaunted, Hideyoshi declared war on China.

By now Hideyoshi was no longer the shrewd, careful commander who had risen to power as Nobunaga's understudy. Possibly infected with syphilis – a disease that Iberian seamen had brought to Japan as to every other accessible nation — he now saw enemies everywhere. The teamaster Sen Rikyu, accused of treason because his statue had been placed above a gate through which Hideyoshi rode, was driven to suicide. A number of Japanese Christians and Portuguese missionaries were executed. The Regent's own nephew and all his family were killed, accused of plotting to capture Osaka castle. Driven by ever-present fears of treachery, Hideyoshi flung his energies into his plan to conquer China, and his affections into a boundless love for his infant son Hideyori, whom he was determined must succeed him despite any plots by his untrustworthy daimyo.

Paranoid he may have been, but he kept his power. Another 100,000 warriors were sent to the war in Korea. They fought heroically — a temple in Kyoto became the repository for the ears and noses of 37,000 Chinese killed in one battle — and by the autumn of 1598 victory seemed to be in sight. By then, however, Hideyoshi knew that he was dying. In his last lucid moments he appointed Ieyasu as the guardian of his cherished son, Hideyori, with a Council of Elders to govern until the boy should be old enough to rule.

With Hideyoshi's death in 1598, the Council of Elders lost no time in abandoning Korea and making peace with China. They knew that all Japanese forces would be needed at home for the power struggle that must inevitably ensue. In this conflict

Kazuko, daughter of the second Tokugawa shogun Hidetada, rides in a curtained carriage out of Nijo castle, the Tokugawa stronghold in Kyoto, on her way to marry Emperor Go-Mizuno in 1620. The scene is shown in a detail from one of a pair of painted screens, decorated with gold leaf, illustrating sights in and around the imperial capital. The marriage was designed to strengthen the ties between the imperial house and the Tokugawa family, thereby tightening the shoguns' hold on power.

Ieyasu had several advantages. The Kanto made him the richest lord in all of Japan; and, having avoided sending any of his troops to Korea, he had men as well as rice fields. With such strength at his command he soon began to receive pledges of support from other daimyo. But Ishida Mitsunari, one of Hideyoshi's most faithful vassals, worked tirelessly to organize a coalition against him. In the early months of 1600, two years after his master's death, Mitsunari felt strong enough to launch an all-out attack on his rival. The fortunes of war seesawed until Mitsunari met defeat and death at Sekigahara. Ten days later, the victorious Ieyasu entered Osaka as the country's military master.

He quickly set about consolidating his position. Eighty-seven daimyo houses were completely extinguished, their lands being absorbed into Ieyasu's holdings and then redistributed to reward his followers. By 1603, he had persuaded the Emperor to make him shogun, and at his castle at Edo – the future Tokyo – he accepted the submission of all the remaining daimyo.

Nor was he content with receiving mere oaths of loyalty. In addition, he required his vassals to provide him with men and materials for the construction of a new seat of government at Edo. During the two years that followed hills were levelled, marshes were drained, canals were dug and great walls were raised to enclose a massive castle, a brooding symbol of power whose white-plastered buildings were adorned with dark tiles picked out in gold.

With Japan's daimyo safely subdued, the only remaining threat to Ieyasu's security was Hideyori, who was still ensconced in the great castle of Osaka that had been built by his father. Yet for years Ieyasu kept the promise he had sworn to the dying Hideyoshi; perhaps he did not feel strong enough to attack the prince whom he had promised to defend, perhaps he hoped that it would not prove to be necessary. Hideyori's guardians for their part also kept the peace, since Hideyori was young and Ieyasu by now was old.

The crisis was postponed until 1614. Aged 74, Ieyasu had little more than a year left to live, and may have known it. Hideyori had been careful to give no offence, but Ieyasu found it all the same. One of the bells in a newly rebuilt Osaka temple bore a Chinese inscription that Ieyasu falsely claimed was insulting to the house of Tokugawa. Scholars, obedient to his command, examined the bell and confirmed that the Chinese symbols were indeed treasonable. Ieyasu's wrath could only be appeased by outright surrender. When the 21-year-old Hideyori refused, Ieyasu took to arms and in December brought 150,000 warriors against Osaka castle.

But the attackers lacked artillery and Hideyoshi had built well. In addition, there were many old enemies of Ieyasu who were more than willing to fight for the young prince. By the end of the winter, Ieyasu's armies had lost many men and had nothing to show for it. When Ieyasu offered favourable peace terms, it seemed that Hideyori had won a famous victory. He was to be allowed to keep the castle and all his lands, and none of the garrison were to be punished. In return, Ieyasu asked only for a few hostages and that, as a face-saving gesture, part of the outer moat of Osaka castle should be filled in.

Peace came, the besiegers and garrison mostly went home, and a troop of labourers – stout, reliable men from the Kanto – arrived at the castle for the symbolic moat-filling. The task proved to be more onerous than expected. To reach the moat the workmen had to demolish the outer battlements. More and more labourers arrived; more of the outer moat was filled in; by some mistake, parts of the inner moat were filled also; and then the inner parapets were brought down. Desperate to keep the peace, Hideyori tried to reason with Ieyasu's officers. They evaded his questions and referred his protests to superior authorities; meanwhile the demolition went on day and night. Eventually they admitted that there might have been some error, but pointed out that walls and moats were of little practical use in peacetime. The workmen eventually left with apologies; soon after Ieyasu returned with his army. Hideyori defended the ruins of his castle from May into June, before finally committing suicide.

In the aftermath, Ieyasu ruthlessly crushed all remnants of opposition: the whole of Hideyori's family was destroyed, save for two small children; the progeny of Osaka's commanders were executed; and the castle's surviving defenders were mercilessly hunted down, their heads displayed in rotting thousands along the road to Kyoto. And lest anyone be in doubt as to Ieyasu's intentions, the daimyo were summoned before him to hear how the country was now to be run.

To the cowed lords he dictated most stringent terms. All opposition parties or factions were to be immediately denounced; traitors were to be expelled from their estates; new castle construction was forbidden and any repairs were to be reported; movements between estates were restricted; samurai were to live frugally and were not to adopt costumes or ornaments inappropriate to their rank; all daimyo marriages were to be sanctioned by the shogun; and strict limits were set on the size of nobles' personal escorts.

These guidelines, which he encapsulated in a document running to 13 clauses, confirmed Ieyasu's position as undisputed master of Japan. He did not have long to savour his triumph, for he died the following year. But his work survived him; the legacy of social peace that he bequeathed to his successors was to keep the Tokugawa dynasty in power for more than 250 years.

By the time of his death, Ieyasu had made the Tokugawa by far the richest family in Japan. His estates, yielding 32 million bushels of rice, accounted for a quarter of the nation's wealth. Ieyasu's eldest son and successor, Hidetada, enriched the clan still further by confiscating the estates of hostile daimyo, and thus bringing his revenues up to 55 million bushels. There were some rumblings of discontent from the nobles, but these were quickly stifled by Hidetada's son, Iemitsu, when he came to power in 1623. The new ruler summoned the great lords to attend his palace in Edo. They arrived, were escorted in, and left alone. They waited, growing colder and hungrier, till after nightfall. Then, with a sudden blaze of torches, Iemitsu appeared and spoke: "I am the shogun by right of succession, and you will henceforward be treated as hereditary vassals. If any man does not like this, let him go back to his estates, and make up his mind; between him and me, battle shall decide." All chose peace. Nonetheless, Iemitsu was subsequently to make further charges of treason the pretext for confiscating yet more land worth an additional 19 million bushels of rice a year, giving the Tokugawa direct control of more than half the entire wealth of Japan.

Under the rule of Hidetada and Iemitsu, Japanese life took on a new shape. Ieyasu had governed in the style of a successful general; his successors created a bureaucracy out of what had been an armed camp. Efficient administration and tight control became the maxims of the new rulers. Every aspect of government was carefully regulated. Any subversive activities were closely investigated by a

FROM RITUAL TO REVELRY

The 17th century saw a revolution in Japanese theatre. At its start, the national tradition was enshrined in the *noh* plays, a style developed at least 200 years before which had its roots in religious ritual. Its highly stylized performances had something of the character of sacred dances. Two or three masked players would act out some sacred historical episode, often involving the appearance of a ghost or a demon, while a chorus commented on the action. Naturalism was far from being the goal; for example, members of the imperial house – even great warriors – were played by small boys, to denote purity.

Although this classic drama continued to be staged in the ensuing centuries, no new plays in the *noh* tradition were composed after the 16th century. Instead, a new style called *kabuki* – literally "the art of singing and dancing" – won popularity. *Kabuki* had its origins in the troupe of an actress named O-Kuni who organized dances and dramatic performances in Kyoto from about 1596. The plays she and her successors favoured were full of devices that were anathema to the refined purveyors of *noh*: buffoonery and melodrama, acrobatic feats and realistic dialogue. Their complex plots, sometimes drawing on recent events, sought unashamedly to entertain. Critics complained of the vulgarity of the new drama, but *kabuki* found an enthusiastic audience in the burgeoning cities, and throughout the Tokugawa period its leading actors were popular heroes, regarded as the incarnations of disreputable glamour.

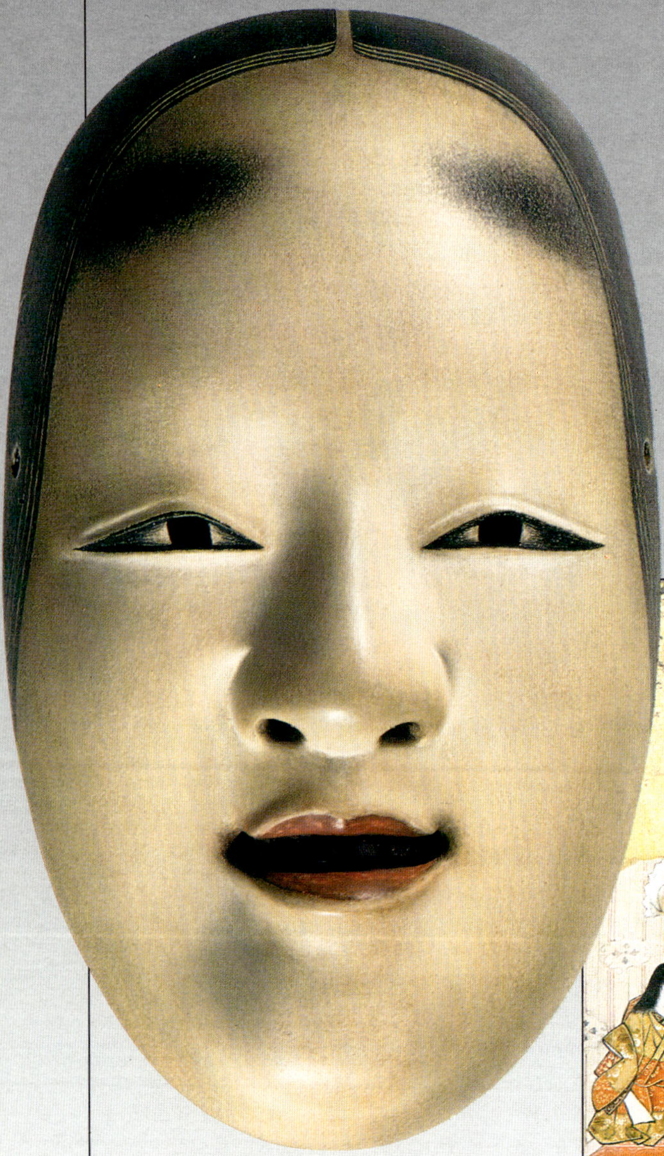

This *noh* mask, made in Edo in the 18th century, would have been worn by a male actor playing the part of a beautiful young girl; there were no actresses in Japan's classic drama. Deprived of the possibility of portraying mood by facial expression, the players had to use gesture and movement to convey emotion.

Noh performers wore demon masks such as this polychromed wood example to portray any of the many evil spirits known to contemporary religious life. The tiny eyeholes of the masks posed problems for actors, who could see very little of the stage.

Backed by an orchestra, three *kabuki* actresses dance for an audience whose attention is divided between events on stage and their own concerns. This painting is a detail from a hand scroll extolling the merits of a popular actress called Uneme who ran a theatre in the Shijo quarter of Kyoto in the early 17th century, before female performers were banned from *kabuki*, as from *noh*, on grounds of public morality.

This fox mask was made for a *kyogen* play: a brief comic interlude that served to relax an audience's emotions after the performance of a serious *noh* drama. In this particular example, an old fox disguises himself as a human in an attempt to persuade the trapper who is pursuing him to give up the hunting life.

Portrayed in a painted wooden statuette, the powerful Buddhist priest Ishin Suden sits enthroned with a staff at his side. Under Ieyasu and his successor Hidetada, Suden – the abbot of a monastery of the Zen sect in Kyoto – was one of the nation's most influential figures, helping to draft the laws prohibiting Christianity and governing the behaviour of the elite warrior class. Zen Buddhism, with its emphasis on individual effort, was popular with Japan's military rulers, who often sought advice from its exponents.

ministry of information, whose findings were swiftly, and usually mercilessly, acted upon by commissioners of police and justice.

As Tokugawa control spread, Japanese society started to ossify into rigid strata. Whatever social mobility had existed during the civil wars now vanished, to be replaced by an inflexible class system. At the top stood the warriors, comprising about five per cent of the population. Beneath them, in descending order, came farmers, artisans and traders. At the bottom of the heap was a floating population of outcasts who carried out such menial tasks as butchery and tanning. In principle, no man could rise above the class into which he was born, although many peasants chose deliberately to downgrade themselves, preferring the comfortable life of an artisan to the hardships of farming the paddy fields. Gradations in status were spelt out in an elaborate code of etiquette governing such matters as dress, precedence and modes of address.

To strengthen their hold on their subjects' minds, the shoguns stressed the ancient Confucian virtues of piety and obedience – traditions which had come to permeate all Japanese thought, whether Buddhist or Shinto, and which, though grossly violated during the civil wars, had always been paid lip service. With its emphasis on loyalty and its attendant obligations, particularly between ruler and subject, Confucianism provided a suitable ethical code for Tokugawa rule.

With the country finally at peace, the only threat to Tokugawa supremacy came from the outside world. Too many foreigners had reached Japan for its rulers' taste, and what the Japanese had learnt from them they did not like. Protestant Dutch and English merchants had alerted the shoguns to the conquests that the Spanish and Portuguese had made all over the world, and as near as the Philippines; the Catholics, for their part, had reported on the faithlessness and rapacity of the Protestant merchants. Furthermore, no foreigner could be trusted to obey the shogun, and the Christianity they brought with them risked corrupting Japanese obedience. Ieyasu had encouraged foreign trade, and had done little to persecute Christians even in the ranks of his enemies. His successors decided otherwise.

The great persecution of Japanese Christians started in 1618. Over the next 16 years all churches were destroyed, and all priests that could be found were executed or expelled. With them perished a multitude of converts. At first the aim was simply to suppress the faith: hundreds were crucified, burnt at the stake, broiled on wooden gridirons or thrown into the sulphurous fumaroles which abounded throughout volcanic Japan. Later, however, persecutors vied with each other to make Christians deny their faith. One popular method was to wrap the victim in a sack, bind him up tightly to impede circulation, and then suspend him upside down over a pit; only the left hand remained free to make the sign of recantation. One priest described the consequences: "Soon blood began to ooze from the mouth, the nose and the ears. For most death came only at the end of two, three and even six days. Care was taken to bleed victims in the temple of the head, to prevent too rapid a congestion and to prolong the pain." Another priest wrote of Christian women being forced to crawl naked through the steets, before being publicly violated and thrown into snake pits. To escape such fates many people – even Jesuit priests – abandoned their faith. Others managed to remain covertly Christian, despite the fact that if a convert was discovered the five nearest families on both sides of his dwelling were executed also, unless they had denounced him to the authorities.

Extreme though it was, the suppression of Christianity formed only part of the campaign to extirpate foreign influences from Japan. Iemitsu, after being taught geography by a French trader, and realizing "the size of the world, the multitude of its countries and the smallness of Japan," was, according to the merchant's account, "greatly surprised and heartily wished his land had never been visited by any Christian". Accordingly, in 1633 he made a remarkable decision. Showing the same thorough application to detail that characterized his internal administration, the shogun resolved to restrict Japan's contact with the outside world, and over the next six years a series of laws was promulgated that put this plan into effect.

Japanese were forbidden to go abroad, and all seagoing ships were destroyed. Citizens caught returning to the country from overseas were killed. No foreigners were allowed to enter either, except at the port of Nagasaki in Kyushu, where an artificial island was built in the harbour to accommodate foreign merchants. The Spanish and Portuguese were barred because of their links with the Jesuits, and the English left of their own accord. Some Dutch were permitted to remain, having impressed the Japanese with their trading vigour and being (on the testimony of the Spaniards) not truly Christians at all, and a colony of Chinese stayed to manage the mainland silk trade, over which the shogun held a monopoly. The only other foreign trade permitted was with Korea and with the Ryuku Islands to the south.

Few Japanese protested as Iemitsu slowly closed the lid on their already boxed-in society. Only in Kyushu, where Christians were most numerous and foreign trade most flourishing, did the population take a stand. In January 1638, some 20,000 peasants, armed with matchlocks and led by a few Christian samurai, captured a castle at Shimabara on the Gulf of Nagasaki, and assembled there with their families. Toughened by adversity, they held out for four months against the shogun's armies and against bombardment from a Dutch warship that came to the government's aid. Their defeat, however, was inevitable; shorn of supplies, the rebels were eventually surrounded by more than 100,000 of Iemitsu's men, and gradually the guns on the ramparts fell silent as their ammunition was exhausted. The climax came at noon on April 11, when the shogun's forces succeeded in breaking through the outer walls. By the following dawn they reached the inner keep. The starving defenders, fighting with anything they could get their hands on – stones, wooden beams and even their rice pots – were massacred almost to a man. Only 105 prisoners emerged from the ruins at Shimabara. Thereafter, apart from the Dutch, there were no known Christians in Japan.

The peasants' revolt at Shimabara was almost the last flicker of opposition to the Tokugawa shogunate. The daimyo, for their part, were kept far too busy travelling to and from Edo to plan revolt, for in 1635 Iemitsu had ordained that his leading nobles must spend four months of every other year within the shogunal capital, leaving their families there as hostages during the intervals. Even the imperial court was not exempt from the decree.

In 1651, however, when Iemitsu died to be succeeded by his 10-year-old son Ietsuna, discontent flared up. The root of the trouble was not the pretensions of the nobility but the exigencies of numerous samurai, veterans of the earlier wars who had lost employment when their masters were dispossessed by the shogun.

These wandering samurai, qualified only for military service, were known as ronin, or wave-men. Rather than drop caste by turning to the land and becoming farmers, many of them set up weapon shops or martial academies, and these establishments became meeting places where discontented fellow samurai could air their grievances. One such ronin, a halberd instructor of enormous strength named Marubashi Chuya, harboured a particular grudge: his father had been killed at the siege of Osaka and he yearned to take his revenge on the Tokugawa family. Another, Yui Shosetsu, was inspired by Hideyoshi's vertiginous rise to power and nurtured hopes of becoming far more than just a humble armourer. When the two went into partnership to run an ironworks, they set about realizing their dreams. Their plan was ambitious: to blow up the main gunpowder store in Edo, burn the city, storm the castle, and eliminate the government.

The plotters gathered support amongst their brethren. A date was set for the coup in June 1651. Chuya, however, fell ill, and in his delirium he began to shout out details of the plan. The government moved swiftly; within weeks the conspirators had been arrested, tortured and executed, along with their wives, children and parents. But the conspiracy of the ronin had alarmed the regents who governed on Ietsuna's behalf. They subsequently took steps to supervise the hordes of wandering samurai, and where possible to teach them useful administrative skills.

For the whole nature of the samurai class was changing. They were still warriors, though by a decision of the shogunate their style of fighting was deliberately antiquated; Japan's rulers had seen what peasants with muskets could do, and did not care for the prospect. Instead, the samurai were encouraged to use weapons that demanded long practice, most notably swords and bows and arrows. Dog-shooting contests, in which mounted archers galloped around an enclosure in pursuit of their agile targets, became a popular spectacle in Edo, and samurai were permitted to practise their swordsmanship on condemned prisoners, or on any peasants who showed disrespect. Measures such as these helped to bolster samurai self-esteem, but without wars to fight they became salaried servants rather than feudal knights. By the middle of the 17th century, samurai were no longer rewarded for their services with grants of land, which might have given them real local power. Instead, they were allotted rations of rice, and made to live in their lords' castles or in cities, where they could be easily watched.

With the great lords tamed and the samurai a dependent salariat, the peasants continued to work the land as they had always done. But now the disruptions of war were replaced by the heavy taxation and strict regimentation of the Tokugawa peace. A village had little freedom except to determine how the tax assessed on the community should be divided among the families; this decision was made by the headman whom the local lord appointed, assisted by the village elders. On these also fell the burden of settling any disputes within the village, and of ensuring that all obeyed the shogun's regulations. Failure in these duties carried diverse and

A painting by an unknown Japanese artist familiar with Western oil-painting techniques shows a massacre of Christians in 1622, one of a series that culminated in the total suppression of the religion in Japan. Fearing that the first loyalties of Christians would lie outside the nation and viewing the message of the faith as incompatible with their warrior ethic, Japan's rulers decided to eliminate it by torturing and killing those who would not renounce their beliefs. In the mass execution depicted here, which took place in 1622 in Nagasaki, 30 Japanese Christians were beheaded *(foreground)*, while at least 22 others, who included nine Spanish missionaries, died at the stake in the fiery pit shown in the centre; "among them," according to an English merchant who witnessed the event, "little children of five or six years, burnt alive in the arms of their mothers".

hideous penalties. Nevertheless, agricultural output swelled and the peasants bred; by the end of the 17th century there were around 26 million Japanese.

An expanding rural population in turn helped feed growing cities. Japan now had three metropolises: Edo, the new capital, made glorious by the shogun's court; Kyoto, the aristocratically elegant seat of the emperor; and Osaka, the thriving hub of coastal trade. Along their streets sprang up a sprawling mass of insubstantial wooden buildings, each two or three storeys high. Earthquakes, typhoons and fires — so frequent that flames became known as "flowers of Edo" — did little to halt urban growth. The flimsy dwellings, so easily destroyed, were just as easily rebuilt, and there was always profit to be made from disaster: many enterprising businessmen grew wealthy from the construction trade.

Such opportunism was just one aspect of the burgeoning commercial spirit that infused the newly peaceful nation. Everywhere goods were on the move. Small boats — truly seaworthy vessels were still not allowed — carried their cargoes along rivers and canals and hugged the islands' coasts, and the excellent roads that spanned the country, originally constructed to give the shogun's armies easy access to every province, were now packed with merchants' wagons.

Rice remained the most prestigious item of trade, but tea, silk, tobacco and cotton were also widely bartered. Timber from the mountain forests was constantly

in demand; fisheries were abundant and profitable; and although the flow of gold and silver that had given such dazzling wealth to Hideyoshi's court diminished as the more accessible lodes were exhausted, copper mining flourished, providing the main export item in the small amount of foreign commerce. Craftsmen produced a range of artisanal goods that were abundant, intricate and carefully made.

Barred from foreign trade, enterprising families found opportunities within Japan. The fortunes of the powerful Mitsui family, for instance, rose through the efforts of a provincial patriarch who became a brewer of rice wine in the 1620s. Turning his hand to moneylending and rice-dealing, he amassed enough money for his son, 50 years later, to set up a dry-goods store in Edo, selling cotton and drapery at fixed prices for cash. Within a decade the Mitsui house had branches in Kyoto and Osaka, and was making a handsome profit from commodity broking. By the 1690s the firm was acting as financial agents for the shogun, the emperor and several leading daimyo. In addition, they managed a large network of wholesale associations, for which their stores provided outlets; operated a speedy courier service between Edo and Osaka; and were heavily involved in the property market.

For the Mitsui and such other merchant houses as the Sumitomo, the 17th century signalled the start of more than 300 years of commercial paramountcy. To the military rulers of the time, however, they were objects of scorn. Segregated in special quarters of the towns, as befitted their low status, they were subject to strict regulations and were forbidden any participation in the running of the nation.

Freed from onerous responsibility and unshackled by social obligations, Japan's merchants found the time to escape the rigours of office and abacus in a round of worldly pleasure. The cities offered endless gratification for those who had the money: rich clothes and food, good conversation in tea and wine shops, the pleasures of paintings, novels, theatres, bathhouses and brothels. In the areas surrounding the merchant quarters, patrons of the numerous restaurants and bathhouses enjoyed the attentions of geisha girls, professional courtesans

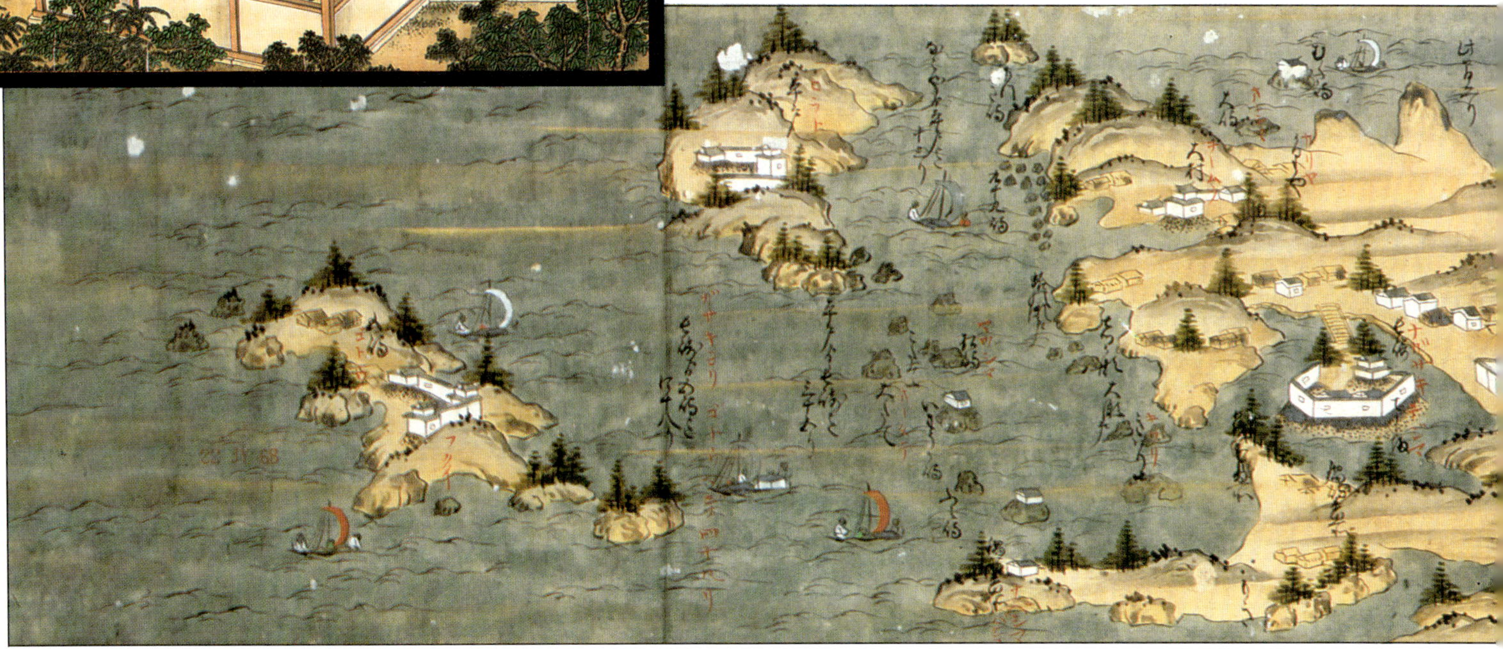

who provided an alternative to the stultification of an arranged marriage or the routine sensuality of the brothel. Theatre-goers hired private boxes where, secluded behind split-bamboo curtains and gold screens, they whiled away the evenings with food hampers and bottles of rice wine. And merrymakers thronged the waterways of such towns as Edo and Osaka, where the wealthy maintained their own luxuriously appointed pleasure boats, fully staffed with cooks, musicians and dancing girls. The poor took along their own supplies and caroused along the canals in more modest hired vessels.

Ukiyo, the "floating world", the Japanese called this urban playground, using a phrase that according to Buddhist teaching signified everything that was transitory and insubstantial in life. Expenditure on these fleeting delights was so lavish that it called forth frequent rebukes from the military government. Nevertheless, many samurai discarded their swords and briefly forgot their principles of frugality and self-control to taste its fruits. One such temporary renegade described a visit to the theatre: "Many went . . . with their faces wrapped in towels, wearing only a short sword so they would look like common people. These disguised samurai broke over the bamboo fence of the theatre, whereas the real common people paid their fees. If the management tried to stop the intruders they uttered a menacing roar and strode on to take the best seats."

The arts were quick to reflect the new urban life style. A new type of prose literature appeared, heroic romances that satisfied the townsman's taste for adventure. Among its greatest exponents was the novelist Saikaku, whose down-to-earth heroes provided a stark contrast to the courtly paramours of traditional tales. He frankly extolled the life of pleasure. "Why offer money to Buddha?" he once wrote. "Is not a land of women paradise? Give your money to women."

In the theatre the popular *kabuki* style came to replace the ceremonial *noh* performances that had bored Nobunaga to distraction. And in the visual arts, carvers and painters used coloured woodcut prints to satisfy a vast market for representations of the floating world: merchants requiring mementoes of their favourite geisha girls, theatres needing handbills, book publishers requiring illustrations. From simple line cuts, the works grew increasingly sophisticated; a series of fine-grained blocks, each one printing a single colour, was kept accurately in register to build up the required image. In their style, the prints also incorporated elements of European art learnt either during the period of open contact or later through the continuing influence of the Dutch at Nagasaki: perspective, dramatic chiaroscuro and modern pigments such as Prussian blue all enhanced the design. Demand swelled and the print runs lengthened. By the end of the century, a few small coins could purchase colourful masterpieces depicting popular entertainers, bustling urban scenes or majestic landscapes.

Native connoisseurs regarded this new fashion as vulgar, preferring the older, established styles of Japanese art that ultimately derived from China. But even for purists, the nation's poetic renaissance had something to offer. The making of intricate, allusive verse had long been a courtly skill in Japan. This tradition had crystallized in the form of the haiku, a three-line verse drawing concise imagery from nature to suggest an emotion. In the 17th century the greatest master of haiku appeared, an ex-ronin named Matsuo Basho. A wandering recluse, Basho studied the doctrines of Zen, a contemplative Buddhist sect whose adepts sought to savour both the uniqueness of every object and moment and the complex web

A page from a late 17th-century map shows the artificial island of De-shima *(walled, centre)* built near the port of Nagasaki to receive Dutch merchants, the only Europeans permitted to trade with Japan. Within the enclosure the merchants enjoyed a comfortable existence, drinking, smoking and playing billiards in well-appointed quarters *(inset)*. But they were allowed only minimal contact with the Japanese; the dark-skinned servant standing just outside the door would have come with the traders from the Dutch settlement in Indonesia.

An important item in the tea ceremony, this cast-iron kettle of an early, restrained style is decorated with etched pines, bamboos and plum trees, symbolizing strength.

THE REFINED PLEASURES OF THE TEA CEREMONY

When the Japanese adopted from China the custom of drinking tea, they imported not only a refreshment but also a ritual. Since the eighth century, the Chinese had made the preparation and sharing of a bowl of the beverage a symbol of inner harmony. Under the influence of Zen Buddhism, with its emphasis on austerity and the renunciation of worldly attachments, this practice was refined into a ceremony known as *wabi*, "simplicity".

In the sparsely decorated surroundings of a humble garden hut, the host would welcome his guests, boil the kettle, whisk the tea powder in a bowl, then offer the drink in a spirit of modesty. This style reached its peak under the 16th-century teamaster Sen Rikyu.

In the 17th century, however, teamasters revived the more ostentatious daimyo ceremony, named after Japan's warrior nobility, which permitted larger surroundings, richly decorated utensils and separate seating for great lords. In later years this style was formalized and codified by tea schools, under whose influence the ritual became a recreation for Japan's burgeoning middle class.

The elegant simplicity of this bamboo tea scoop belies its creation at the hands of Kobori Enshu, a 17th-century teamaster who developed the luxurious daimyo ceremony. By tradition, the scoop was carved by the master himself.

The *natsume* style of tea caddy, shaped like a jujube fruit and made out of dark lacquer, was a favourite of Sen Rikyu. This 17th-century example, decorated with golden feathers, is in a later and more ornate style.

A ceramic tea bowl, bearing an enamel pattern of fish scales and waves, epitomizes the courtly grandeur of the later daimyo style. The height of the ceremony was reached when the master ladled hot water from the kettle on to the powdered tea in the bowl from which the guests were to drink.

The most formal type of ceremony calls for two servings of tea; the first "thick", or unwhipped, and the second "thin", whisked up to a foam. The tea whisk is made from a single piece of bamboo, carefully split into tines at one end and bound round with silk thread at the base of the tines. This example was bought by a Dutch merchant at De-shima.

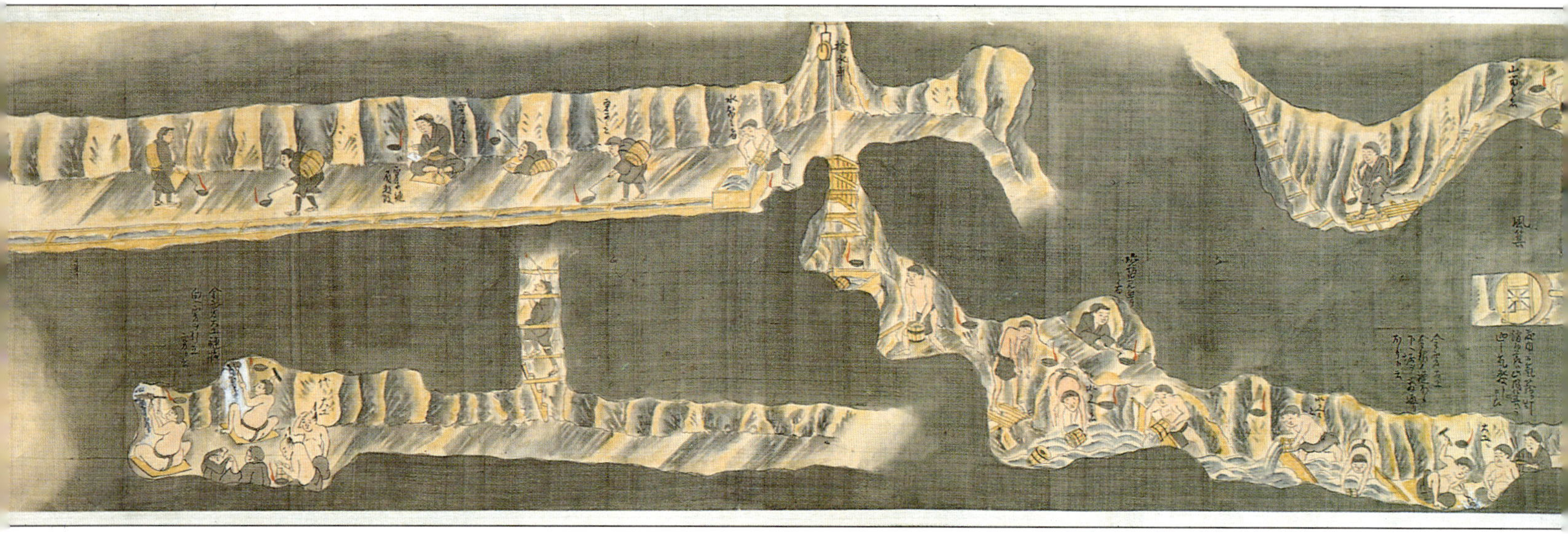

of destinies linking them. Far removed in spirit from the venality of the floating world, Basho's terse, allusive poems were tinged with a contemplative melancholy:

On a withered branch
a crow has settled;
autumn nightfall.

Basho himself died in 1694, but his works had a lasting influence. In years to come he would be honoured as Japan's greatest poet, and as the hectic existence of the towns began to pall, many followed Basho in seeking meditative repose in nature. Shortly before his death, Basho composed his last haiku:

On a journey, ill
and my dreams o'er withered fields
are wandering still.

Tokugawa culture developed in seclusion. Iemitsu had forbidden the handful of Dutch traders penned in on the island of De-shima to import books, and Japanese interpreters were only allowed to discuss with them the commonplaces of trade. In time, however, such intellectual isolation proved unsustainable. The eighth Tokugawa shogun, Yoshimune, had scientific leanings, and he was aware that in earlier centuries much learning had come from abroad. In 1744, he reversed his predecessor's ruling. Japanese scholars were sent to learn Dutch, and Western books were permitted so long as they made no mention of Christianity.

Through this narrow crack in the wall of isolation, Western influences began to trickle into Japan. Daimyo collected clocks and field glasses and drank out of glass goblets. Japanese artists experimented with Western oil-painting techniques, while individuals of a more scientific bent studied Western medicine, experimented with asbestos and electricity, peered at the heavens through telescopes and discussed European advances in the fields of agriculture and botany. Even the shogun's

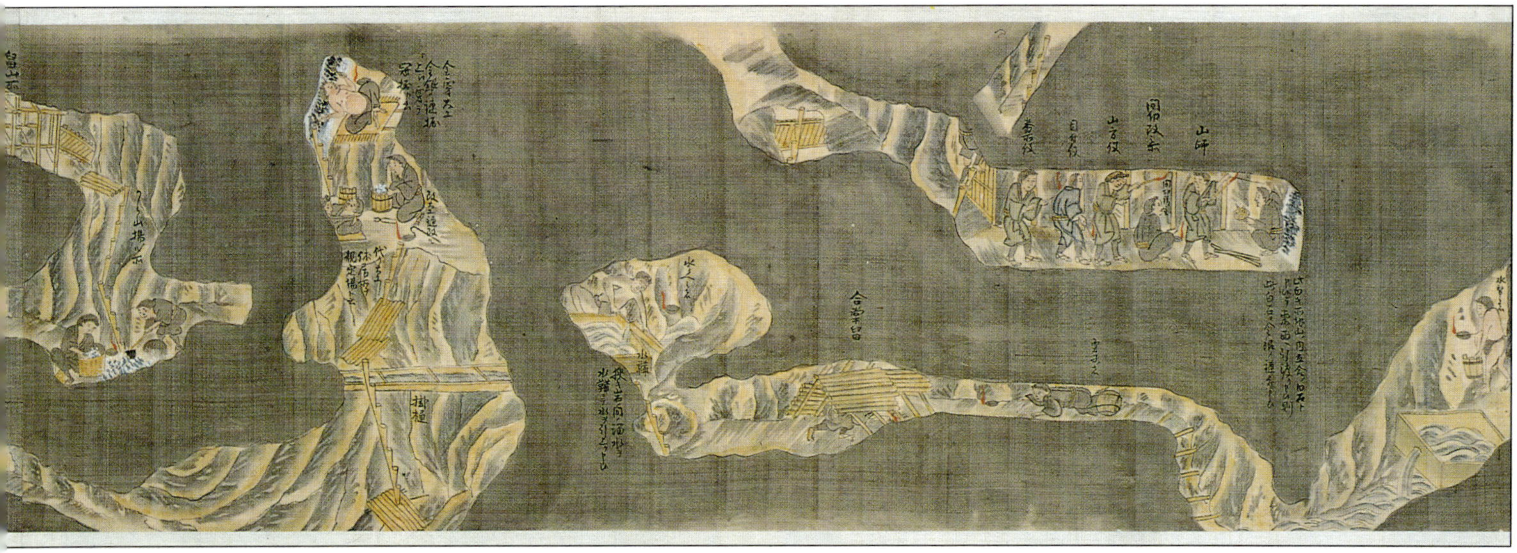

Shown in an 18th-century copy of an earlier scroll, Japanese miners toil underground to win the precious metals of the mines on Sado Island, off northern Honshu. While some miners work on the rock face, others repair scaffolding supporting the tunnel and remove underground water by means of buckets and a pulley. To the right, officials inspect a newly excavated shaft; on the left, porters carry the mined rock back to the pit entrance. Also shown is a circular device *(centre)* that served as a rotary ventilator to freshen air made smoky by the oil lamps that many of the miners carry. The ores of Sado were a valuable asset for the shoguns; the gold, silver and copper that they produced were the nation's main export.

palace was embellished with imported meteorological equipment. His subjects balked, however, when Yoshimune ambitiously proposed replacing the traditional Chinese calendar with the Gregorian version.

Such interests were limited to a tiny minority of the population. Still, the seeds of doubt were being sown, and by the turn of the 19th century educated Japanese were growing uneasily conscious of the threat posed by more advanced nations overseas. In 1807, Russian raiders attacked the northern islands of Sakhalin and Yezo (later named Hokkaido). The following year, a British warship sailed into Nagasaki and threatened to bombard the port unless the governor gave it supplies.

During the decades that followed, such incursions were repeated with alarming frequency. The shoguns found themselves struggling against forces they could not control, and the passing of sumptuary laws intended to promote frugality – the banning of barbers, the arrest of prostitutes, the prohibition of gambling – did little to invigorate an economy that was rapidly deteriorating. Crop failures and famines sent prices soaring, creating growing unrest amongst the peasantry. Attempts by the shogunate to curb the rampant inflation by debasing the coinage merely incurred the enmity of the samurai. And increasingly, local daimyo broke away from the tottering central government and took charge of their own affairs.

The long Tokugawa peace was thus already failing when, in 1853, Commodore Matthew Perry of the U.S. Navy put the final nail into the coffin of Japanese isolation by sailing with four gunboats into Edo harbour and, despite Japanese protests, demanding that his country be given trading rights. The shogun had neither the military nor economic strength to resist. Assailed by foreigners from without and attacked by contemptuous daimyo within, the shogunate limped on for another 15 years. Then, in January 1868, the bubble burst. A group of rebel lords from the western provinces announced that thenceforth the country would be ruled by the emperor. The discredited Tokugawa government disintegrated almost without a struggle. For two centuries Japan had lagged behind the Western powers. Now, in the name of their emperor, Japan's samurai prepared to rectify the situation.

CHINA'S MANCHU OVERLORDS

2

The Kangxi emperor of China was in a rather satirical mood. When Monsignor Mezzabarba, legate from Pope Clement XI, appeared before his throne towards the end of his long reign, which spanned the years from 1662 to 1722, the Emperor held up three different pieces of cloth that lay on a table before him. "If anyone should maintain that this red stuff is white, and that the white is yellow, what would you think of it?" he asked. Mezzabarba understood with perfect clarity that his host was mocking the way in which successive popes had contradicted themselves in edicts regarding religious worship in China. He attempted to explain to the Emperor the infallible nature of papal authority, but Kangxi would have none of it. "Is it possible," he abruptly demanded of the Monsignor, "that the Pope can judge of the nature of the rites of China, which he has never seen, or had any personal knowledge of, any more than I can judge of the affairs of the Europeans, who are unknown to me?" With this confident challenge Kangxi dismissed his suitor. He was beginning to lose patience with Europeans who lectured him. "How can they presume to talk about 'the great principles of China'," he wrote. "After all, they know only a fraction of what I know."

Kangxi had every reason to be self-assured. He presided over the largest and wealthiest empire on earth, a fact that even the most culturally confident European visitors were forced to acknowledge. From the forests of Manchuria to the jungles of Southeast Asia, bounded on the west by Tibet and the plains of central Asia and on the east by the South and East China seas, this vast country was at peace both with the European powers and with its immediate neighbours. Nowhere else on earth did so many people enjoy the benefits of such a prosperous life. One hundred and fifty million or more subjects of the Celestial Empire, as the Chinese called their country, were experiencing an economic and cultural renaissance that would have seemed inconceivable just 50 years earlier.

Yet the Emperor who had helped to create this peace — the man venerated as the Son of Heaven — was not even Chinese. He was a Manchu, whose grandparents had lived in the wild lands situated to the north of the Great Wall. This "barbarian" people had poured into China in the mid-17th century, replacing the corrupt and moribund Ming dynasty with their own Qing administration. How the Manchus managed to establish their authority, cope with the ever increasing attentions of the Western powers and revitalize China's ancient civilization is one of the most remarkable stories of the 17th century.

China was an old and enfeebled state when the Manchus swept down from the north towards the imperial capital of Beijing in 1644. The Ming dynasty, which had assumed power nearly three centuries earlier in the wake of a hundred years of Mongol occupation, had grown increasingly inward-looking over generations of

Dignitaries of the city of Suzhou in eastern China crowd the banks of the Grand Canal to welcome the Kangxi emperor in 1698. This detail from a contemporary scroll painted on silk shows an honour guard dressed in imperial yellow uniforms lining up before an elaborate altar; a groom waits with the Emperor's white horse. Kangxi was the greatest ruler of the Manchu Qing dynasty, which replaced the decadent Ming regime in 1644.

timid, inefficient rule. Ming officials relied upon agriculture for national revenue, generally mistrusting the motives of merchants who might subvert the state with foreign ideas. By the dawn of the 16th century, isolationist policies had brought to an end the wide-ranging expeditions in mighty, ocean-going ships that had marked the early, more confident years of Ming rule. As the once proud Chinese fleet dwindled to a collection of coastal junks, maritime trade was increasingly left to foreigners, while the Turks and Mongols continued to dominate commerce across the landmass of central Asia.

Despite the dead hand of official policy, the industrious Chinese people invested the Ming economy with a surprising vitality. Fresh land was continually being brought into agricultural production, while the planting of faster-growing strains of rice allowed farmers to harvest two crops in a season. In some regions that were particularly favoured agriculture was shifting from subsistence farming to the production of cash crops such as tea, cotton, citrus fruits, and mulberry trees for the silk industry. Fish ponds supplied the hungry cities, while some pioneering farmers even experimented successfully with newly introduced crops from the Americas, including peanuts, maize and sweet potatoes.

Industry, too, progressed and made steady advances, although it received little encouragement from the central government. Chinese silks, cottons and particularly ceramics were items which were all highly prized in Europe. It was not until

The Manchu people came from a small homeland to the north of Korea, in the region later called Manchuria. They took advantage of Ming weakness to burst through the Willow Palisade, a defensive line separating China from the "barbarian" lands to the north. Using mounted bowmen *(above)* as their main strike force, they took advantage of civil war within the country to enter Beijing in 1644. Once in power, they quickly asserted control over the whole nation, and then set about pushing back its frontiers. By the century's end they had incorporated Outer Mongolia and lands north of the River Amur. Korea had been a vassal of China since early in the century; and after 1683 even Taiwan, which had never previously been part of imperial China, fell into their hands.

the early years of the 18th century that Europeans learnt the secret art of manufacturing porcelain, and even then authentic Chinese ceramics remained the envy of collectors throughout the world.

In one essential industry, the Ming authorities reluctantly enlisted Western aid. Although the Chinese were excellent metallurgists in their own right – more knowledgeable in some respects than the best smiths of Europe – they admitted Western superiority in the manufacture of firearms. Undoubtedly the most advanced cannon and handguns were either imported from Europe or made under the supervision of Western experts. The Ming had, in fact, been purchasing European matchlock muskets and light artillery from the Portuguese in Macao since the 16th century, as well as encouraging the manufacture of Chinese copies. As the threat of rebellion and frontier warfare grew and became even more menacing during the 17th century, the Ming government relaxed its deep-seated suspicion of Western barbarians and sought assistance in the manufacture of weapons from an apparently unlikely source – Jesuit missionaries.

The Jesuits had been accepted at the imperial court in Beijing since the beginning of the 17th century. Although they had come to China with the prime purpose of winning converts to Christianity, Chinese intellectuals were less interested in their faith than in the news that they brought with them of Europe's recent scientific and technological discoveries. These highly educated clerics were natural diplomats, who quickly realized that Catholicism was unlikely to win the hearts of the people unless the emperor himself blessed their work with his approval.

As a consequence of their insight, the Jesuits adapted totally to Chinese society, learning the language and assuming Chinese dress. On June 21, 1629, a Jesuit astronomer astonished his hosts by successfully predicting a solar eclipse. This apparent prophetic magic led to the employment of Jesuits at the Imperial Board of Astronomy, where they were to remain for nearly two centuries. When embattled Ming officials found that they needed more fire power to fight off the growing menace of the Manchus, they naturally invited the holy fathers to supervise the casting of heavy artillery.

But guns alone could not preserve the failing dynasty. As cash crops turned farming into a lucrative business, land had become concentrated in the hands of wealthy landlords. Powerful local landowners could defy government tax collectors, while an increasing tax burden fell upon the smaller peasant farmers. The result was a wave of peasant uprisings in almost every province of China. Some of these blazed into full-scale regional rebellions; others sputtered into banditry, the plague of life in provincial China in the early 17th century.

Quick to exploit the opportunity for easy plunder, China's neighbours harassed her from all sides. Japanese pirates ravaged the coast. Massive Japanese armies invaded the Ming vassal kingdom of Korea, involving the Ming in years of costly warfare. To the northwest, the Mongol nations began a disturbing revival, while beyond them a further threat was developing: Cossack adventurers were spearheading an expansion that would extend the boundaries of Russia eastwards to the Pacific Ocean by the middle of the century. Meanwhile along China's northeastern frontier the newly established Manchu state steadily and efficiently developed its military and political organization.

Despite having the advantages of superior technology and vast manpower, the Ming government was slow to defend itself against these challenges. Decades of extravagance and neglect of the economy had left the Chinese state unable to pay for an adequate army. Private militias supplemented the undermanned national force, half-heartedly defending the realm in campaigns that often threatened to degenerate into banditry and rebellion.

Natural disasters added to the catalogue of China's woes. A series of bad harvests during the 1620s led to devastating famines in the impoverished northwest region. Plagues accounted for the lives of millions of people between the years 1639 and 1644, further weakening the Ming armies.

At the heart of this smitten empire was the dissolute and self-absorbed court at Beijing, whose emperors had virtually abdicated from all political responsibility; after 1582 they even refused to conduct court business or meet with government ministers. Power consequently fell into the hands of eunuchs. A prominent feature of Chinese court life for more than two millennia, these household servants had frequently seen their influence on affairs of state wax as the imperial fortunes waned. Now, with their private armies, secret police and factional rivalries, they terrorized the Chinese administration and people alike.

Court life reached a nadir between the years 1620 and 1627 during the reign of the Tianqi emperor, an illiterate who withdrew entirely from the political sphere in order to devote his life to carpentry. In his absence the state was effectively ruled by the Emperor's former nursemaid Mistress Ke and a cruel and self-seeking eunuch by the name of Wei Zhongxian. Wei's great influence and untrammelled delight in torture and murder silenced the majority of his critics. One brave court officer, however, presented the uncaring emperor with a list of Wei's "twenty-four great crimes". "Can your majesty employ as your right-hand man a creature whose flesh the whole empire desires to eat?" the anguished official demanded. He received an unambiguous reply two years later when he was savagely tortured on Wei's commands and left to die in prison.

On the death of Tianqi, his 17-year-old brother assumed the imperial throne, taking the reign title of Chongzhen. This young man attempted to restore some degree of integrity to Ming politics. The eunuch Wei found an easy escape for himself in suicide. However, his companion in misrule, Mistress Ke, suffered death by slicing, a prolonged form of torture in which the victim was slashed with sharp knives and each wound was quickly cauterized with a hot iron to prevent too painless a death through loss of blood. But such purges and reforms were by now too late. Internal rebellion was soon to tear the state asunder, while an enemy at the gate had grown too powerful to be denied.

During the steady collapse of the Ming regime, the Manchu nation rapidly increased in power, as if feeding off its effete southern neighbour. This energetic people lived in the mountains north of Korea in the region that was subsequently named Manchuria after them. They were one of three Tungusic tribal groups collectively called Jurchen, distantly related in language to the Mongols and Turks to their west. In the 12th century the Jurchen had burst into history by conquering much of northern China, where they established their Jin or "Golden" dynasty before falling prey to Chingis Khan's Mongols. The Jurchen subsequently withdrew to their homeland in the north, but their brief ascendancy over China remained a proud and inspiring memory for them.

Under the centuries of Mongol and then Ming suzerainty, the people of Manchuria remained generally at peace with their overlords. Chinese officials used the age-old policy of "divide and rule" to dominate the tribes, while Chinese settlers were confined within the Willow Palisade, a largely symbolic frontier defence around southwestern Manchuria. Nevertheless, some Chinese did move beyond the Willow Palisade, offering their expertise to tribal rulers and playing a major role in the establishment of a local arms industry.

The Manchu – the branch of the Jurchen people who lived closest to the Chinese frontier – set about unifying Manchuria towards the end of the 16th century under the rule of a vigorous leader called Nurhaci. They seized Chinese territory within the Willow Palisade, setting up a new capital in 1625 at Shenyang, which they subsequently renamed Mukden.

From this new capital Nurhaci, having already thrown off nominal Ming suzerainty, declared the creation of a new Jin state, recalling the "Golden" empire that had existed five centuries earlier. He built up an efficient government that was organized along partly Chinese and partly nomadic lines, and he ensured strong economic foundations for the state by monopolizing the pearl, fur and ginseng trades. In addition, Nurhaci simplified the complex Mongolian script previously used by the Jurchen. And most importantly of all, he replaced the existing tribal

Decorated with gems, pearls and kingfisher feathers on a base of gold, a crown made for one of the two queens of the Wanli emperor, who ruled China from 1573 to 1620, suggests the extravagance of the later years of Ming rule. At a time when the empire was committed to major military campaigns in Korea against Japanese invaders, the treasury was further burdened by massive expenditure on the repair of royal palaces and the upkeep of a court entourage that by now included 70,000 eunuchs and 9,000 women attendants, as well as on lavish spectacles celebrating such occasions as the investiture of imperial princes.

military organization with the famous banner system, which provided him and his successors with one of the most formidable armies in Asia.

At first the banner organization was quite simple: Nurhaci's troops were divided into four companies each with its own colours – yellow, white, blue or red. In fewer than fifteen years the number of companies expanded to 200, forming eight larger "banners", their flags now fringed with red or white. Eventually each of the banners in Nurhaci's army included 7,500 men in five regiments, each comprising five companies. As the Manchu state expanded, Chinese and Mongol divisions would be added to the ranks. Leadership of the banners was, and remained, largely hereditary, although officer ranks in later years had to be confirmed by the Manchu government. Most troops were tribesmen, but captives, slaves and serfs all came to be enlisted in the ranks of one or another of the banners for administrative purposes.

These early banner armies did not receive any payment for their services; the troops were expected to support themselves from the revenues of their own lands or else with loot, as the old Mongol hordes had done. In their fighting style, however, they preferred to use Chinese as opposed to Mongol tactics, relying heavily upon foot soldiers. Their vanguard consisted of armoured infantry, the first rank being armed with pikes, the second with swords and the third with bows. A much smaller cavalry force remained in the rear, ready to support the infantry and deliver a decisive blow if the need or the opportunity arose.

Such military tactics left the Manchus extremely vulnerable to firearms, of which Ming Chinese garrisons had an increasing number. In 1626, the

The Jesuit Presence

China seemed to be promising territory to Christian missionaries in 1600. Challenged by no single dominant faith like Islam in the Middle East, proselytizers nurtured a dream of Christianizing the entire country through the conversion of its ruler. With that hope in mind, the Italian Jesuit, Matteo Ricci, travelled to China in 1582 and set about studying Chinese culture. His example was followed by other members of his order, men of great learning who made themselves welcome at the Chinese court, where they won many souls to the faith.

Towards the end of the century, however, Dominican friars arrived in China. They found Jesuit toleration of Chinese traditions, such as the discharge of firecrackers during Mass, deeply shocking. They appealed to the Pope, who condemned the practices, thereby alienating the Kangxi emperor, who subsequently expelled most of the missionaries, Jesuits and Dominicans alike.

Made of ivory, this pocket sundial was the work of Adam Schall, a German Jesuit who became head of the Imperial Board of Astronomy under the first Manchu emperor. In addition, the device incorporates a compass.

This portrait of a Jesuit missionary in China is thought to be of Matteo Ricci, who spent his last 30 years in China trying to provide a link between Chinese and European culture. The book in his hand bears the title *Holy Teaching of the Heavenly Ruler* – the Chinese term for Catholicism.

Manchus suffered a notable reverse against Ming artillery at the Battle of Ningyuan; Nurhaci himself died of wounds that he received in the encounter. But within the space of a few years the Manchus had firearms of their own – Russian guns presented as tribute by Mongol tribes. The still-primitive matchlock musket was less accurate and had a far slower shooting rate than the bow, but competent archers took years to train while the guns required no great skill of the user.

Even before establishing the Manchu capital at Mukden, Nurhaci had forced the eastern Mongols into submission. His son and successor Abahai brought more Mongol tribes into the expanding Manchu realm, and also extended his authority northwards into the River Amur valley, which today forms the frontier between China and the Soviet Union. Meanwhile, the steady decline of the Ming dynasty's power in China turned Manchu attention southwards once again. China, even in its state of decadence, was so much vaster than the Manchu homeland that its conquest could only be contemplated if the invaders could count on substantial Chinese support. In this respect the name of Jin that Nurhaci had given to his state was counterproductive, for it carried bitter memories of defeat and foreign domination for the Chinese. So Abahai coined the new name of Qing or "pure" for his dynasty, which had wholly different associations.

Two pictures of the Annunciation – the announcement of her divine mission to the Virgin Mary – show how the Jesuits adapted European material for a Chinese audience. The original engraving *(far left)* by Hieronymus Wierx was published in Antwerp in 1595. The copy *(left)*, made by a local artist for a Chinese edition of *The Life of the Lord in Pictures* by the Jesuit missionary Giulio Aleni, uses an identical composition, but the style has been changed to suit Chinese tastes.

Despite experiencing occasional setbacks, Abahai continued to wear away the northern defences of Ming China. In 1629, a Manchu army managed to reach the gates of the city of Beijing before withdrawing north of the Great Wall. Success bred success, and an increasing number of Chinese administrators, soldiers and craftsmen came to serve the new Qing state which, since it was organized along acceptably Confucian lines stressing the importance of education and public service, offered them rich rewards and even high office. In fact the Manchu state was in the process of becoming more and more Chinese all the time; Abahai even set up six government ministries, mimicking the Ming administrative system. In this manner the foundations were laid for the cooperation between Manchu and Chinese that was to govern China for more than two and a half centuries.

An illustration from a Manchu chronicle depicts mounted bowmen overrunning a Ming camp in 1619, one year after Nurhaci, the first great leader of the Manchus, had invaded China. Several of the fleeing defenders carry firearms, while abandoned cannon litter the ground behind them. Although they were initially dismissive of guns, the Manchus soon came to realize the value of the weapons, and after their conquest of China they proceeded to build up the musketry contingents in the imperial armies.

It was not, in the end, the Manchu state that delivered the fatal blow to the tottering Ming regime. By the early 1640s a series of powerful uprisings were tearing the country apart. In central China a one-eyed rebel by the name of Li Zicheng attracted a huge army of disillusioned peasants, the victims of famine and poverty. Ruthless and ambitious, Li firmly believed that the "mandate of heaven", which alone entitled an emperor to rule, was destined to descend upon him, and he suffered nothing at all to stand in his way. When the city of Kaifeng resisted a siege that he had mounted, he proceeded to cut the banks of the Yellow River, drowning hundreds of thousands of innocent civilians – together with a great number of his own followers – in the resulting flood.

The road leading to Beijing lay open to Li Zicheng's army by the spring of 1644. The imperial city itself was defended by an inadequate army of eunuchs, which quickly melted away in the face of the rebel horde. Informed of the fact that the insurgents were actually within the walls of his capital, the Emperor muddled his senses with wine. Dressing his sons in rags so that they would escape recognition, he ordered them to flee from the palace. Having done this, he summoned the ladies of the court to his presence. "All is over. It is time for you to die," he announced. He felled his senior concubine, killing her with a single blow from his sword. Trying similarly to dispatch his 15-year-old daughter, the Princess Imperial, he succeeded only in chopping off her arm. Then, dressed in his ceremonial robes and attended by a loyal eunuch, the Emperor wandered out into the palace grounds. The bodies of Emperor and eunuch were subsequently discovered hanging from a rafter in a grand pavilion known as the Imperial Hat and Girdle Department. A despairing farewell note was found pinned to the Emperor's robe. "I die unable to face my ancestors," it concluded.

"May the bandits dismember my corpse and slaughter my officials, but let them not despoil the imperial tombs nor harm a single one of our people."

This last imperial command was signally ignored by Li's army of rebels. The people of Beijing had eagerly poured out of their houses and thronged the streets on their arrival. "Long live the new emperor," proclaimed the posters that were strung the length of the route. But the warm welcome rapidly turned to terror as the undisciplined army embarked upon a wholesale orgy of looting and murder. "Hands were amputated, legs severed, stomachs ripped open, ears sliced off, hair cut away . . . No one dared oppose them," wrote an anonymous survivor.

It was now that the Manchus finally descended upon Beijing. Their soldiers met with no resistance this time, for Wu Sangui, the Chinese general who had previously barred their way, took the decision to join forces with these disciplined foreigners rather than allow Li's murderous army to preside over the capital. In the face of this irresistible alliance the rebels fled, and the Manchu conquerors proclaimed their Qing dynasty as the rightful successor to the Ming. Abahai had died the year before. His five-year-old son became the first Qing emperor, in the Chinese manner taking the name of Shunzhi, "Obedience and Good Order Established", for his reign title; the boy's uncle, Dorgon, was the principal regent.

The most pressing task for China's new rulers was to assert control over the vast land that had fallen so effortlessly into their hands. "If there are those who disobediently resist us," proclaimed the regent Dorgon in his very first edict, "then the stones themselves will be set ablaze and all will be massacred." This was no idle threat; when Yangzhou, a walled city near the River Yangtze, attempted to offer resistance, thousands of men, women and children, in the words of one survivor, "went to their graves like beds".

The Ming resistance in fact presented little serious threat to the Manchu armies. During the course of the next 10 years a succession of Ming claimants to the imperial throne made continued attempts to rally loyalists to their cause, but their courts retreated steadily into the southwest, where the last serious pretender to the throne met his death by execution in 1662.

An altogether more formidable challenge to the new dynasty presented itself in the form of a half-Japanese nobleman by the name of Zheng Chenggong, known to Westerners at the time by the name of Coxinga. Steadfastly refusing to recognize Manchu authority in spite of the offer of generous peace terms, Coxinga amassed an army consisting of more than 100,000 men and dominated the coast of central and southern China with his large, swift fleet. (So enraged was the Shunzhi emperor by Coxinga's continued successes that he is said to have hacked a throne to pieces with his sword in sheer frustration.)

Like a great number of heroes who have since passed into folklore, Coxinga was finally betrayed by a human weakness. In 1659 his army seemed on the point of capturing Nanjing, the largest city of the empire. Flushed with the prospect of a tremendous victory, Coxinga and his soldiers lavishly celebrated his birthday, staying up for the entire night. The morning after

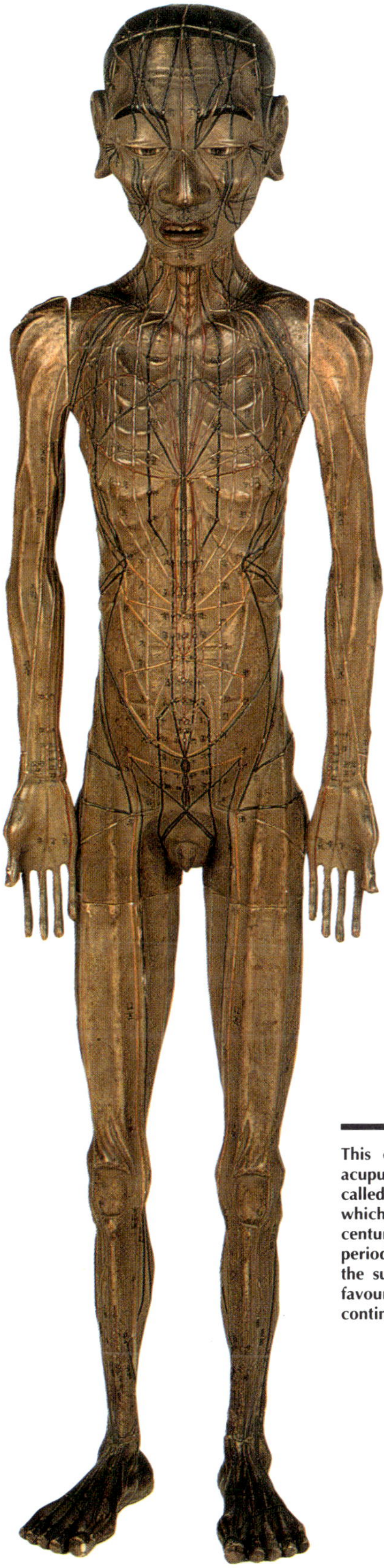

This carved 17th-century figurine shows the main acupuncture points along with the imaginary lines, called meridians, that link them. Acupuncture, which had been used in China since at least the third century BC, was widely practised in the late Ming period, when two of the most celebrated books on the subject were written. It subsequently fell out of favour, and in 1822 was officially banned, though it continued to be practised surreptitiously.

"so inappropriate a ceremony" – as a censorious Dominican friar put it – "his troops were careless with sleep and wine". Set upon by the enemy at this unhappy moment, the rebel army fell back to the sea in confusion.

Even after suffering this demoralizing defeat, Coxinga continued his defiant rebellion from the offshore islands of Xiamen and Jinmen. Attempts to starve him into submission by evacuating a long coastal strip of mainland China caused a great deal of suffering for thousands of dispossessed Chinese civilians; "Along the coast we have nothing but ruined cities and villages," lamented one Chinese official, commenting on the situation. Two years after their defeat at Nanjing, Coxinga's army succeeded in overwhelming a small Dutch garrison on the island of Taiwan and established a permanent base there.

Coxinga himself died the following year, and leadership of his forces passed to his son. As tensions gradually eased, mainland inhabitants slowly began to trickle back to their former homes along the coast, but the rebels continued to pose a lingering threat to the Manchu dynasty for another 20 years. It took a Qing invasion of Taiwan in 1683 finally to put an end to resistance and incorporate the island – for the first time – into the Chinese state.

In asserting their rule over China, the Manchus were greatly assisted by the wide cultural and social gulf that separated the gentry from the peasants, thereby making it difficult for the two to join together in resistance. Imbued as they were with the Confucian principle of reverence for authority, a majority of the existing elite found that it was easier to transfer allegiance to their new rulers, particularly as the Manchus made considerable efforts to respect China's ancient codes of justice. Ming officials were welcomed back into the administration and were even allowed to retain their distinctive costumes. One new regulation did, however, cause widespread resentment. From the outset the Manchus insisted that all officials shave their foreheads and pull back their hair into Manchu pigtails. This humiliating symbol of their subservience to a foreign culture never ceased to rankle with Chinese nationalists. In fact, the removal of such pigtails became a symbol of revolt against Manchu rule.

In the Manchu efforts to ease the transition from the Ming dynasty to the Qing, the Shunzhi emperor played an extremely important role. This scholarly young man mastered classical Chinese, actively encouraged Confucian scholarship, and attempted to stamp out corruption wherever he found it. As a boy he was fortunate enough to fall under the influence of Adam Schall, a German Jesuit who had been appointed head of the Imperial Board of Astronomy with the title "Master Who Searches Out Celestial Secrets". Schall was both spiritual and political adviser to the Emperor, who called him *mafa* or grandpa. "Father Schall exercises an influence with the Emperor possessed by neither viceroy nor prince," commented a Jesuit colleague. Despite his strong influence, however, Father Schall was unable to persuade his young protégé to accept Christianity. Shunzhi became increasingly attracted to Buddhism, and by the time of his death from smallpox at the age of 22 he was a devout follower of the Zen sect.

Shunzhi was succeeded by his third son, a boy of seven at the time of his father's death. This child was designated heir to the imperial throne partly because he had survived an attack of smallpox and so had acquired immunity to the disease that had killed his father. Shunzhi himself had scarcely met the boy – like all imperial children he had been brought up by nurses and eunuchs – but the choice proved

The Kangxi emperor sits cross-legged to read in this portrait on silk by an unknown artist, possibly a Jesuit missionary. Kangxi was one of the most successful of all Chinese rulers. For the duration of his 60-year reign he not only brought stability and prosperity to his realm, but also worked long hours, took firm personal control of government and avoided the corruption that had marred the later Ming period. Despite his heavy workload he retained a lifelong devotion to learning, and even when he was ill from overwork did not stop reading books.

to be an inspired one. The child possessed prodigious curiosity, energy and intellect, absorbing Confucian classics and dynastic history as avidly as he practised riding and archery. Assuming the reign title of Kangxi, he was destined to rule for over 60 years and become one of the greatest figures of the 17th century.

Because the new emperor was too young to assume power in person, another regency ensued. Under the harsh domination of Oboi, who was a leading Manchu nobleman of the time, the fair and conciliatory pro-Chinese policies of Shunzhi were abruptly overturned. In a series of stringent measures, Chinese officials were forbidden to criticize the government; those suspected of anti-Manchu sentiments were arrested and tortured. Oboi's influence would have lasted much longer had these high-handed policies not been offensive to Kangxi, who formally assumed power in 1667 at the tender age of 13. Two years later, finding himself unable to control his former regent, Kangxi arranged for his death. The circumstances are obscure, but according to one picturesque account, Oboi was seized and killed by a group of boys who were playing hide-and-seek in the palace courtyard. They were, in fact, youths who had been trained in the martial arts, acting under orders from their emperor.

This audacious coup marked the effective beginning of Kangxi's long and autocratic reign, in the course of which China reached a pinnacle of power, prosperity and cultural achievement. An able military leader, a careful administrator and an enthusiastic scholar, Kangxi set out a list of 16 moral principles which became known as the *Sacred Edicts*. These ranged from calls for filial piety and brotherly love, to exhortations for citizens to cooperate in the protection of property. The Emperor himself strove to follow these guidelines throughout his own life, as far as was possible for the ruler of a great empire. He cultivated China's own intellectual class and controlled trade with the outside world to China's advantage. Under Kangxi's leadership, Manchu rule was not only legitimized in China but was consolidated across the entire country, while his conquest of Mongolia began the process of Manchu expansion across what is now the Chinese People's Republic and beyond.

Kangxi adopted a demanding and rigorous daily routine. He rose before dawn to give himself time to study the Confucian classics. Imperial audiences began as early as five o'clock, although officials who lived some distance from the palace were permitted to attend a little later. Kangxi then discussed government issues with directors of the main boards and departments, next receiving the high government officials known as Grand Secretaries to discuss other problems. "It is the constant attention to detail that is of the greatest importance," he once wrote. Towards the end of the morning, officers of the imperial household, provincial officials and finally foreign ambassadors were received. In the afternoon the Emperor read reports from lesser officials who, because of their rank, were not permitted a personal audience. What little time remained was devoted to his own studies, family matters, writing poems or practising calligraphy. Tutored by Jesuit missionaries, the Emperor extended his interests beyond traditional Chinese scholarship to encompass European science, mathematics, cartography, medicine and chiming clocks, which had a particular fascination for him. He studied Euclid's geometry and learnt to play simple tunes on the harpsichord. "There is not a science of Europe that ever came to his knowledge, but he showed an inclination to be instructed in it," wrote one admiring Jesuit. Not surprisingly, it was said that Kangxi rarely got to bed before midnight.

Throughout the early years of his reign, Kangxi had to fight hard to secure his huge empire under Qing rule. The first major campaign he conducted was a bitter civil war that lasted for nearly 10 years. In the south and west of the country three powerful Chinese generals – one of whom was the same Wu Sangui who had assisted the Manchus in taking Beijing – presided over provinces that they had transformed into virtually independent states. Their original task had been to help the Manchus crush Ming resistance, but by 1674 that job was virtually completed. Not surprisingly, however, the Three Feudatories, as they were referred to, resented the Emperor's attempts to bring the provinces back under firm imperial control. When Kangxi moved against one of the generals, who was entrenched in Guangdong in the deep south, all three rose in revolt, their numbers reinforced by an army dispatched from Taiwan under the son of Coxinga. This powerful rebellion very nearly succeeded in driving the Manchus out of the country, but with the assistance of loyal Chinese generals Kangxi eventually prevailed in 1681. Two years later he invaded Taiwan, successfully defeated Coxinga's grandson and thereby stamped out the last spark of civil war.

Another military problem faced Kangxi as soon as he had crushed the Three Feudatories and occupied Taiwan. This took the form of a growing Russian presence along the River Amur in northern Manchuria. The Manchu emperor obviously would be foolish to ignore a rival so close to the birthplace of the Manchu dynasty. For their part, the Cossacks were attracted to this relatively fertile area after their epic conquest of the harsh Siberian wastes. Beyond the Amur lay the Pacific Ocean and the lure of the Asian riches that were already bringing great wealth to various European naval powers.

At the heart of the Manchu-Russian confrontation was the fortress of Albazin, erected by Cossacks on the northernmost bend of the River Amur in the year 1655. The very existence of the fortress was a provocation, but in addition Cossack atrocities led the local tribes to demand help from their Manchu overlords. Fighting flared on and off until, after 1680, Kangxi set about the systematic consolidation of Manchu control throughout the Amur region.

He established a system of postal communications along roads and rivers from the south, and set up bases, granaries, river fleets and military colonies. Kangxi's armies proved themselves well able to deal with European troops, destroying Russian positions and Cossack colonies until, by 1686, only the fortress of Albazin itself remained in enemy hands. Now at last negotiations began. A fleet of 90 ships sailed up the Amur in order to strengthen the Manchu's bargaining position. In 1689 the two sides signed the Treaty of Nerchinsk – the first formal agreement that existed between China and a European power. Both sides made concessions. China held on to the Amur valley and Russian expansion came to an end, but the newcomers maintained a base from which to trade with Beijing, a city which had in the past been loath to grant such privileges.

The army that achieved these successes was still based on the banner system, although this had changed somewhat since the Manchu conquest of China. Bannermen, who received government pensions and land grants, now included Mongols and Chinese, but these outsiders were paid less than Manchus. Banner companies were now of three types. Most bannermen came from the "external companies" based in a cordon around Beijing. Next came the garrison companies stationed in various Chinese or Manchurian cities, near the borders or along strategic roads. Somewhat separate from the main garrisons was the green banner army. This substantial but scattered force of largely Chinese constabulary was primarily concerned with the suppression of banditry.

Manchu mounted bowmen still formed the military elite, but the role of the infantry continued to grow and expand its scope. Most of the foot soldiers fought with a shield and short sword or with a long axe-like halberd. Archers and musketmen provided fire support, while a crack force of so-called "shield-bearers" served as an aggressive assault force.

Despite initial reservations, the Manchus were increasingly reliant upon firearms. Jesuit missionaries were persuaded to cast cannons in China, while additional artillery was purchased from the Portuguese and other European traders. Russian prisoners of war were enlisted to fire the new weapons, and eventually were incorporated into the banner system. In 1683 the Emperor ordered that every banner

In one of a series of paintings of "The Four Pleasures of Bo Juyi", the artist Chen Hongshou shows his subject, a celebrated ninth-century poet, in meditation. In choosing his theme, Chen may have been drawing a parallel with his own day, for both poet and painter lived in times of upheaval – Bo in the latter years of the Tang era, while Chen saw the collapse of the Ming. The change of dynasty severely disrupted intellectual life; many Ming scholars killed themselves rather than serve the new masters. Chen himself abandoned his government post to become a Buddhist monk, but remained torn between the inward-looking ideal of Buddhism and Confucian notions of public duty. His uncertainties were reflected in a series of pseudonyms he chose for himself, among them Huiseng (Repentant Monk) and Laochi (Old and Too Late).

in his army should include a musketry battalion, these apparently being formed of Chinese soldiers who had shown themselves to be poor horsemen.

The adoption of firearms did not mean the immediate abandonment of armour. In fact China's traditional body defences made of overlapping scales were probably as well able to resist 17th-century firearms as the plate armours of Europe. The protective scales were not always made out of metal. Lightweight but extremely resilient paper armour remained in use, those consisting of 10 to 15 sewn layers still being proof against all but musket balls.

In an effort to sustain their formidable fighting skills, the main combat banners regularly took part in enormous hunting expeditions. The soldiers on such exercises formed circles many kilometres in diameter which then gradually closed in around deer, bears, tigers and any other hapless game that was unable to escape. Hunts improved coordination among fighting units and in addition sharpened the bannerman's skill with a bow. In 1683, Kangxi led 100,000 horsemen and 60,000 infantry on one such excursion north of the Great Wall. He exulted in escaping the confines of Beijing. "It is when one is beyond the Great Wall that the air and soil refresh the spirit," he wrote.

An expert bowman who could shoot either right or left-handed, Kangxi boasted of having killed 135 tigers, 96 wolves and 132 wild boars "as well as hundreds of ordinary stags and deer". But he derived equal joy from the simple outdoor life, cooking stag's liver over an open fire or chatting informally to local herdsmen. Even when out in the wilds Kangxi found a means to exercise his nearly obsessive love of learning. "Many of the officials could not even recognize the basic 28 constellations," he complained after one trip.

For all his enthusiasm for scholarship and the hunt, Kangxi never neglected his duties to the empire. In the 1690s a tribe of Mongols under the leadership of a man called Galdan began stirring up trouble on the northwestern frontier, and at one point advanced to within 300 kilometres of the city of Beijing. The Emperor personally led his armies in pursuit of the invader, and he took enormous pride in the defeat of this elusive enemy – the last man to threaten Beijing for more than a century. When Galdan finally committed suicide in the year 1697 Kangxi was exultant. "My great task is done," he wrote to a eunuch. "In two years I made three journeys across deserts combed by wind and bathed with rain, eating every other day in the barren and uninhabitable deserts . . . The constant journeying and hardship have led to this achievement."

Victory in this war enabled the Manchus to establish a protectorate over the land that now forms present-day Outer Mongolia. Nevertheless Mongol-Manchu competition would surface again in the early years of the 18th century, when both sides struggled to dominate Tibet. Victory eventually went to the Manchus, and by the mid-18th century even the westernmost Mongols of Dzungaria and the Tianshan Mountains had lost their independence.

The civil administration of the Manchu empire was as complex, and as traditional, as its military organization. From the outset the Manchus paid particular attention to ensuring that the new dynasty was acceptable to their Chinese subjects. Accordingly, they chose the course of least resistance, taking over the existing Ming administration virtually intact. Having no long tradition of imperial rule themselves, the Manchus readily accepted Ming political institutions. The advantage of this smooth transition was that many Chinese transferred their allegiance from a Ming to a Qing emperor without question; the mandate of heaven had merely passed from one ruling family to another.

Although they were perfectly willing to adopt the Ming system of government, the Manchus – who represented only about two per cent of the entire population – were understandably afraid of losing their national identity. In an attempt to prevent total assimilation and to ensure their continued control over the state, they enshrined in law their separation from the Chinese. The Manchu elite was governed through a special department and had its own grades of social rank. Manchus were barred from both commerce and labour and in addition they were forbidden to marry ethnic Chinese. Chinese immigration into Manchuria, beyond an extended Willow Palisade, was still banned. The Manchu and Chinese languages were jointly used for official purposes.

In taking over much of the Ming administrative system wholesale, the Manchus also implemented several improvements of their own. They split up some of the provinces to the south of the Great Wall into smaller units, making a new total of 18 such regions within China. Although the system of local government remained virtually unchanged, the tax burden on the poor was considerably lightened and there was a widespread decline in the practice of serfdom. In 1681 the

An engraving of Chinese beggars *(above)* shows one man who has lit a small fire on his head to rouse sympathy and another beating himself with a stone, while a third wears a wooden collar; a group of street entertainers *(right)* includes a man suspended on a pole and another demonstrating performing rats. The pictures illustrate an account by the Dutch traveller Jan Nieuhof of a journey to China in the 1650s. Nieuhof was much struck by the beggars, whom he called "not only bold, but troublesome". He described how some beggars mutilated themselves "to stir up a commiseration in such as pass by", and reported an encounter with one man, naked but for a loincloth and armed with spears, who threatened to kill himself unless he was given money.

Kangxi emperor banned the practice of selling serfs along with land in at least one province; and his successor Yongzheng abolished all hereditary servile groups in 1727, thus effectively liberating the serfs.

Under the new dynasty the basic social unit remained the family, which itself formed part of a wider clan under an acknowledged clan head. Though rather weak in the north, the clan structure was a powerful social influence in southern China, where the state rarely interfered with an effective system of internal clan justice. The role of women also remained unchanged. Wives continued to be treated as subservient to their husbands. Girls of good family still had their feet bound in childhood to shape them into the "golden lily", which measured no more than seven centimetres from heel to toe. This practice confined a woman's movements, while supposedly enhancing her erotic appeal.

Although such ancient traditions continued to exert a powerful influence, Chinese life was changing, sometimes quite dramatically. The population was again growing and agriculture was expanding, to the benefit of the peasantry who comprised about 80 per cent of the population. The proportion of large landowners declined as the importance of moderately prosperous peasants – their interests protected by the state – increased.

Urban industries such as the manufacturing of textiles and ceramics overcame the disruption that had been experienced during the 1630s and 1640s to reach and even surpass their previous levels of production. By the end of the 17th century an expansion of the cloth, ceramics, salt production and mining industries was accompanied by increased capital input. The great wealth that was generated by these considerable economic changes encouraged a levelling tendency in China's hitherto very stratified society. It became increasingly difficult to judge a person's social class merely by observing his dress.

The Kangxi reign also witnessed a considerable expansion in China's overseas trade. The principal exports were channelled through Canton in the south, from

where tea, silk, fine cotton textiles, porcelain and lacquerware were shipped to Europe. Yet despite all this, the attitude of the Manchu government to commerce with foreigners remained somewhat equivocal. Merchants who journeyed from neighbouring countries such as Korea, Indo-China, Thailand and Burma were regarded merely as the bringers of tribute. Russian merchants were obliged to fulfil their business obligations under the guise of conducting political missions, even after the Treaty of Nerchinsk had theoretically opened the border for trade. Traders who arrived from western Europe were generally dismissed as barbarians – and reckless and uncultivated many of them undeniably were.

Amid the burgeoning economy, the ancient tradition of Chinese scholarship continued to flourish. A sophisticated upper class still cultivated formal gardens, collected antiques, wrote poetry, practised painting or calligraphy and patronized the theatre, as they had for centuries past. These scholar-gentlemen formed a pool of talent from which the government could recruit its administrative bureaucracy.

At the same time there emerged a trend towards what was called "practical scholarship", which emphasized the gathering of evidence from as wide a range of sources as possible, followed by the making and subsequent testing of new theories. These remarkably modern intellectual principles were generally applied to the study of language and literature rather than science or technology, but one exception was the work of the widely travelled scholar Gu Yanwu, who turned his attention to the practical problems of geography, frontier defence, agriculture and trade. This gradual shift away from traditional forms of scholarship took place at the same time that European learning was beginning to alter China's view of the world outside the Celestial Empire.

The Jesuits flourished under the new dynasty, adding greatly to the intellectual life of the Manchu court. They enjoyed their finest hour during the middle decades of Kangxi's long reign, playing the part of courtiers and enjoying positions of high rank in the Emperor's entourage. They performed the necessary Manchu rituals

A section from a scroll painted by the artist Wan Wei shows sights along China's Grand Canal including the popular tourist resort of Tiger Hill *(left)*, the village of Shantang *(centre)*, and a troupe of travelling players performing in a floating theatre *(right)*. The 20-metre-long work was commissioned to commemorate the Kangxi emperor's journey down the canal in 1698. Perhaps because of its official origins, there are no beggars to be seen, and all of the hundreds of figures that people it are in their best clothes. In other respects, though, it gives a startlingly vivid and realistic view of life in 17th-century China, down to such details as the three berobed central Asian merchants shown directly below, walking down a village street where stalls sell, among other goods, children's toys, baskets, teapots and miniature trees or shrubs.

without any trace of embarrassment, in the full knowledge that their position depended solely upon the Emperor's good favour. These included the ceremonial kowtow, in which a kneeling supplicant touched his forehead to the ground until the Emperor invited him to come forward.

Despite such seeming indignities, they were enthusiastic apologists for their adopted country. "China offers an enchanting picture of what the whole world might become, if the laws of that empire were to become the laws of all nations," wrote one enthusiastic missionary. They helped familiarize the West with Chinese ceramics, textiles and lacquerwork, all of which were to influence European baroque and rococo art. They also helped to draw Chinese civilization to the attention of the great thinkers and writers of Europe, including Spinoza, Voltaire, Goethe, Diderot and Adam Smith.

Although it was prepared to borrow much from Europe in return, China – unlike many other traditional civilizations when faced with the power of Western technology – did not find that its own heritage was obviously outmoded. In fact Chinese scholars generally regarded European achievements as representing a "new science", complementing but not superseding their own. They sought to learn from both traditions in a broad-ranging effort to achieve a universally valid system of scientific thought.

In the latter part of the Kangxi reign, however, the Jesuit influence was lessened by divisions within the Christian camp. Missionaries from other orders were increasingly critical of what they saw as Jesuit sycophancy towards the Emperor. Their complaints were sympathetically received in Rome, and the papacy's subsequent critical messages to the Chinese court led to a cooling in relations with the Emperor. The Pope's claim to universal spiritual jurisdiction, even over the Son of Heaven, further undermined the Christian cause.

For Kangxi was not used to disagreement. He ruled with absolute authority, paternal benevolence and unflagging energy. A man of action, he was intolerant of officials who thought physical involvement in the course of duty beneath their dignity. When a fire broke out in the Chinese quarter of Beijing, he was furious to observe Manchu officials standing by "with their hands folded in their sleeves". "We'd be better off with less talk of moral principles and more practice of them," he once wrote.

Among China's most important exports during the 17th and 18th centuries was porcelain made for the European market. As the two examples here show, these wares were often quite unlike the traditional Chinese ceramics, being shaped and decorated specifically to appeal to Western tastes. The plate on the left copies a French print of a *fête champêtre*, or outdoor entertainment, but surrounds the scene with typical Chinese landscapes; the pot on the right bears images of both Chinese and Western ships. Many millions of such pieces were shipped from Canton and, along with other examples of Chinese decorative art, had a profound influence on the European rococo style.

To observe the problems of his domains at first hand, Kangxi made several tours throughout China, inspecting public works, pardoning criminals, listening to grievances and sometimes reading the examination papers of aspiring state officials. According to one astonished Jesuit he permitted "even the meanest workman or peasant to approach his person", speaking to them "with so much affability and sweetness, as charms them to the heart". Perhaps as a result of these internal encounters, Kangxi learnt to identify dialects from 13 of the 18 provinces. Life on tour was not all business. On at least one occasion the Emperor demonstrated his Manchu skill at mounted archery, a common touch that would have been inconceivable to his Ming predecessors.

Kangxi was less successful in governing his family than in ruling the empire. Of his 20 sons who survived into adulthood, it was Yinreng, the second, upon whom the Emperor lavished all his attention and hope. This young man, however, repaid his father's devotion with extravagance and disobedience. Worse still, he became involved in the traffic of boys as homosexual companions. Kangxi was outraged. "He is dissolute, tyrannical, brutal, debauched – it's hard to even speak about it," he wrote. He dismissed Yinreng as his heir, later reinstating him only to dismiss him again. In growing paranoia, he executed several associates of the former heir apparent; at one point three of his own sons were under arrest. "I cannot overcome my anger and sorrow," he wrote at the height of the crisis. As a result of this domestic turmoil, the embittered emperor refused to designate a successor.

In 1717, fearing that he would soon die, Kangxi expressed the extent of his weariness and disillusionment in a document known as the *Valedictory Edict*, which he had read out to his sons and to leading officials. "I have prepared these notes to make my own record," he wrote "for fear that the country may not know the depth of my sorrow." Fifty-five years of rule had taken their toll on the Emperor: "Now that I have reached old age I cannot rest easy for a moment. Therefore I regard the whole country as a worn-out sandal, and all riches as mud and sand. If I can die without there being an outbreak of trouble, my desires will be fulfilled."

Five years later the Emperor indeed fell ill and died. The succession passed to his fourth son, who was at his bedside during his last days. Suspicion that Kangxi was murdered by his heir remains mere speculation.

The era of wealth and prosperity that had been established during the reign of Kangxi did not come to an abrupt end with his death. The Manchu empire continued to expand, reaching its maximum extent in about the year 1760. By then it included all of modern China and Mongolia, in addition to parts of Soviet central Asia, India and Pakistan. The later 18th century, however, saw the beginnings of a decline which, within the space of 50 years, had become an irreversible slide towards dissolution. The European powers, by then entering their colonial heyday, would quickly take advantage of China's internal weakness to win commercial advantage. In so doing, they set the stage for the end of imperial rule itself; on his abdication in 1912, the last of the Manchus was also to become the last emperor.

THE GREAT SHAH OF PERSIA

3

In the summer of 1628, unusual visitors arrived at Ashraf, the Shah of Persia's pleasure palace situated in thick forests three kilometres south of the Caspian Sea. The strangers were the first royal envoys to be sent to Persia from England; and before being granted an audience, they were left to kick their heels for four days, probably as a result of the Shah's habit of consulting astrologers over favourable days for receiving important guests.

One of the Britons, Sir Thomas Herbert, later wrote an account of their reception. He noted that "the palace is large and looks into very pleasant gardens, albeit the building itself be not very regular, but rather confusedly divides itself into four *mohols* or banqueting houses, which be gorgeously painted." When the visiting party was finally admitted, they proceeded down a long audience chamber where they passed between rows of functionaries sitting cross-legged against the walls and sidestepped pages who ran about with flagons of wine. At last they stood before the man they had come to meet – Shah Abbas, "beloved at home, famous abroad and a terror to his enemies".

Abbas – whom Herbert referred to oddly as "Potshaw", apparently an English rendering of the Persian *Pad-i-Shah*, or chief ruler – was probably the most powerful and effective Persian king to ascend the throne from the fall of the Sassanian dynasty in AD 642 up to the present day. He was the greatest monarch of the Safavid dynasty which, between 1499 and 1736, restored to the nation something of the lustre of its earlier glories. Confronted by enemies to east and west, he managed to restrain both: his armies held their own against the fearsome Ottomans of Turkey, and defeated the Uzbek tribesmen of the central Asian steppes. Meanwhile at home, Abbas encouraged a revival of commerce and the arts, and left as his memorial the splendid city of Isfahan.

It was in pursuit of foreign aid to support him in his various campaigns that the Shah, who at the time of Herbert's visit had no more than eight months left to live, had agreed to receive the emissaries from England. The envoys duly congratulated him on his recent victories against the Ottoman Turks, and the Shah received their congratulations genially. By now a number of his front teeth were missing, but he was still vigorous and he conducted negotiations with a mixture of bullying and teasing. After some solemn talk about the possible future prospects for Anglo-Persian trade, Abbas pulled Sir Dodmore Cotton, the head of the delegation, down to sit beside him, deriving considerable amusement as he did so from the English ambassador's inability to sit cross-legged in the oriental fashion. Abbas called for a bowl of wine and drank the health of Cotton's sovereign, King Charles I of England. At the mention of the royal name, Sir Dodmore immediately removed his hat as a mark of respect. Much struck by the gesture, the Shah

Backed by barren mountains, a ceramic-tiled dome crowns the sanctuary of Isfahan's Royal Mosque, built on the orders of Shah Abbas I, the greatest ruler of Persia's Safavid dynasty. When Abbas seized the throne in 1587, Isfahan was in decay. In 1598, however, the Shah decided to make it his capital and, urged on by a mixture of piety and dynastic pride, commissioned many new buildings. The splendour of the monuments he created gave substance to his subjects' boast that "Isfahan is half the world".

promptly removed his own turban in clownish imitation of this foreign ritual. Abbas was always fond of jokes, good wine and luxury.

His behaviour was a far cry from that of the founder of his dynasty, his great-grandfather Ismail. In 1494, at the tender age of seven, Ismail had inherited the guardianship of a holy shrine in Ardabil in northwest Persia, and with it the leadership of the Safavid order of Muslim mystics, whose holy place it was. He thereby also inherited the unquestioning loyalty of many of the Turkoman tribesmen who roamed across the pastures of eastern Turkey, northern Syria and western Persia. These doughty warriors were known as *qizilbash* – "redheads" – from the red hats they wore as a sign of their partisanship for the Safavid house.

The *qizilbash* regarded Ismail with more than the normal respect accorded by believers to their spiritual leader. The tribesmen were the most significant surviving supporters of the once-mighty Shiite branch of Islam, then fallen on hard times; and as Shiites, they believed that Ismail belonged to a line of imams, spiritual leaders drawing their authority directly from the Prophet Muhammad via his son-in-law, Ali. This belief put the *qizilbash* at odds with the established Muslim regimes in Turkey, Egypt, Transoxiana and India, all of which subscribed to the Sunni branch of Islam, which followed a different pattern of succession from the Prophet.

In a minority for most of their history, the Shiites had developed their own religious rituals and law. They also tended to espouse doctrines that were mystical,

The Safavid empire was created in the first two decades of the 16th century by Shah Ismail, leader of an Islamic mystical order based at Ardabil in northwestern Persia. At the head of an unruly army of tribesmen, he conquered a realm that included all of modern Iran as well as territories between the Black and Caspian seas now in the U.S.S.R. The Safavid domain was subsequently challenged by the Ottoman Turks to the west and by Uzbek tribesmen to the east, and in the early, difficult years of Shah Abbas' reign it seemed that his territories might fall apart under the strain of waging war on two fronts. The Shah, however, made peace with the Ottomans in order to deal with the Uzbek threat; then, having defeated the Uzbeks, he reopened the war in the west and retook the provinces previously surrendered to the Ottomans.

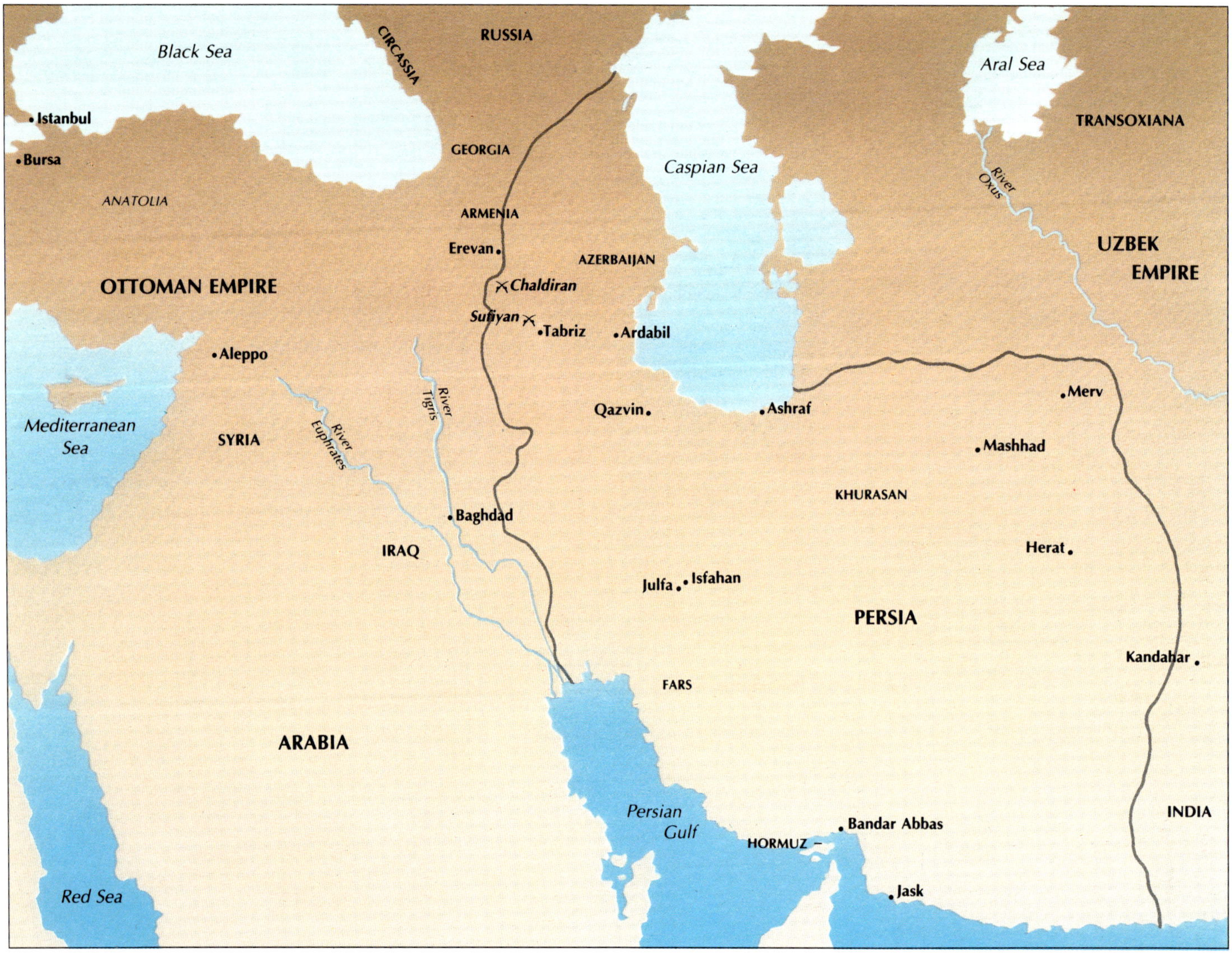

cabbalistic, revolutionary and messianic. Many Shiites, for example, maintained that the 12th and last imam claiming direct descent from Muhammad, who had disappeared in mysterious circumstances in the year 874, had not in fact died but had gone into a mystical form of concealment known as occultation. This was the man the Turkomans took Ismail to be; and they believed that his return to earth signalled the coming of the Last Days, in which the resurrected imam would lead the true believers to victory and establish the rule of perfect justice.

The chieftains who guided the boy Ismail drew on such expectations as these to assemble armies of the dedicated faithful, who rode into battle believing that they were invulnerable thanks to the protection of their mystical leader. Their early victories were gained at the expense of the rulers of much of Iran, the White Sheep Turkomans (so called to distinguish them from a rival, Black Sheep, clan). In 1501, Ismail entered the White Sheep capital of Tabriz, where he was proclaimed king. Subsequently Ismail and his followers campaigned vigorously against the Sunni Muslim regimes that dominated the Middle East: the Ottomans of Turkey, the Mamluks of Egypt and Syria, and the Uzbek rulers of Transoxiana. Though not always successful – his forces were humiliatingly defeated by the Ottomans at the Battle of Chaldiran in 1514 – Ismail had by the time of his death in 1524 succeeded in carving out a Safavid empire that incorporated all of modern-day Iran and Iraq and some areas of Afghanistan, as well as parts of the southern Caucasus which are now in the U.S.S.R.

Moreover, the empire that Ismail created was firmly Shiite in faith. Although Persia had been predominantly Sunni towards the end of the 15th century, a mixture of fierce proselytizing and even fiercer persecutions dragooned most of the population into adherence to the *qizilbash* creed – a legacy that was to endure through the centuries to come.

Although the great majority of the Safavid shahs' subjects were Persian, the armies that defended them continued to consist mainly of Turkomans, immigrants from Turkey and Syria who at first had little in common with the civilians they protected. Grouped in tribal confederacies, the *qizilbash* spoke Turkish rather than Persian, and followed a nomadic life style.

There were religious differences, too. Although the *qizilbash* were firm, even fanatical Shiites, their version of the faith sometimes verged on heterodoxy, incorporating some ill-digested borrowings from shamanistic Turkic folklore. They were sometimes referred to as "grass-worshippers" from their pantheistic tendency to see God in natural features and in natural omens. Their *dedes*, or spiritual gurus, were so venerated that devotees would reverently sweep up and preserve the dust from their horses' hoofprints. The *dedes* had the pick of the young women of the tribes, whom they blessed by ritually deflowering them. The tribesmen also practised ritual cannibalism on the bodies of their slain enemies. A *qizilbash* tribesman wore an earring in his left ear as an outward sign of his devotion to chastity; nevertheless, hostile chroniclers accused the nomads of participating in orgies that involved both homosexuality and incest.

Though wild, the *qizilbash* army was nonetheless an invaluable resource for the Safavid rulers. The shahs needed cavalry to defend the extended frontiers of their empire against enemy attack, and there was no doubting that the *qizilbash* were splendid mounted warriors. They rode into battle equipped with a small armoury of weapons that included bows and arrows, swords, daggers, battle-axes, and by

Shown here in a portrait by an Indian miniaturist, Shah Abbas was of less than average stature and in later life was physically unimpressive. But he was robust – hunting was his favourite activity – and observers commented on his keen eye and quick intelligence. He followed the fashion of the time in allowing his moustache to droop, as it was considered presumptuous to point the tips upwards to heaven. Abbas' court dress was thought simple by the showy standards of his day; he discouraged ostentation as a matter of principle, and always made a point of making himself accessible to his subjects.

the late 16th century arquebuses, which they fired from the saddle. Often their zeal and élan won the day against more numerous enemies.

The shahs garrisoned the tribesmen in the dangerous frontier provinces, and rewarded their leaders by giving them provincial governorships. Although Persian civilians dominated the Safavid bureaucracy, *qizilbash* chieftains held a near-monopoly of military and court offices. At times when the shah was weak, the Turkomans took the opportunity to meddle in politics. Some of them even aspired to become kingmakers. Such ambitions were encouraged by the Safavid practice of putting the young princes of the ruling dynasty under the tutelage of Turkoman chiefs who acted as their guardians.

On Ismail's death in 1524, his 10-year-old son Tahmasp became shah, and for a decade or so the empire fell prey to the ambitions of contending *qizilbash* chiefs. But Tahmasp grew into a capable warleader and politician, and he was able to bring his unruly subjects under control. On his death in 1576, however, the Turkomans reasserted themselves. The tribesmen formed factions around two of Tahmasp's sons, Haydar and Ismail. First, Haydar was murdered; then, after a short and bloody reign, the drug-addicted, alcoholic Ismail died, perhaps also assassinated. A third brother, the languid and half-blind Muhammad Khudabanda, was placed on the throne in 1577, but real power continued to lie with the rival *qizilbash* factions that contended for control of the country. Not only was Muhammad Khudabanda an ineffective ruler; to many of his subjects, his near-blindness amounted almost to a formal disqualification for the throne, for Islamic tradition held that a ruler must be in full possession of all his senses.

Accordingly, when the *qizilbash* chieftain who acted as guardian to Muhammad Khudabanda's son, the 16-year-old Abbas Mirza, raised the banner of revolt in 1587, the insurrection quickly gathered strength. Born in February 1571, Abbas had survived a dangerous childhood during the troubled years after the death of Tahmasp. His mother was murdered by tribesmen resentful of her influence over state affairs. His first guardian, the governor of Herat (now in Afghanistan), was killed when he was five. Another Turkoman chieftain was then dispatched to Herat by the young prince's uncle, Shah Ismail II, with orders to execute the boy, whom he considered to be a dangerous rival. The envoy chose to disobey the order, however, and in the chaotic circumstances of the time contrived to take over both the governorship of Herat and the guardianship of the prince. He subsequently lost Abbas to a rival chieftain as part of the spoils of war; the victor, Murshid Quli Khan, was the instigator of the 1587 rebellion.

By that time it was plain for all to see that Muhammad Khudabanda was not fit to rule. Ottoman armies had invaded western Iran, and the rest of the country was prey to tribal strife. As Murshid Quli Khan and his royal protégé moved steadily westwards across the country, their advance soon turned into a triumphal progress. The prince eventually reached Qazvin, the town in northwestern Persia that Tahmasp had chosen as the Safavid capital, in mid-1587. On October 1, he was proclaimed ruler of Persia as Shah Abbas I.

If Murshid had expected Abbas to be merely a pliant puppet ruler, he was fatally mistaken. Just nine months after his accession, the young king arranged for the assassination of his overmighty subject. He had already, following a common Middle Eastern tradition, had his brothers blinded to remove any threat to the throne from

A miniature illustrating a 17th-century manuscript of Persia's historical epic, the *Shahnama*, shows warriors of the legendary past fighting in costumes familiar in Shah Abbas' day. Over their armour, the soldiers wear surcoats of cotton to keep the metal cool; vambraces, or arm-guards, are attached over the coat sleeves to protect the forearms. Although the warriors carry only swords and bows, their real-life counterparts would also have had firearms, the use of which Abbas encouraged. The horsemen wear pointed helmets of a style long familiar in the Middle East; the example on the right, more likely intended for ceremonial use than for battle, boasts a lengthy curtain of mail.

that quarter. The young shah also conducted a purge of the tribesmen who had been responsible for his mother's death. There were revolts in the provinces, but these were ruthlessly suppressed.

Despite these sanguinary measures, Abbas continued to feel insecure. In August 1593 he was advised by his astrologers that the stars boded ill for the ruler of Persia, since Mars and Saturn were in quadrature in the ascendant. Resourcefully, Abbas stepped down from the throne and had a condemned heretic, an adherent of a small, outlawed religious sect, proclaimed shah in his place. The heretic ruled under close surveillance for three days. On the fourth day, when the zodiacal aspects were declared to have become more favourable, the substitute shah was executed and Abbas resumed his reign once more.

Persia's external enemies provided further cause for alarm, and the problems that they posed were less easily solved. The continuing threat from the Ottomans and Uzbeks, dating back to the reign of the first Ismail, had grown in the time of troubles following the death of Shah Tahmasp. The Ottomans represented the more serious danger: Abbas inherited a war against them that had begun some 10 years before his accession. The territories at issue were Iraq, Armenia, Azerbaijan and the

Caucasus, and much of the fighting took place in the two latter areas. For the most part, the Ottoman army had the upper hand. Its strengths were its large and tightly disciplined infantry forces, its many artillery pieces and its sophisticated logistical backup. Time and again the Ottoman battle tactic of placing artillery and musketeers behind carts linked together by chains thwarted the charges of the Safavid cavalry. In 1587, the Ottomans captured Baghdad.

Given the limitations of his army, there was little that Abbas could do to regain lost ground. In order to buy time, he agreed in 1590 to conclude a humiliating peace. By the terms of the Treaty of Istanbul, he acknowledged Ottoman control of Iraq, Georgia and most of Azerbaijan. To placate the Sunni Ottomans, he also swore to prohibit his subjects from cursing Umar, Abu Bakr and Uthman, who were the first three caliphs to lead the Muslim community following the death of the Prophet Muhammad; in Shiite eyes they were usurpers, and the devout liked to demonstrate their religious loyalties by execrating them.

Abbas needed peace with the Ottomans so as to confront the Uzbeks, who were pressing hard on Persia's eastern province of Khurasan. Uzbek forces had sacked the cities of Herat and Merv, and had desecrated the Shiite holy place of Mashhad. Unlike the Ottomans, however, the Uzbeks had a relatively unsophisticated military machine, consisting of levies of nomadic tribesmen. Under Abbas' leadership his *qizilbash* cavalry proved more than a match for them. Mashhad, Herat and Merv were all recaptured during 1595 and 1596, and Safavid cavalry went on to cross the River Oxus, taking the war into Uzbek Transoxiana. The Uzbek leader Abdullah Khan II died in 1598; later that year a large Uzbek army was defeated in a battle fought near Herat. In the decades that followed, skirmishing continued and Uzbek raids still posed a menace to the towns and agriculture of Khurasan, but the sorties no longer threatened the safety of the realm. Abbas felt secure enough to redirect his attention to the Ottomans.

Taking her ease in a flower-bedecked garden, a lady clasping a flagon of wine considers whether to accept the shawl offered to her by an admirer; the painted and glazed tiles that carry the scene probably once adorned a pavilion in Shah Abbas' palace in Isfahan. Strict Muslims in 17th-century Persia denounced the mingling of the sexes and consumption of alcohol, as well as the portrayal of human figures in art which, they claimed, was proscribed by the Koran. Yet despite their fulminations, languorous and willowy men and women, picnicking, daydreaming and getting drunk in verdant orchards, were part of the stock-in-trade of the painters and poets who sought to cater to the hedonistic tastes of the Safavid court.

Conscious of the earlier failure of his army, Shah Abbas sought to remedy its weaknesses. In pursuit of this aim he looked northwards to the Christian territory of Georgia, which had nominally been in Ottoman hands since the Treaty of Istanbul. Along with the neighbouring Christian states of Circassia and Armenia, Georgia had for long been the favoured hunting ground of white slavers, who culled the flower of its youth to sell at the great Islamic courts. The women were esteemed for their beauty, and were favourites in the harems of the shahs. The men had, at least since the reign of Shah Tahmasp, been organized into a military corps; the best of them were hand-picked to enter palace service.

These were the people to whom Abbas turned for help. Despite their nominal subjection to the Ottomans, the semi-independent Christian rulers of Georgia resumed their old practice of sending slaves as tribute to Persia in the 1590s. Their lowly origin notwithstanding, the Georgians came in the course of Abbas' reign to constitute a third ethnic element in the ruling elite, and they competed for office with Turkomans and Persians.

The Georgians' most significant role was in the army. Abbas may not have been the first ruler to make use of Georgian troops, but he was the first to deploy them on such a large scale. Hitherto the shahs had supplemented the intimidating but undisciplined tribal forces of *qizilbash* cavalry with a much smaller standing army which was also recruited from the *qizilbash*, but organized on a nontribal basis. Now Abbas began to form regiments composed of the military slaves from Georgia and other regions of the Caucasus. Among them was an elite force of cavalrymen, 10,000 strong, who owed their loyalty not to any tribe but to the Shah alone. Abbas also formed a bodyguard of 3,000 slave-soldiers.

He innovated further by creating a regiment of musketeers and a corps of artillerymen. Abbas recruited Persians into these infantry regiments, and in so doing became the first of the Safavid shahs to give the native people of his realm a role in the defence of their own country. The guns themselves came at first either as spoils of war from the Ottomans and Uzbeks, or from the Portuguese, who maintained a naval and mercantile base on the island of Hormuz in the Persian Gulf. Later, Abbas set up his own gun foundries.

Abbas' military reforms, which drew upon the Ottoman example both in the use of slave-soldiers and of massed fire power, carried with them important implications for the internal politics of Persia. With a regular standing army of around 37,000 men, the Shah was no longer totally dependent on the Turkomans to repel foreign invasions or to suppress internal disorder. The power of the *qizilbash* at court and in the provinces declined accordingly. Although *qizilbash* chiefs continued to hold the majority of the provincial governorships, Abbas now felt strong enough to dispatch them to provinces that were far from the lands of their own tribes, the sources of their strength. The leading offices of state were increasingly given to palace servants and to Georgian officers, and some favoured Georgians were even given provincial governorships.

One such placeman, the Georgian Allahverdi Khan, owed his tenure of high office to his participation in the murder of Murshid Quli Khan in 1588. He was rewarded in the first instance with the governorship of a small town, but by 1595 he had become commander of the slave regiments and governor of the important province of Fars. Later he was appointed commander in chief of all the Safavid armed forces, and in that role he was the principal architect of Abbas' army reforms. Abbas valued Allahverdi Khan's military ability and favoured him for his readiness, repeatedly demonstrated, to act against enemies of the Shah.

For all the advantages, both military and political, that the standing army brought, it had one major disadvantage: it had to be paid regularly. To meet the extra expenditure involved, Abbas presumably increased taxation, although no detailed records of this survive. He certainly increased the extent of the crown lands. Under his predecessors, most of the revenue from land in Persia had been collected by the tribal chiefs, who had tenure of estates that could be as large as a whole province. They then sent a portion of the money collected to the central government. Abbas, however, did away with these middlemen in many areas, claiming the land directly in his own name.

After 10 years on the throne, Abbas felt sufficiently confident of his position to start on a great work that was for ever after to be associated with his reign. He decided to create a new capital city to replace Qazvin, which was uncomfortably close to the Ottoman war zone and, besides, was in a region that was dominated by the *qizilbash* warlords and their tribesmen.

Seeking a new location closer to the heart of his empire, Abbas settled on the small town of Isfahan, situated on the high central plateau of Iran. The site had been occupied since before the time of Muhammad, and during the 11th and 12th centuries the town had briefly been the nation's capital, though subsequently it had declined in importance. Now Abbas planned to extend and transform it into a garden city that would advertise his rule and his empire's prosperity.

Advice on the layout of the city was sought from the Lebanese poet and engineer, Baha al-Din al-Amili. (Al-Amili is alleged once to have designed a bath-house whose pool was kept hot by the flame of a single candle burning under its water tank.) The royal astrologers were also consulted regarding the time at which the building work should begin. Construction finally started in October 1598; it was to continue throughout Abbas' reign and beyond it.

The city that the Shah and the poet created was splendid indeed. Its principal axis was provided by the Chahar Bagh, a 50-metre-wide avenue built along a central canal, which was spanned by little bridges and flanked by fountains and pools. The street was shaded by plane trees and poplars and lined with palaces, mosques, shops and gardens. At the end of the day, princes and populace alike would ride or stroll down the avenue to enjoy the tranquil pleasures of the evening. Shah Abbas himself liked to mingle with the crowds, cracking jokes with the street entertainers and examining the goods for sale in the booths.

To the east of the Chahar Bagh was a warren of pavilions, courtyards, harem quarters, reception chambers, administrative offices, service rooms, stables, imperial workshops and storehouses that together made up the royal palace. This edifice was no monumental pile in the European manner; rather it was a small village of separate buildings scattered among shady gardens, on the lines of the Ottomans' Topkapi Palace in Istanbul.

Beyond the palace was the Maidan or town square. Covering eight hectares, this was the main communal space in the city. When no special event was being staged there, it was covered with market stalls; at night there was a lantern-lit funfair. At other times, it might be used at the Shah's behest for parades, public executions of criminals, or sports such as wolf-baiting, for which a live wolf would be loosed into the square while it was crowded with young men eager to show off their courage. Though one or two people might get bitten, no serious harm ever came to any of the participants other than the wolf.

No sport played on the Maidan pleased the Shah as much as polo, the pre-eminent game of the Safavid court and its military elite, prized both as a recreation and as a training for mounted warfare. A French visitor, noting that it was the favourite exercise of the ruler and his retainers, observed that "their horses are so well trained to it that they run after the ball like cats". The royal orchestra accompanied the game, sounding a fanfare every time Abbas hit the ball.

The dominant feature of the northern end of the Maidan was the archway that led into the great covered bazaar, a maze of shops and workshops extending over almost four square kilometres. Within the bazaar, tradesmen were grouped into separate quarters, for carpet weavers, textile workers, metalsmiths and so forth. The royal mint and the royal caravanserai (providing lodging and protection for dealers in luxury goods) were located close to the bazaar's entrance. Elsewhere small enterprises prospered, for though the Shah himself was the nation's wealthiest individual, enjoying a near-monopoly on the expanding silk trade in addition to the growing fruits of customs duties, others flourished too in the prosperity that was generated during his reign.

Among the greatest beneficiaries were the Armenian merchants and craftsmen encouraged by the Shah to settle in the Christian suburb of Julfa, just south of

Isfahan proper, which enjoyed tax privileges and a degree of self-government. With Abbas' compliance, the Armenians came to dominate the overland trade in luxury commodities, and especially in raw silk. Julfa-based entrepreneurs dispatched caravans across the Syrian desert or the Anatolian plateau to the cities of Aleppo, Bursa or Istanbul, where fellow Armenians, subjects of the Ottoman sultan, would handle the sale of the merchandise. Apart from finished commodities, popular trading goods included natural substances such as opium, civet (the richly perfumed secretions of the civet cat) and bezoar, a stone secreted in the stomach of the wild goat that was valued at the time as an antidote to poisons.

The Shah's policy of toleration encouraged Christian missions from western Europe to use Julfa as a base. Augustinians, Carmelites and Capuchins all established houses there. In the light of the Shah's friendly attitude towards Europeans and their faith, a number of missionaries managed to persuade themselves that the ruler himself was on the verge of converting to Christianity. The error was fostered by Abbas' mischievous sense of humour; on one occasion he joined a band of Portuguese Augustinian friars in their tent, singing psalms with them and serenading them on the lute. But the truth was that Abbas had no inclination to abandon Islam; he valued Europeans primarily for the military assistance that they could give him against the mutual enemy, the Ottomans.

Merchants and traders were not alone in benefiting from the internal peace of Abbas' reign. The arts also revived. Miniature-painting, in particular, flourished under royal patronage. Some of the greatest Persian painters held posts in the Safavid royal library, for a librarian in 17th-century Persia was not just supposed to look after books and assist readers' access to them: he was also expected to add to their number by creating original manuscripts.

One such was Abbas' first royal librarian, Sadiqi Beg, who described himself without false modesty as "the rare man of his time". Contemporaries regarded him as ill-tempered, self-seeking and above all arrogant, while conceding that he had much to be arrogant about. Sadiqi Beg was born into one of the leading *qizilbash* tribes, and at first pursued the military career that was expected of him, distinguishing himself by feats of foolhardy bravery. Then, in his early thirties, he took the unprecedented step of giving up warfare for painting. He studied under the poet and calligrapher Mir Sani, and subsequently was employed as court artist by Shah Ismail II. In the turbulent times that followed Ismail's death, he took up the life of a wandering dervish before returning to a military career. Finally, on Abbas' accession to the throne, he became royal librarian and returned to his painting and writing, composing poetry in Persian and prose in the Chagatai dialect of Turkish. Among the work for which he was to be remembered was *The Assembly of Worthies*, a biographical dictionary that took great pains to establish the inferiority of most of his contemporaries to himself.

For many years Sadiqi Beg's pre-eminence among Persian artists was universally, if somewhat reluctantly, acknowledged, but then a newcomer named Ali Riza appeared in Isfahan and, in the words of one contemporary critic, "snatched the ball of precedence from his forerunners". For a time the two painters worked together at the court, but relations between them were probably tense as the Shah came to prefer the hair-fine brushwork of the younger man. Abbas held Riza's work in such reverence that, it is said, he would hold a candle for him while the painter worked. In the long run, however, Riza fell into bad company. He became

A miniature dating from 1626 shows a wandering dervish announcing his presence by blowing a horn. Holy men vowed to a life of poverty, the dervishes survived by begging food, which they carried with them in baskets like the one shown. Such men helped the first Safavid shah, Ismail, to seize power, and their support was an important prop for the dynasty in the 16th century. Abbas, however, distrusted his dervish following, and during his reign the itinerants were occasionally persecuted.

an aficionado of wrestling, and spent much of his time in the company of the lowlife that practised and admired the sport. He took to dissipation and boasting, and fell out of favour with the Shah. By that time Sadiqi Beg was dead; outshone by his younger rival, he had been dismissed from his appointment at the library, apparently for stealing a precious illustrated book.

The demand for such luxury items as miniature paintings was stimulated by the hectic diplomatic activity of Abbas' court. Indeed, the exchange of diplomatic gifts with monarchs in Europe and India was on such a grand scale that it amounted virtually to a self-contained import-export trade. Ambassadors flocked to Isfahan in the hope of swaying the Shah to further their nation's interests. Envoys from Moscow tried vainly to touch him for money. Missions from the Mughal court at Delhi came with extravagant presents. Papal emissaries talked enthusiastically but vaguely about a grand alliance against the Ottoman Turks. A legation from Spain sought to protect the Portuguese base on the island of Hormuz in the Persian Gulf. (From 1580 to 1640, Spain and Portugal were jointly ruled by one king.)

Among the diplomats clustered at Abbas' court were a couple of Englishmen who were to have a significant influence on the latter part of his reign. Though not officially accredited by Queen Elizabeth, Anthony and Robert Sherley had been dispatched by her favourite, the Earl of Essex, to explore informally the possibility of an alliance with Persia against the Ottoman Turks. The two brothers arrived in Qazvin in November 1598, shortly after the Shah's victory over the Uzbeks. The returning *qizilbash* cavalry streamed into the town wearing necklaces made of Uzbek ears and carrying the earless heads aloft on their lances. The two Englishmen thoughtfully surveyed the scene, then hastened to congratulate the Shah on his victory.

They were well received. Anthony Sherley was sent back to Europe by the Shah with letters for the Holy Roman Emperor, the King of Spain, the Pope and other monarchs, including Queen Elizabeth. Sherley carried off his mission flamboyantly, but no grand alliance was forthcoming.

The Shah's relationship with Robert Sherley, who stayed behind virtually as a hostage during his brother's travels, was ultimately to prove more fruitful. Abbas rapidly found a use for him as a military adviser, in which capacity the Englishman's knowledge of artillery and tactics proved to be invaluable. Abbas carried out his successful reorganization of the Persian army with the help of Sherley, who served as an officer and won for himself the title of "Master General against the Turks".

In 1611, Robert Sherley was sent back to England to see if he could interest Elizabeth's successor, King James I, in

Ali Qapu Palace
Maidan
N
Royal Mosque
Lutf-Allah Mosque

A SPACIOUS NEW CAPITAL

Backed by a residential district that stretched southwest towards the Zagros Mountains, the Maidan or open space – shown diagramatically in the inset – was the centrepiece of Abbas' planned city of Isfahan. Measuring 512 by 159 metres, it was surrounded by low arcades of shops and workplaces, as well as by trees and water channels. Soaring high above its southern end, the Royal Mosque, with its great dome and four minarets, was the centre of public worship. The lofty balcony of the Ali Qapu Palace – in the right foreground of the main picture – gave the Shah and his intimates a commanding view of all that happened below. The threshold of the royal residence was regarded as sacred ground, and any criminal who managed to reach it and kiss its gate was safe from arrest. Behind the palace lay spacious royal gardens.

A great deal of Isfahan's public life was transacted in the Maidan. On most days it housed a public market, and all the square, except for the immediate vicinity of the palace, was covered with stalls. But the great open space also served by turns as a parade ground, as an execution yard, and as a sports arena for polo matches, horse races, archery tournaments and wrestling. Sunrise and sunset were marked by concerts from the imperial orchestra.

At night 50,000 lamps illuminated the square, which was transformed into a funfair thronged with hucksters, water-sellers, prostitutes, preachers, jugglers, acrobats and animal tamers. Shah Abbas himself, contemptuous of European sovereigns who in his view "always sat indoors", liked to walk about in the evenings, sampling the goods on display and admiring the performances.

Profits from Silk

The splendours of Shah Abbas' court could not have been paid for without the revenues that came from the cultivation and export of silk and the artefacts made from it, principally carpets and textiles. Carpet-weaving had traditionally been a cottage industry, but Shah Abbas set up royal workshops for their production adding the revenues from them to the monopoly he already enjoyed on silk production. The carpets were distinguished not only by the intricacy of their designs but also by the density of the knotting made possible by the use of fine silk thread; a rough and ready way of judging their quality was to press a thumb against the edge to gauge how many threads were covered by the thumb's breadth.

The chief silk-producing regions were in the southern Caucasus and near the Caspian coast. Both areas were contested between the Safavid shahs and the sultans of Ottoman Turkey, but production went on despite the wars. So for the most part did the overland carpet trade, which was carried by camel caravan to the Ottoman domains for shipment to Europe, where the goods consequently became known as "Turkey carpets". Shah Abbas, however, also encouraged English and Dutch merchants to buy and export silk directly by sea from the port of Bandar Abbas on the Persian Gulf.

opening up direct trade with Persia via the Gulf, thereby freeing the Shah from the necessity of exporting his silk overland through Turkey. Although the Levant Company, which controlled English trade with the eastern Mediterranean, preferred not to imperil its traffic with the Turks through making a deal with Persia, officials of the British East India Company, based in India, showed an interest in the idea. The company subsequently established a base at Jask on the Persian Gulf, and the British eventually came to supplant the Portuguese as Persia's principal European trading partner. In 1622 a joint Anglo-Persian force attacked and captured the Portuguese base at Hormuz. The island entrepôt subsequently fell into ruins – its streets were torn up by bounty hunters seeking nonexistent buried treasures – and its place as a commercial centre was taken by a new port on the mainland that the Shah named, after himself, Bandar Abbas.

The testing-time for the Shah's reforms came in the early years of the 17th century, when he resumed hostilities against the Ottomans with the aim of reversing the humiliating Treaty of Istanbul. The time was propitious, for the Ottoman empire had been weakened in the intervening years by growing internal dissent. From the 1590s on, much of Anatolia had passed into the hands of rebellious tribesmen and unemployed soldiers whom the government in Istanbul stigmatized as bandits. As the Ottomans struggled to reassert their control, refugees streamed into Persia by

Languid youths drinking wine decorate a coat of Persian velvet that in 1644 was given by the Tsar of Russia to the Queen of Sweden. A great deal of raw silk was required to create the smooth, dense pile characteristic of true velvet.

the tens of thousands to put themselves at the service of Abbas. Many of the rebels harboured Shiite sympathies, for throughout the Ottoman lands there were groups of religious dissidents who favoured the faith of the Safavid shahs.

In the autumn of 1603 the Shah set off on what he claimed was a hunting trip, though it was noted that his retinue seemed overlarge for the purpose. Suddenly he swooped on Tabriz, recapturing the Safavids' original capital from the Ottomans. After a prolonged winter siege, the strategically important fortresses at Erevan in Armenia were also taken. In 1605 the Turks attempted to regain Tabriz, but they were heavily defeated at the Battle of Sufiyan. The Sufiyan debacle led to further revolts in Anatolia, and for a while the Persian armies were able to advance into eastern Turkey before being forced to withdraw. Eventually the two nations agreed on peace in 1612, on the basis of the frontiers that had been established in the mid-16th century. Though both parties to the treaty tried to improve on the agreed terms by raids and skirmishes, a temporary status quo had in fact been reached, and this was recognized by the formal reaffirmation of the 1612 agreement six years later.

Yet Abbas' conflict with the Turks was still not at an end. In 1622, the Ottoman governor of Baghdad rebelled against his Sultan. In conjunction with yet another rebellion that took place in Anatolia, this event persuaded Abbas to reopen the anti-Ottoman offensive. In 1623 he invaded Iraq, recapturing Baghdad in November of that year. The Sultan subsequently sent an army to besiege the city. Though the Shah did not dare attack the Ottoman forces, he blockaded them. Doubly besieged, the starving inhabitants of the city were reduced to eating palm leaves. It seemed so certain that the beleaguered city must fall that when Abbas' astrologer predicted that its defenders would successfully hold out, he was for once not believed. Yet his forecast proved correct. The Turks were forced by the chronic shortage of supplies to abandon the siege. Abbas' forces allowed them to march back to Turkey, leaving their cannon and their sick behind them. The recapture of Baghdad was Abbas' last great military triumph, though the war continued to smoulder for the rest of his reign and beyond.

Meanwhile, Abbas had other troubles to concern him closer to home. In the course of his reign he fathered five sons. At first he followed the practice of his predecessors in

Exotic birds and beasts decorate this silken *kilim* – a patterned cloth in which coloured weft threads are interlaced with warp threads only where required to form the pattern. The textile, too delicate for use as a carpet, might once have graced a Persian divan.

sending the children to live in provincial capitals to learn the arts of government under the guardianship of *qizilbash* chiefs. In 1589, however, the governor of Mashhad, guardian of Abbas' second son, attempted to follow the example of the kingmaker Murshid Quli Khan by raising the standard of rebellion.

Abbas put down the uprising, but henceforth kept his sons in the royal palace, where they were reared in the harem under the supervision of eunuchs. Ever mindful of the security of his throne – such was his fear of conspiracy that he moved from bedroom to bedroom in the palace to confuse potential assassins – he had his children closely watched. In 1615 he arranged for the assassination of his eldest son after certain courtiers had accused the young man of plotting against his father. Suffering remorse, he subsequently forced the man who had carried out the deed to kill his own son. Six years later, Abbas fell dangerously ill, and his oldest surviving boy made the dangerous mistake of prematurely celebrating his forthcoming accession. When Abbas recovered, he had the youth blinded. Five or six years later he condemned his last remaining able-bodied son, Imam Quli Mirza, to the same fate, again on suspicion of conspiracy. A Carmelite missionary reported that Abbas "was wont to say that he would have killed a hundred children in order to reign alone for a single day".

Soon after the blinding of Imam Quli Mirza, Abbas began to dream of his own death. Then a fever came upon him. Despite the sickness, he continued to hunt until he was too weak to leave his bed. As it became clear that the Shah was dying, his courtiers turned their attention to the task of finding a successor. All of Abbas' sons were either dead or were disqualified by blindness, but there were several grandsons. Abbas died on January 19, 1629; nine days later, his eldest grandson, Safi Mirza, was installed on the throne.

Abbas' ruthless treatment of his sons revealed the darker side of his character. Throughout his reign, he had made terror effectively one of the instruments of his government. His adoring chronicler, Iskandar Munshi, reported that no-one dared disobey the Shah: "For instance, should he command a father to kill his son, the sentence would be carried out immediately, even as the decree of destiny; or should the father, moved by parental tenderness, make any delay, the command would be reversed; and should the son then temporize, another would slay both. By such awful severity the execution of his commands attained the supreme degree of efficiency and none dared hesitate for an instant in the fulfilment of the sentence as inevitable as fate." Thomas Herbert, in his account of the Persians, thought that "to record the variety of tortures here too much used by men-eating hags of hell, cannibal hounds . . . and their death-twanging bowstrings, ripping up men's guts and the like – what could be the effect but an odious and unnecessary remembrance?" Yet despite the horrors, the sovereign always remained popular with the crowds and with foreign visitors, Herbert among them.

In other respects, however, Abbas was a model of prudent kingship. He made little or no use of the messianic trappings that had carried his great-grandfather Ismail to power. Instead he preferred to reign as a secular monarch, employing the force of arms, the persuasive power of money and the lavish use of spectacle as well as terror to command the obedience of his subjects. He was not a great innovator, but he was a wise reformer, many of his best moves being developments of policies that were first initiated by his grandfather Tahmasp. In other areas Abbas copied the institutions and practices of his neighbours, the Ottoman and Mughal

Seen here giving audience to ambassadors from Mughal India, Shah Abbas II was not of the same moral or intellectual stature as his great namesake. Acceding to the throne as a boy in 1642, thirteen years after the death of Abbas I, he allowed the army to decline in numbers and quality in the course of his 24-year reign. Addicted to opium and alcohol, he died, probably of syphilis, at the age of 33. His successors were no more impressive; but such was the strength of Abbas I's legacy that the Safavid dynasty remained in power until well into the 18th century.

sultans. He also took full advantage of the growing European interest in Persia, and of the technological and economic opportunities that ensued.

Abbas' successors, brought up in the rarefied atmosphere of the harem, lacked experience of the real world and were often the pawns of factional intrigue. None of them possessed his flair and flamboyance, yet the strength of his legacy was such that the Safavids were to remain in power, using mostly the institutions which he put into place, for almost a century after his death.

It was not until the early 18th century that the lack of decisive leadership took its toll. Sultan Husayn, the last Safavid, was a debauchee and heavy drinker who paid little attention to affairs of state. The neighbouring Baluchis and Afghans took advantage of his negligence to invade and seize border provinces already alienated by Husayn's attempts to enforce rigid Shiite orthodoxy throughout his realm.

Finally one Mahmud, a former vassal of the Safavids from Afghanistan, besieged the ruler in his splendid capital of Isfahan. The starving citizens were reduced to cannibalism before finally surrendering to the rebel warlord, who then took for himself the title of shah. Husayn was murdered in the *madrasah* or mosque-school that had been built in his mother's name. The Shiite faith survived; but once more Iran found itself under the rule of foreigners.

Soldiers Looting a Farmhouse

AGONIES OF THE THIRTY YEARS' WAR

"For what can war but endless war still breed?" When the poet John Milton posed that question in 1648, he was addressing the civil war that was then devastating his native England. Yet he could have found an even apter illustration of his aphorism across the Channel where parts of Europe were being devastated by a conflict more enduring, more widespread and more savage than any they had previously known. History was to call the struggle the Thirty Years' War, but to those whose lands it laid waste and whose children it butchered, it must have indeed seemed endless. It was a conflict that fed upon itself, destroying agriculture and creating a class of beggared peasants whose only hope of survival lay in joining the ranks of the pillagers who had reduced them to ruin. This was war absolute and total, and it transformed some of the continent's wealthiest provinces into wasteland.

The conflict started as an internal dispute within the Holy Roman Empire and swelled to involve most European nations. Its outcome was hardly inconsequential: it established the status quo in Europe for almost a century. But the Thirty Years' War was to be remembered by later generations not so much in terms of battles won but as an orgy of violence, a glimpse of the hell that man could create on earth.

It was a war which saw terrible advances in methods of mass destruction. Muskets and cannon became less unwieldy and more deadly. New, shallow formations exposed more soldiers to fire and to hand-to-hand fighting and death. Unprecedented numbers of soldiers fought, and over the 30 years around a million of them died.

Nor was the suffering confined to the military. The huge numbers of soldiers bled dry the countryside over which they fought, creating mayhem on a par with that inflicted by the Mongols 400 years earlier. It led the most celebrated German poet of the time, Martin Opitz, to write:

The trees stand no more
The gardens are desolate
The sickle and the plough are now
a cold, sharp sword

And its horrors inspired a French artist, Jacques Callot, to produce a famous series of engravings called *The Miseries of War*, some of which are reproduced here.

Although the Thirty Years' War was fought by many nations, most of the carnage took place on the soil of the Holy Roman Empire, a loose collection of about 1,000 semi-independent statelets nominally controlled from Vienna by its emperor, Ferdinand II. Ferdinand was a member of the Habsburg family, which collectively ruled nearly half of Europe, including Spain and sections of Italy and the Netherlands. Ferdinand's share included present-day Germany, Czechoslovakia and Austria, as well as parts of Hungary, Poland and Yugoslavia; it stretched from the Baltic Sea in the north to the Adriatic in the south, from the Rhine in the west to the Carpathian Mountains in the east.

The force that set off the destruction was religion. In medieval times a source of unity throughout western Europe, Christianity had been transformed by the Protestant Reformation of the 16th century into a cause of conflict between and within nations. Parts of the Holy

Enrolling the Troops

Roman Empire, together with the Scandinavian countries, England, Scotland and most of Switzerland, had gone over to Protestantism, chiefly of the Lutheran or Calvinist varieties; Italy, Spain, most of France and the remainder of the Holy Roman Empire – and the Emperor himself – had remained Catholic, retaining their loyalty to the Pope. The new pattern cut across old diplomatic links; traditional allies such as Spain and England now found themselves at odds over religion. Moreover, religious affiliations did not neatly follow national boundaries. All major states found themselves confronting an enemy within – a religious minority whose first loyalty was to its creed.

Within the Holy Roman Empire, the religious rift had upset what had always been a precarious balance between the individual principalities and their would-be rulers in Vienna. When, in 1618, Ferdinand tried to assert his imperial authority by debarring Protestants in Bohemia from public office and by closing two of their churches, the balance was not so much upset as destroyed. An anti-imperial revolt broke out in the Bohemian capital, Prague. This started a chain reaction whereby not only German states but also a number of neighbouring powers were drawn into the conflict.

They ranged themselves at first primarily by religious affiliation. Protestant England, Sweden, Denmark and the Dutch Republic came in on the Bohemian side, Catholic Spain, Poland and the Pope on the Imperialist front. But the motives of the individual combatants – especially the German ones – varied between the spiritual and the secular, the aggressive and the defensive; between self-assertion and self-preservation. The prime secular issue was the desire of the German princes and dukes and the rising nation states neighbouring the Holy Roman Empire to counteract the multinational power of the Habsburg family.

The struggle fell into two phases. In the early years, local issues were paramount and the most heartfelt of these were religious. But after 1635 naked politics took over; the goal of the warmongers was primarily to alter the balance of power in Europe. The war had created a momentum of its own. With all Europe divided into two camps, diplomatic initiatives were difficult: there were no neutral parties to serve as mediators. Fighting was the only way of resolving the conflict, and the fighting was inconclusive. So the war dragged on.

Since no state received sufficient tax revenues to support a large permanent army, their rulers had recourse to the crude and ultimately ineffective method of hiring mercenaries. The notion of fighting purely for financial gain had entered Europe towards the end of the Middle Ages, when the old obligation of feudal vassals to fight for their lords began to wane. The use of mercenary soldiers had grown steadily, and by the 17th century they were indispensable.

The job of running these temporary armies fell to private businessmen-generals, such as the ambitious and

The Battle

unscrupulous Count Ernst von Mansfeld. The illegitimate son of a minor Catholic prince, Mansfeld began his career in the Habsburg army. The stigma of his birth held back his progress, however, and at the start of the war he transferred his allegiance to the Habsburgs' Protestant opponents. In the first eight years of the conflict, he led armies on behalf of Savoy, France, Britain, the Netherlands and a variety of German states; a contemporary engraving showed him preparing a steambath in which the German states were portrayed sweating money.

While some of the men led by Mansfeld and his ilk had a religious or political commitment to their cause, the majority were no more idealistic than their leaders. Many were forcibly conscripted; others joined the army to escape destitution or the gallows. Few fates, however, were so terrible as to make soldiering seem a desirable alternative. The men, clothed in lice-ridden uniforms, lived constantly under threat of death from disease or battle, in that order. Mutiny and desertion were savagely punished.

Under the mercenary system, all wages were channelled through the regimental commanders. The soldiers' allegiance accordingly lay with these men rather than with the cause for which they were fighting. If a commander swapped sides, his men would follow him. But their loyalty was poorly rewarded. The commanders, and the officers who served under them, regularly skimmed off a percentage of the already low pay provided by the rulers who hired them. Quite often, the supply of cash dried up altogether. "Neither they [the soldiers] nor their horses can live on air," Mansfeld complained when funds were cut off by one of his employers, the Duke of Savoy.

If the revenues did run out in mid-campaign, rulers would authorize army commanders to extract payment from the local citizenry, either in the form of taxes or of free board and lodging. Such impositions were made all the heavier by the community of servants, wives, children, freebooters, prostitutes and traders that accompanied every army. And the countryfolk suffered even more acutely from the acquisitive instincts of individual soldiers. For the one attraction that a soldier's life did offer was the hope of booty. Each soldier became a small, property-acquiring industry at the expense of the local populace.

A contemporary novel, *Simplicius Simplicissimus* , by the German writer Hans von Grimmelshausen, described how thieving from local farmers became a way of life for the book's anti-hero, a musketeer in the imperial forces. "If I was not on patrol," says Simplicissimus, "I went out looting, and neither horses nor sheep were safe from me in their stalls, which I raided for miles around. To avoid being trailed, I knew how to put boots or shoes on cattle and horses until I brought them to a much-used highway." For pigs, "I made a well-salted porridge with meal and water, and soaked a sponge therein, to which I had tied a strong rope, and let those that I wanted to keep swallow the sponge full of porridge, keeping the rope

The Maimed and Wounded Seek Refuge in a Hospital

in my hand, whereupon they followed patiently without further dispute, and paid the bill with hams and sausages."

Simplicissimus was driven to soldiering when his father's farm was raided; the invaders killed some of its occupants and tortured others with thumbscrews or by roasting them over a fire. Such incidents were far from being products of Grimmelshausen's imagination. One well-attested brutality inflicted by marauding bands of soldiers and their camp-followers was to force-feed local farmers with liquid excrement, either out of wanton cruelty or as a means of getting them to divulge the whereabouts of valuables.

In some parts of Germany, particularly along river supply routes, the ravages of soldiers were a regular occurrence. Hans Heberle, a shoemaker who kept a diary of the war years, described how on 30 separate occasions plundering soldiery drove him and his family from their village to take refuge in the nearby city of Ulm. Yet even if they escaped with their lives, Heberle and his like would often be left penniless in a countryside stripped of all its crops. An Englishman named William Crowne, who journeyed through Germany in 1636 as a member of a diplomatic mission, gave an eyewitness account of their sufferings. At Neustadt, on the River Aisch, he wrote of "wretched children sitting at their doors almost dying of hunger". And he recorded that in the village of Bacharach, on the Rhine, "the poor people are found dead with grass stuffed in their mouths", in a final, desperate bid to escape starvation.

Unsurprisingly, villagers sometimes retaliated against their oppressors. "The boores [peasants] on the march cruelly used our soldiers," a Scots officer noted, "in cutting off their noses and ears, hands and feet, pulling out their eyes, with sundry other cruelties which they used; being justly repayed by the soldiers in the burning of many dorpes [villages] on the march, leaving also the boores dead where they were found."

In this way civilians and soldiers alike were drawn into an accelerating spiral of violence. The bloodletting could only end when every permutation of national and international hostility had been exhausted, and when sufficient destruction had been done to have drained every emotion except the desire for peace.

By 1643 that process was well under way. The population of Germany as a whole had fallen by perhaps 20 per cent. In areas directly affected by the fighting, the figure was higher; up to three quarters of the population had disappeared, due to disease, war and mass migration to the cities, whose walls and protection money kept most armies out. In the much-fought-over southern duchy of Württemberg, the number of inhabitants fell from 450,000 in 1620 to 100,000 in 1639.

Nor was the depopulation confined to Germany alone. In Sweden, conscription stripped the land of adult males; once shipped off to fight in Germany, a man was unlikely to come back alive. Many died within a year of enlistment. "We may indeed say that we have conquered lands from others and to that end ruined our

The Hangman's Tree

own," wrote a depressed member of the Swedish government.

By the 1640s the mood was conducive to peace; achieving it, however, turned out to be a cumbersome process, requiring an international conference that dragged on for four years and met simultaneously in two different cities. The French and their Catholic allies negotiated with the Emperor in Münster, while the Swedish and Protestant delegations met him 50 kilometres away, at Osnabrück. The delegates stuck to their task, and the result was the triumphant announcement, on October 24, 1648, of the long-awaited Peace of Westphalia.

To guarantee a lasting peace, the negotiators had determined to obtain the agreement of all the parties, not just some. For as the Swedes' perceptive ambassador Count Johan Salvius put it: "The first rule of all politics is that the security of all depends on the equilibrium of the individuals." And all the individual states did indeed get enough out of the peace to ensure a new equilibrium.

Sweden won financial compensation and a strategic slice of northern Germany, while France secured sufficient territory on her eastern border to break what had threatened to become encirclement by the Habsburgs. The Emperor (now Ferdinand III) kept his title and most of his territory, but the German states within his empire won recognition of their supreme power in their localities. The concessions to the German states not only diminished the concern of other countries over the excessive power in Habsburg hands; it also resolved the tensions within Germany – and there was general agreement by this time that a stable Europe depended on a stable Germany.

The treaty included some specifically religious clauses, but they were not of enormous moment. Since 1555, the rulers of the German states had had the right to determine whether their subjects should adhere to the Catholic or to the Lutheran church; now Calvinism became another option. The treaty also decreed that future religious disputes in the empire should be settled by "amicable" agreement between the Catholic and Protestant members of the Imperial Diet, or parliament. The clause was a measure of how far down the list of priorities spiritual considerations had sunk; never again was religion to spark off a European war.

Now that the threat of Habsburg domination had subsided, it was the turn of other European nations, notably France, to kindle their territorial ambitions. Not for another two centuries would the diverse states of Germany be welded together, under William I of Prussia, into a power sufficiently unified to threaten the continent's stability.

And for the best part of a century, the war-weary German people were left largely in peace to rebuild their lives and livelihoods. They did so with surprising speed. By 1700, some areas had returned to prewar housing and population levels. But the memories were not so easily erased. For centuries to come, the Thirty Years' War would endure in European minds as a byword for calamity.

CIVIL WAR IN ENGLAND

4

On February 23, 1642, the warship *Lion* set sail from England for Holland. Its most distinguished passenger was Henrietta Maria, the 33-year-old, French-born wife of the English king, Charles I. Ostensibly the Queen was taking her 10-year-old daughter, Mary, to join the 15-year-old Dutch prince, William of Orange, to whom she had been married 10 months earlier. In fact, however, Her Majesty had even more important business to accomplish. Her luggage contained the crown jewels of England and most of her own jewels as well, and she was on her way to pawn them in Europe and use the money raised to buy arms. The King of England was preparing to go to war against his own subjects.

The conflict which was about to erupt was to be the first and the most critical act in a long-drawn-out drama that changed the balance of power in England. At a time when most of the continental European nations were subjected increasingly to the will of absolute monarchs, the English would forcibly resist the claims of their king to rule by divine right alone. During the course of the century, two separate rulers of the Stuart dynasty would be driven from the throne, one to face execution, and the other exile. As a result, the English nation would enter the following century set firmly on the path of constitutional monarchy, and would provide a model for the rest of the world of the checks and balances that could be used to shackle royal absolutism.

The Stuarts had succeeded to the English throne in the year 1603, when the last ruler of the preceding Tudor dynasty, Queen Elizabeth I, died childless. By the laws of succession, the throne passed to her cousin, James Stuart, who had by that time been ruling in Scotland as King James VI for 20 years. In stature tall and broad-shouldered, though with thin legs and a tongue that seemed too big for his mouth, James had a reputation as an intellectual; before his arrival in England he had published *The True Law of Free Monarchies*, a scholarly if unoriginal treatise on political theory that argued the case for the divine right theory of kingship. But he was also conceited and lazy. A bisexual, he showed a penchant for worthless favourites, the last of whom, George Villiers, he addressed as "sweetheart" and "wife". In his character good and bad qualities were mixed together in such a way that his fellow monarch, Henry IV of France, was led to describe him as "the wisest fool in Christendom".

Nevertheless, to the English in 1603, James had much to recommend him. He subscribed to the Protestant faith of his predecessor, and he had an established reputation as a ruler. Though Scotland retained its status as a separate country with its own distinct constitution, the fact that one king would henceforth reign in both Edinburgh and in London seemed to hold out the promise of a period of peace between the two nations, which had often in the past been at loggerheads. And

Dressed in ceremonial armour, King Charles I of England gazes proudly from a portrait by his court artist, the Flemish master Anthony Van Dyck. Charles's regal bearing in the painting was more impressive than his demeanour in real life – he was a short, slightly built man with a stammer – but it accurately reflected his exalted conception of kingship. This was, he believed, bestowed by divine right, making kings answerable to nobody but God. This view brought him into conflict with the elected representatives of his people in Parliament, a struggle that ended in civil war.

despite his penchant for handsome young men, James was married to a daughter of the King of Denmark, who had borne him two sons and a daughter; the succession seemed assured. As he travelled south in April 1603, his future subjects turned out in crowds to greet him.

By inheriting the English throne, James also became king of Ireland, a largely Catholic country that had been established as a separate kingdom under the rule of the English monarch by Elizabeth's father, Henry VIII. Yet for all its appurtenances, James's new throne was not as rich as he might have hoped. For their daily expenses, the monarchs of England were expected to "live of their own", which for the most part meant off the income from the revenues of the royal estates and the fines that were imposed by their courts. In addition, Parliament traditionally voted customs duties known as tunnage and poundage to each monarch for life at the beginning of his reign. These resources had at one time been sufficient to support a royal household, but their value had recently diminished. Although Queen Elizabeth had been an extremely thrifty ruler in everything but the cost of her wardrobe, she had still been forced to reduce the income that would accrue to her heirs by selling off large tracts of royal land in order to pay for the long war she had waged against Spain.

Even if James had been as careful as Elizabeth, he would still have had difficulty in making ends meet. In fact, he was impetuously profligate. He spent lavishly on

At the start of the Civil War in 1642, Royalist forces loyal to King Charles controlled the north of England, Wales, the west Midlands and Cornwall, while supporters of Parliament held the richer south and east of the country *(shaded yellow)*. Since London was in Parliamentary hands, the university city of Oxford became the Royalist capital. Most of the major battles of the conflict, from Edgehill in 1642 to Naseby in 1645, were fought in the disputed territory near the boundaries of the two hostile zones.

new buildings, on gifts to courtiers, on splendid balls and spectacular theatrical productions written and designed by Ben Jonson and Inigo Jones, respectively the leading playwright and architect of the day. Fortunes were squandered on jewellery and clothes for his queen, Anne of Denmark, a lady of extravagant fancies who once came to a Christmas ball dressed as a mince pie.

In an effort to meet his debts, James exploited the royal prerogative. He sold titles, imposed new import duties and rewarded his courtiers with grants of monopolies, to the cost of the populace at large; and despite the fact that most of his reign was spent at peace, he too sold off royal estates.

The only other way in which James could raise substantial sums of money was by seeking approval from Parliament to impose additional taxes; and herein lay the seeds of future conflict. This institution, which had parallels in every other major western European country, had evolved from the habit of medieval kings of summoning consultative assemblies of their subjects. At first such gatherings had consisted exclusively of the great nobles and the leaders of the Church; later, however, some lesser landowners and representatives of the cities had also been included. Since the 14th century, the English kings had conceded to this body the right to approve the raising of taxes.

In the ensuing centuries, Parliament had split into two separate chambers: the Lords, which was for the bishops and hereditary nobility, and the Commons for the representatives from the cities and shires. Certain guarantees of the right of free speech had also developed. One was that the king never entered the debating chamber in person; in his place, the House of Commons elected a Speaker to preside over its debates and speak on his behalf.

Although the House of Lords had originally been the dominant parliamentary body, it gradually lost its pre-eminence during the course of the 16th century when the Commons had consolidated its influence, on the whole by loyally supporting the Crown. Under the Tudors, the House of Commons had developed certain powers and privileges that were real, although limited. It had the right to petition and protest to the monarch, and in addition provided an important arena for the airing of grievances. The Commons was expected to debate such measures as were proposed by the king, and its consent was part of the formal process by which new laws were enacted. But neither it nor the House of Lords had any authority to dictate matters of policy or to take part in the executive government of the kingdom, except in authorizing the raising of taxes.

Nevertheless, the Parliament which James inherited was very different from the docile gathering which had assembled under the early Tudors. The country gentlemen who made up the bulk of the Commons had benefited greatly from a wave of economic expansion, based on wool and the textiles made from it, that had enriched England in the previous century. The boom had raised the price of land and increased the rents paid by tenants to landowners. The beneficiaries of the new wealth were not politically sophisticated, but they were resolute, ambitious and eager to protect their own interests.

Many of them also held religious opinions that divided them from the King. Ever since Henry VIII had broken with Rome in the 1530s and established an independent Church of England, the nation had been torn by theological controversy. Henry's church owed allegiance not to the pope but to the English monarch, but in other respects differed little from the Catholic model it had supplanted. Yet the upheaval engendered by the English Reformation, and the anti-Catholic rhetoric it encouraged, inevitably fostered the Protestant doctrines being preached by Martin Luther on the continent at the time. An attempt by Queen Mary Tudor in the 1550s to restore the Catholic faith did not survive her death.

Under Elizabeth the Church of England had finally begun to find its identity as a compromise between the conflicting parties. In dogma it was Protestant, but its liturgy continued to be reminiscent of Catholicism, and furthermore it was still organized under a hierarchy of bishops and archbishops. Loyalty to the Church was strictly enforced. The Roman Catholic faith was proscribed, and priests were condemned to the gallows. There were still Catholics living in England, numbering among their ranks some of the greatest families in the land, but now they were forced to practise their faith in secret.

The Catholics' bitterest enemies were the strict Protestants known as Puritans – devout and serious-minded men who wanted to "purify" the Church of England by removing from it all remaining traces of popery. Many of them took their ideas from the French reformer, John Calvin, whose austere insistence on salvation through faith alone had already come to dominate the Scottish church. A radical Puritan minority belonged to a variety of dissenting or nonconformist sects, which were to grow in strength as the 17th century progressed. All these groups had in common a distaste for ecclesiastical show or ostentation of any kind. Believing the important part of any act of worship to be the word of God, pure and unadorned, they tended to favour religious gatherings of equals held in bare rooms where the Bible could be read and explained without distraction. These men were strongly represented in the House of Commons.

Since Scotland had moved much further in the direction of ecclesiastical reform than England – its Church was organized along largely Presbyterian lines, being run by the clergy and by lay elders who were known as presbyters rather than by bishops – the Puritans in England hoped that James would be a supporter of their cause. But he had already learnt by bitter experience. Exasperated by the interference of Scottish synods in affairs of state, he was unwilling to encourage similar developments in his new kingdom. His refusal was unequivocal. Although he agreed reluctantly to impose penalties on Roman Catholics, his gesture did little to appease the Puritans and only served to earn him some additional enemies among the Catholics, a few of whom went so far as to hire a fanatical explosives expert called Guy Fawkes, who very nearly managed to blow up both King and Parliament in the Gunpowder Plot of 1605.

After their disappointment, the Puritans in Parliament were inevitably unsympathetic when their spendthrift king asked to be voted more money. The House of Commons demanded in exchange a statute forbidding any further imposition of customs duties, and in addition the abolition of certain feudal privileges such as wardship – the king's right to the custody, and property, of an infant heir of a feudal tenant – and purveyance, the royal right to requisition provisions. Negotiations on these matters collapsed in 1610 and again in 1614. By then a pattern of confrontation had been set that was to be repeated in the ensuing decades, and that would finally culminate in civil war.

In 1621, the members of a subsequent Parliament summoned by the King even attempted to influence his foreign policy. Fearing rightly that James was hoping to heal the wounds of Christian Europe by marrying his son Charles to the daughter of the Catholic king of Spain, they refused to grant him the money that he needed unless he promised to declare war on Spain and marry his heir to a Protestant.

In a fury, James dismissed Parliament and ripped the offending pages from its records. When his efforts at matchmaking foundered, however, he turned to Parliament again. This time the members did at least grant him sufficient funds to embark on a new conflict, on behalf of the Protestant cause in the Thirty Years' War, although they laid down certain conditions as to how the money was to be spent. But by then the King had only a year to live.

Under the 24-year-old Charles I, who succeeded to the throne in 1625, the relationship between King and Parliament deteriorated further and faster. Charles shared his father's indolence and his faith in the divine right of kings, but in other repects he was a very different man. He was short in stature, and by temperament he was pious, devious and indecisive. In order to hide his deep-rooted insecurity, he adopted a pose of earnest and often pompous formality, and like most insecure men he did not always keep his word.

Besides James's kingdoms, debts and war with Spain, Charles also inherited the dubious influence of his father's last and most cherished favourite, George Villiers, who had been created duke of Buckingham. Widely resented for his arrogance, the duke by now virtually dictated English foreign policy. After the failure of the planned Spanish marriage, the extrovert duke arranged a match between Charles and Henrietta Maria, the ardently Catholic sister of the King of France. The couple were married by proxy; when the big-eyed, buck-toothed queen, then aged 16, finally came over to England with several priests in her entourage, she burst into tears at the sight of her husband. She hated Buckingham; and she despised Charles for his weakness as much as he disliked her for her frivolity. For their first three years together, until the death of Buckingham, their mutual antagonism was so great that some said the marriage was not consummated.

As part of the marriage contract, Charles had promised to relax the penal laws against Roman Catholics and had lent the King of France some English ships, which

Shown in a contemporary engraving, conspirators plan the failed coup of 1605 known as the Gunpowder Plot. Roman Catholics incensed by an edict banishing priests, the group sought to blow up Parliament on November 5, 1605, when the King and members of both Houses would have been assembled for its ceremonial opening. Enlisting the help of a soldier and explosives expert named Guy Fawkes, they rented the cellars that ran beneath the House. Fawkes installed barrels containing almost two tonnes of gunpowder in the vaults and covered them with firewood and iron bars. But one of the plotters aroused suspicion by warning his brother-in-law not to attend the ceremony. The cellars were searched, Fawkes was arrested, and before his execution he revealed under torture the names of his fellow plotters.

Oliver Cromwell, seen here in a miniature by Samuel Cooper, was one of England's greatest soldiers and statesmen. Until 1642 he was simply a country gentleman with Puritan religious inclinations who sat as a Member of Parliament and more than once had considered emigrating to America. After the outbreak of the Civil War, however, he became the best cavalry commander in the entire Parliamentary army, and his disciplined and dedicated troops, nicknamed "Ironsides", played a key role in its victory.

were subsequently used against the French Protestants – the Huguenots. Deeply suspicious of the new king's intentions, Parliament failed to vote him adequate taxes for an expedition to Cadiz, which had been planned by Buckingham as part of the ongoing war with Spain and which subsequently ended in fiasco. Worse still, they refused to grant the traditional tunnage and poundage. Charles had no choice but to raise the money himself. His methods, however, went far beyond anything that his father had tried.

He levied tunnage and poundage without the proper parliamentary consent and thereby incensed the merchants. He also imposed a forced loan to the Crown on property holders and imprisoned all those who refused to pay, which infuriated the landed gentry. And, having fallen out with his brother-in-law and having decided to send an expedition to the aid of the Huguenot rebels in France, he angered everyone living along England's southeast coast by billeting his men in the houses of the local population and in addition imposing martial law on soldiers and civilians alike.

When Charles summoned Parliament in 1628, there was hardly a man in it whose family had not suffered from the exercise of the royal prerogative. Despite the anti-Catholic swing in his foreign policy, both the House of Lords and the House of Commons refused to supply him with any money until he had unwillingly assented to a document known as the Petition of Right, which outlawed forced loans, compulsory billeting, martial law and imprisonment without cause.

Some months later, the hated Buckingham was assassinated by a disgruntled Puritan naval officer who had served on his unsuccessful foreign expeditions. Nevertheless, Parliament remained hostile when it met again after a six-month-long recess. In the first place the members were angry because the King was still collecting unauthorized tunnage and poundage. In the second place they were deeply concerned about the future of the English church, which was being modified in a Roman Catholic direction by the churchmen whom the King was appointing to bishoprics, particularly by the new bishop of London, William Laud. To the passionate reformers in Parliament, it seemed as though the differences between the Church of England and the Church of Rome were being reduced almost to vanishing point.

A confrontation quickly materialized. On March 2, 1629, a member from Cornwall, Sir John Eliot, proposed a motion that was bitterly critical of the Crown. When the King ordered Parliament to be dissolved, the members barred the door, forcibly held the Speaker down in his chair so that their proceedings would still be legal, and then passed resolutions condemning as enemies of the state all those who collected or paid tunnage and poundage or furthered popery.

Next day, when Parliament was dissolved at last, Eliot and the other leaders of the debate were arrested and imprisoned in the Tower of London, where Eliot subsequently died. For the next 11 years Charles ruled England without summoning another Parliament. Under Laud, who became archbishop of Canterbury, altars were restored to the churches, and a series of strict regulations banning dancing, archery and other amusements on Sundays, which had been introduced in James's time to placate the Puritans, were rescinded. Many disillusioned Puritans gave up hope and emigrated to America.

By avoiding war and living frugally, the King managed to keep his expenses to a minimum. Like his father before him, he granted monopolies, and he imposed new taxes and resurrected old fines. But at the end of those 11 years his need for money suddenly increased dramatically.

An ill-advised attempt to impose a new Laudian prayer book on Scotland resulted in the eruption of a full-scale rebellion. In the spring of 1640, Charles summoned what was to be known as the Short Parliament and asked it for the money to finance an army. Inevitably, both Houses refused to grant him a single penny until he redressed their many grievances. On May 5, after making little serious effort to negotiate, the King simply dissolved Parliament and began to muster as much as he could of the militias – the volunteer regiments which all the counties in England were required to maintain for the defence of the realm. These troops were both ill-equipped and ill-prepared; they seldom trained for more than a few hours each year before retiring to the nearest tavern.

The sullen militiamen, many of whom had been press-ganged unwillingly into the King's service, were no match for an angry, well-armed Scots force led by professional officers who had served in continental armies. The English were put to ignominious flight. In the treaty that followed, Charles allowed the Scots to occupy part of northern England and agreed to pay the expenses of their army until a full peace was arranged.

That autumn he summoned another Parliament. It was to sit for the next 20 years, winning for itself the title of the Long Parliament. One of its earliest enactments prevented it from being dissolved without its own consent.

The humiliated king could do nothing but accept its terms. The Scots were waiting, and the citizens of London were rioting in protest at the popish innovations of his bishops. He submitted meekly to the curtailment of his prerogative, particularly with regard to the imposition of duties and taxes. By the time the Scots had been paid off, he had seen his archbishop imprisoned in the Tower of London and had signed a death warrant for his closest adviser, the Earl of Strafford, who had been attainted for treason by Parliament.

Despite everything, a majority of the members of both Houses were intent on reform, not revolution. But there was a growing body of Puritans, led by a landowner called John Pym, who had set their sights not merely on bishops and the Book of Common Prayer but also on the King's monopoly of executive power. Once the immediate problems of the war against the Scots had been resolved, they began to argue their case for limiting the royal prerogative. As the ensuing heated debates rose to a climax, fate played straight into their hands. The news reached London of another rebellion.

This time the insurrection was in Ireland. Despite the country's nominal allegiance to the English king, its sovereign, the island's impoverished inhabitants were for the most part bitterly hostile towards their foreign rulers. In an attempt to make the nation more governable, King James I had dispossessed thousands of Catholic farmers in the northern province of Ulster, granting their land instead to Scottish Protestant settlers. The simmering grievances that were left behind by the Plantation of Ulster, as it was called, now burst into outright rebellion. Some four or five thousand of the newcomers were massacred, and many more fled to the hills, where they faced starvation.

There was no longer any good reason for Parliament to refuse the finance for an effective army. But once the King had control of such a force, there was a real possibility that he would use it not to crush the Irish rebels as intended but to overpower his foes within the House of Commons. Many members were already alarmed by rumours of royal plots, and the extremists exploited their anxiety. John Pym persuaded the members of both Houses to protect themselves by requesting the right to appoint the army's senior officers. When the King adamantly refused to surrender any more of his sovereignty to Parliament, Pym and his supporters introduced the Grand Remonstrance.

This document consisted of a long list of all the wrongs which the English church and state had suffered at the hands of the King, followed by a summary of Parliament's accomplishments and a number of specific proposals. One of these demanded that a synod should be summoned to supervise a religious reformation in England, and another insisted that in future all the King's appointed ministers should be approved by Parliament.

The Commons was divided in its attitude towards the Remonstrance. The prospect of radical religious reform was too much for many members. After a fortnight of fierce debate the Remonstrance was adopted, but only by 159 votes to 148; a third of the House had abstained.

If the King had only waited, the missing members might well have rallied to his cause and the Remonstrance might subsequently have been overturned. Instead, he overreacted violently. Urged on by the taunts of his contemptuous queen, he ordered his attorney general to impeach his leading opponents in both Houses of Parliament. On January 4, 1642, he went down to the Commons himself at the head of a contingent of armed guards to arrest five of its members. It was the first time that an English monarch had entered the premises in person. But when he sat down in the Speaker's chair and looked around the astonished house, he saw that the five members had already departed. One of the Queen's ladies-in-waiting had warned them of the impending raid.

London rose in outrage at the King's blatant breach of parliamentary privilege. The city's 6,000-strong citizens' militia, known as the Trained Bands, was mobilized to protect Parliament; and unlike other volunteer forces around the country, the Trained Bands took their soldiering very seriously and drilled regularly under experienced professionals. A contingent from the Royal Navy, who had long been

A sequence of illustrations from a 17th-century military manual shows the correct way to fire a musket. Such works helped familiarize English officers with the new drill and tactics then being employed on the continent of Europe in the long-drawn-out conflict that became known as the Thirty Years' War. The strategic innovations were designed above all to get maximum benefit from the use of firearms, which were available in ever-growing numbers but which still generally lacked finesse. The musket seen here was a heavy, hazardous weapon fired not by a spark from a flint but by a match made from cord boiled in vinegar, which was kept permanently burning.

discontented over their pay and conditions, marched up mutinously from the docks to join them. Fearful for his own safety, King Charles abandoned his capital on January 10. He was never to return to it as a free man.

Negotiations continued for a while, but the King would not accept the terms of his Parliament, and Parliament would not trust the word of its King. On a wet and windy English summer's day in 1642, King Charles I raised his standard at Nottingham. His herald could hardly read the declaration of war because the King had altered it so many times, and during the night, when the wind increased, the standard was blown down into the mud. The English Civil War had begun with an unpropitious omen for the Royalist cause.

The English did not divide by class to fight the war. They chose sides in accordance with their consciences, their own personal loyalties and the demands of self-preservation. Nevertheless, a majority of the greater landowners fought for "King and Country", while there was a tendency for those who had grown rich in the booming cloth industry to support "God and Parliament". In general the Royalists were strongest in the north and west, while the Parliamentarians were dominant in the richer south and east. But in every town and in every county – even within some families – there were supporters of the two parties. There were also many who hoped to stay neutral and let the war pass them by. At the outset, according to the Earl of Clarendon who wrote a famous history of the conflict, "the number of those who desired to sit still was greater than the number of those who desired to engage in either party". As the war dragged on, however, more and more were forced to choose either one side or the other in order to protect themselves from plunderers, press gangs or persecution.

Even within Parliament the divisions were not clear-cut. Although a majority of the members of the House of Lords were Royalists, there were around 30, more than a quarter of the total, who sided with Parliament and who provided it with its first generals; and over a third of the House of Commons, more than 170 of its members, remained loyal to the King. Most of them had been his opponents since the Long Parliament was first summoned, but when it came to war they could not bring themselves to fight against him. Sir Edmund Verney, who became the King's standard-bearer and saw his own family divided by the conflict, spoke despondently for many of them. "I have eaten his bread and served him near 30 years, and will not do so base a thing as to forsake him; and choose rather to lose my life (which I am sure I shall do) to preserve and defend those things which are against my conscience to preserve and defend."

PARLIAMENT VICTORIOUS

The Battle of Naseby, fought on June 14, 1645, was the decisive encounter of the Civil War. The disposition of troops at the start of the engagement was subsequently depicted in the engraving shown here, which was published two years after the battle. It shows the Northamptonshire village of Naseby in the foreground, with the Parliamentary baggage train on its left and spectators on a hill to its right. Below them, the cavalry of Oliver Cromwell, on the right flank of Parliament's New Model Army, faces the Royalist cavalry of Sir Marmaduke Langdale. On the other wing, the horsemen of Cromwell's son-in-law, Henry Ireton, confront the high-spirited troopers of Charles I's nephew, Prince Rupert. Although the artist depicted the King in front of his infantry, Charles in fact commanded his army from the group at the rear, near the top of the hill.

The battle opened with a charge by Rupert's horsemen. Despite a devastating musket volley from Parliamentarian dragoons who had dismounted and hidden in a hedge, his men kept going and chased the bulk of Ireton's cavalry back as far as the baggage train. Behind them, the two advancing lines of infantry engaged. But it was Cromwell's men who won the day. As their front ranks drove off Langdale's horsemen, the hindermost wheeled to attack the flank and rear of the Royalist infantry, who were surrounded when the dragoons from the hedge rode across to attack their other flank. Returning to the field after only an hour, Rupert's men were too late to save the day.

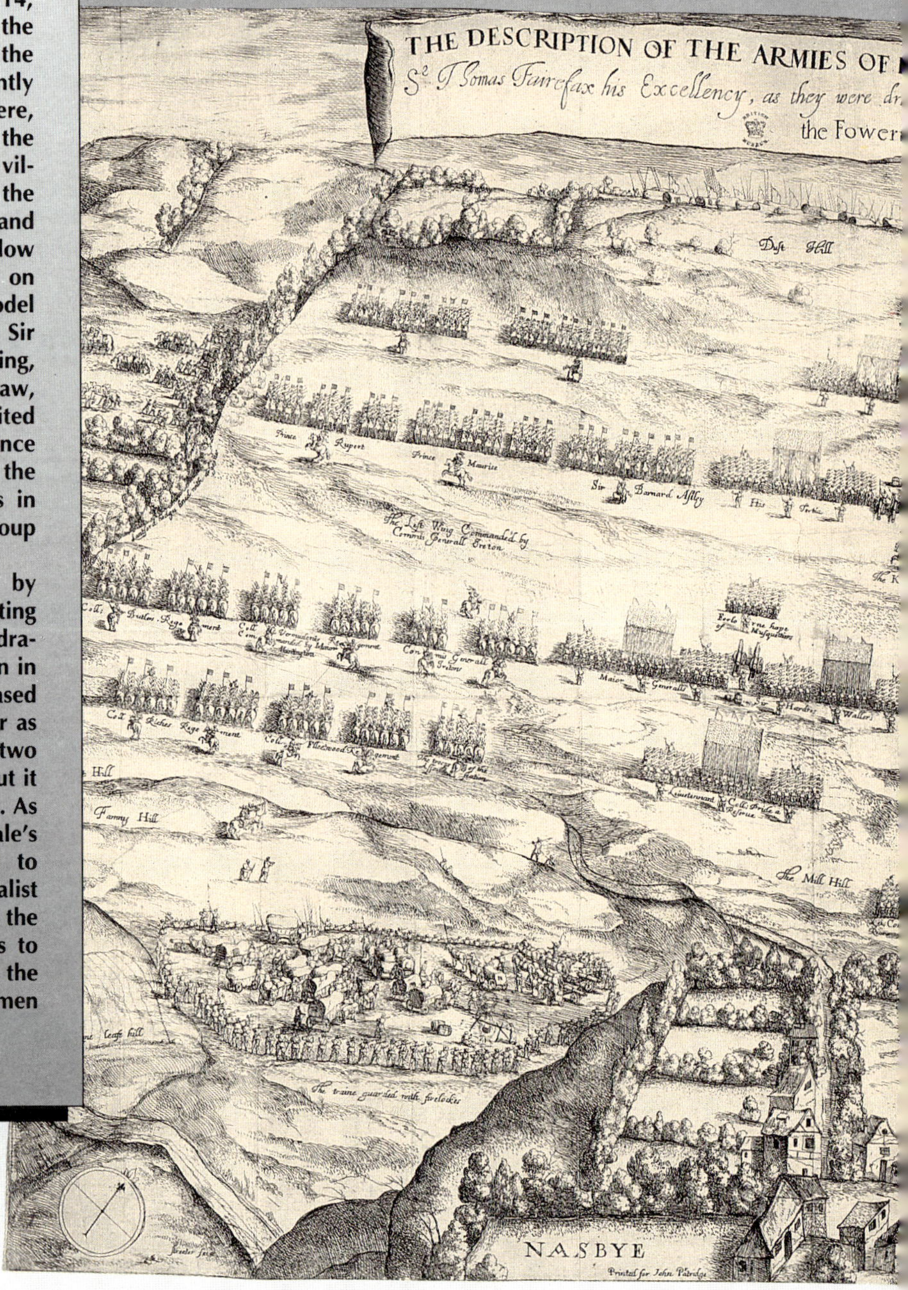

The standard of King Charles I, who commanded the Royalist army at Naseby, combines symbols representing England, Ireland, France and Scotland. Although personally brave, Charles was not a good general; he gave battle when his men were outnumbered, and failed to commit his cavalry reserves when there was still a chance of saving his infantry.

The standard of Sir Thomas Fairfax, commander in chief of the Parliamentarian army, flew over his headquarters. A scholar as well as a soldier, Fairfax fought for Parliament from the outset. Never a radical, he was shocked by the execution of the King and played a leading role in arranging the restoration of his son, Charles II.

The first volunteers to join up with the Parliamentary army were the apprentices of London, who wore their hair cropped short; as a result, the dour, determined Parliamentary soldiers were given the nickname "Roundheads". The carefree and reckless Royalists, on the other hand, were called "Cavaliers" after the brutal Spanish *caballeros* or horsemen who had oppressed Protestants in the Netherlands during the Dutch struggle for independence. Despite the nickname's connotations, King Charles himself authorized its use, commenting that it signified "no more than a gentleman serving his king on horseback".

In the beginning both sides recruited and paid for their armies in the same way. Their rich supporters sold their silver plate and other treasures – Queen Henrietta Maria's jewels among them – in order to provide the sort of wages that would induce men to enlist, and some large landowners even raised entire regiments from among their own tenants. But as time passed and the resources of the rich began to run out, the financial advantage tended towards the Parliamentarian cause. Parliament was able to borrow from the bankers in the City of London. Parliament introduced systems of assessment and imposed taxes on land and property which

A contemporary depiction of Charles I's execution shows a woman fainting as the executioner holds up the head of his royal victim. The beheading was carried out on January 30, 1649, outside the Banqueting House of Charles's own palace of Whitehall. Although this painting shows the King kneeling at a large block, he in fact had to lie with his head on a low one, so that he could have been tied down if he had chosen to struggle. The crowd that assembled to watch the proceedings was held well back by soldiers. Once the axe had fallen, however, some people scrambled onto the scaffold to dip handkerchiefs in the royal blood to keep as sacred relics.

were more efficient than any that had previously been imposed by the Crown. And since Parliament controlled not only the navy but also almost all the nation's ports, it was able to impose import duties.

With very few ports left at his disposal, and with his former navy blockading them, the King found it difficult enough to obtain supplies from the continent, let alone impose duties that would yield the money to pay his soldiers' overdue wages. But, at the outset of the war at least, the King did have the advantage in the quality of his recruits. The Welsh hills and the moors of Cornwall provided him with hardy and tenacious infantry; and the great landowners and their followers provided the perfect raw material for first-class cavalry. Long experience gained in the hunting field had made them expert horsemen. Trained and led by the King's 22-year-old German nephew, Prince Rupert of the Rhine, they became the first effective shock troops of the war.

At the end of August 1642, the Parliamentary army marched north from London to Nottingham under the command of the Earl of Essex. By then, however, the King had gone west to collect his Welsh recruits, and by the time that Essex caught up with him he was already marching towards London. On October 23, Charles halted his army and turned to face his pursuers on the crest of Edgehill near Banbury in the Midlands. As the two armies prepared for the first great battle of the war, Sir Jacob Astley, the 63-year-old commander of the King's infantry, uttered a prayer that became celebrated: "Oh, Lord! Thou knowest how busy I must be this day: if I forget thee, do not thou forget me."

Both armies numbered around 13,000 men, and each was drawn up for battle in a similar formation. Units of steel-helmeted cavalry stood ready for action on either wing. The centres were made up of alternating squares of musketeers in large felt hats and helmeted pikemen bearing pikes that were anything from three to five metres in length. Both armies also had a few cannon, but the big guns were to prove of more use in siege warfare than on the battlefields. After each shot fired, it took a full five minutes to cool their barrels and reload them – and cavalry could cover a great deal of ground in five minutes.

The Roundheads wore orange sashes and the Cavaliers red ones, but apart from this distinction the regimental uniforms on either side were very much the same. The red coats worn by the King's Lifeguards, for example, were echoed in the Roundhead regiments of Lord Robartes and Denzil Holles. On several occasions during the Civil War the similarity in uniforms, particularly among the officers, enabled commanders to pass unnoticed through the enemy lines; more often, however, it led to fatal mistakes.

The battle opened with a brief and ineffective exchange of fire from the artillery. Then Prince Rupert led the cavalry on the Royalist right in a massed charge against the Roundhead left. After long argument, he had succeeded in persuading the Royalist commanders to abandon the traditional system, in which cavalry rode up to the enemy in a column, halted rank by rank to fire their pistols and then rode away again. Instead he followed the tactic introduced by Sweden's King Gustavus Adolphus during the Thirty Years' War, which was then raging in Germany. His men charged in line abreast and drove home their attack with their swords as they slammed into the enemy at full gallop.

The effect was dramatic. The horsemen on the Roundhead left broke and fled, and so too did the infantry next to them. Soon afterwards a charge from the

Royalist's other flank had a similar effect on the Roundhead right. But although Rupert had taught his men how to fight, he had not managed to instil discipline in them. Now, instead of rejoining the battle, they set off in pursuit of the fugitives and attacked the Roundhead baggage train.

When at last they rallied and returned to the battlefield, they were only just in time to avert complete disaster. Unsupported by any other cavalry, the Royalists had been forced back by a strong frontal assault from the Roundhead infantry and by flank attacks from their mounted reserves. Their guns had been captured, and the enemy had come so close to the King himself that his standard-bearer, the sad Sir Edmund Verney, had been killed. What could have been a crushing victory in the Royalists favour had ended in a bloody stalemate.

The Earl of Essex and the Parliamentary forces withdrew towards the west. The road to London now lay open to the King. But the Royalist commanders were in no doubt that the capital would be well defended against them. Ignoring the pleas and arguments of Prince Rupert, they advanced no farther than the university city of Oxford, situated some 80 kilometres to the northwest of the capital, which became their headquarters for the duration of the war.

The colleges of Oxford were turned into courts, council chambers, billets, arsenals and stables. Their quadrangles became sheep pens, playhouses and duelling grounds. The whole atmosphere of the ancient seat of learning changed as

THE RELIGIOUS RADICALS

In the chaotic years of the Civil War, a diverse group of nonconforming sects made their appearance in England, to the general alarm of the moderate Puritans who made up a majority of Parliament's supporters. Among the groups who are satirized in the pamphlet illustration shown here are the Arians, who rejected the doctrine of the Trinity; Soul Sleepers, who denied the afterlife; the Family of Love, who kept no sabbath; Seekers, who sought a personal relationship with God; and also the advocates of easier divorce, whose number included the poet John Milton. For good measure the pamphlet's author included two old enemies, associated in Parliamentarian minds with the Royalist cause: the Catholic Jesuits, and the Arminians, who supported the High Church Anglicanism of Charles's archbishop of Canterbury, William Laud.

The Great Seal of England, which was fixed to official documents to guarantee their authenticity, shows the Speaker *(centre)* presiding over a session of Parliament in the year 1651. Three years earlier the House had been purged of moderate members opposed to the execution of the King. The "Rump Parliament" that remained set up the special court that condemned Charles I to death. It subsequently did away with the House of Lords and abolished the monarchy, proclaiming in its place a republican regime known as the Commonwealth.

the city became filled with fashionable women and ill-paid fighting men who lived mostly on plunder and sought to the best of their abilities to present themselves as the very opposite of their pious enemies.

With the opening of armed conflict between the two sides, the war of words also intensified. Puritan pamphlets accused the Royalists of various atrocities. One suggested that Prince Rupert was a witch and that his dog Boye was his familiar. Others tried to destroy morale by printing false lists of Royalist casualties, in response to one of which the following appeared in the Royalist newspaper, *Mercurius Aulicus*: "Sir Jacob Astley lately slain at Gloucester, wishes to know was he slain with a musket or a cannon bullet?"

While the Roundhead generals mounted sieges and manoeuvred aimlessly, the Cavaliers planned a three-pronged attack on London, with one army coming from the north, one from Oxford and one from the southwest. But at the same time the Parliamentarian leaders were making plans of their own. On September 25, 1643, little more than six weeks before his death from cancer, John Pym triumphantly concluded a crucial alliance with the King's Scottish opponents. The two parties accepted the Solemn League and Covenant: in return for a promise to bring the churches of England, Scotland and Ireland "to the nearest conjunction and uniformity in religion", and also a payment of £30,000 a month, the Scots agreed to send an army to England in support of the Parliamentarians.

Events in eastern England were equally auspicious for the Parliamentary cause. The big, clever, melancholy Member of Parliament for Cambridge, Oliver Cromwell, had been in the thick of the fighting at the Battle of Edgehill and had seen how the Roundhead horsemen, whom he described as "old decayed serving men and tapsters", had fled in the face of Rupert's Cavaliers. He had returned filled with a determination to build the best regiments of cavalry in England from the ranks of the nonconformist local yeomanry, men he described as being "of greater understanding than common soldiers". "I had rather," he wrote, "have a plain russet-coated captain that knows what he fights for and loves what he knows than what you call 'a gentleman' and is nothing else."

He dressed his recruits in red coats, and provided them with the best armour and weapons that were available. Believing passionately that every man had the right to find his own way of God, he tolerated his soldiers' differing and unorthodox Puritan faiths. But he also used their religious zeal as the basis on which to build stern moral and military discipline. And he taught them the Swedish tactics that the Royalists had already learnt.

At the end of June 1644, Cromwell and his newly trained troopers joined forces with a combined army of Scots and Roundheads that had been forced to abandon a siege of York by a relief column under the command of Prince Rupert. On July 2, the Puritan allies met Rupert and his army at Marston Moor, 10 kilometres to the west of the city. There were 27,000 Roundheads and Scots, against only 18,000 Cavaliers; but Rupert had received a letter from the King specifically ordering him to fight, and he obeyed the order.

All that day the armies faced each other, and then, in the evening, when Prince Rupert had stood his men down and gone to the rear to have his supper, Oliver Cromwell led his troopers in a charge against the cavalry on the Royalist right. After some initial success, they fell back when Rupert joined in with his reserves, but the Cavaliers were then overwhelmed by the Scots cavalry which appeared on their flank. For the first time in the war Rupert's horsemen retreated; and as the Scots set out after them, Cromwell's disciplined soldiers turned back to rescue the hard-pressed Roundhead infantry.

By nightfall a Parliamentary victory had been assured. The Royalist cavalry's reputation for invincibility had been destroyed, and 4,000 of the King's soldiers lay dead on the battlefield. In the thick of the fighting, Cromwell himself had been wounded. Rupert, much impressed by his enemy's stubborn strength and courage, had referred to him as "Old Ironsides". It was a nickname that was soon to be applied to all Cromwell's cavalry.

Northern England was now at the mercy of Parliament. But the success was offset by disaster in the southwest, where the Earl of Essex had been forced to surrender all his infantry at Lostwithiel after advancing too deep into Royalist Cornwall. It was time for the russet-coated captains to take over from the gentlemen.

At Cromwell's urging, the House of Commons now agreed to reconstitute the Parliamentary army. During the winter of 1644 to 1645 the old, personally raised regiments were disbanded and the men were incorporated into new, highly trained and disciplined units. Local conscription was imposed to increase their numbers. Overall command was put in the hands of Sir Thomas Fairfax, and command of the cavalry was given to Oliver Cromwell.

On June 14, 1645, the last great battle of the war took place at Naseby in Leicestershire. On one side, there were 7,000 Royalists commanded by the King. On the other, there were 11,000 soldiers of Parliament's New Model Army.

Once again Rupert and his Cavaliers charged the horsemen on the Roundhead left and, although outnumbered, chased them from the field. But Cromwell was on the right. In their own charge, his new troopers broke the cavalry on the King's left; and since he had superior numbers, he was able to hold the rear ranks back from the pursuit and wheel them to attack the flank and rear of the Royalist infantry, most of whom surrendered. By the time that Rupert's men finally returned to the battlefield, the day was lost.

The Parliamentary victory at Naseby was not as bloody as at Marston Moor. Only 1,000 Cavaliers were killed, but more than 4,000 of them were captured, along with their cannon, 8,000 muskets and all of their ammunition. In addition, the righteous troopers of the New Model Army slaughtered a hundred of the women whom they found in the King's camp, and they branded several hundred more as prostitutes by slitting their noses or scarring their faces.

After Naseby the New Model Army set about mopping up the remaining opposition and taking Royalist towns with bombardments and storming parties. Rupert, who had been sent to hold the vital west-coast port of Bristol, became convinced that the King's only hope was to agree terms with Parliament. By early September he had barely a thousand men left, and a plague was spreading among the citizens. He agreed to surrender the city to Fairfax, who allowed the Cavaliers to keep their colours and march away as free men.

It was not long before the King too had to accept that his cause was lost. In April 1646, the last Royalist army left in the field was defeated at Stow-on-the-Wold in Gloucestershire. Rather than give himself up to his Parliamentarian enemies, Charles chose to surrender to the Scots. Rupert tried desperately to dissuade him from this course, but the King ignored him. On April 27, 1646, Charles left his nephew at Oxford and set out in disguise for the Scots camp at Newark. Eight

A Dutch painting of 1660 commemorates a ball held at The Hague to celebrate the departure for England of Charles Stuart, son and heir of the executed Charles I, to be crowned as Charles II. After the death of Oliver Cromwell in 1658, army leaders and other influential figures came to see the restoration of the monarchy as the only way to avoid large-scale civil disorder. In the painting, the King is shown dancing with his sister Mary, princess of Orange. Two other future kings of England are also featured. Behind Charles, in a cloak, stands his brother James, duke of York, who was to succeed him as James II; and beyond the dancers, with the ladies of the Dutch court, stands Mary's nine-year-old son, Prince William III of Orange, who later married James's daughter and ruled jointly with her in her father's place.

weeks later, Oxford surrendered to Fairfax, and once again the commander of the New Model Army was chivalrous, allowing Rupert and his brother Maurice to leave England with their servants.

At Newark, the astonished Scots made the King their prisoner. But Charles behaved as though he was a guest and negotiated haughtily with Parliament. In August, Parliament offered to restore him to his throne in return for the imposition of Presbyterianism in England, the punishment of his chief supporters and the surrender of control of the army. When Charles refused to comply, the Scots, who had approved the terms, handed him over to the English in return for a down payment of half the £400,000 which Parliament still owed them. As the Scots marched northwards to the border, the King, who had mocked them for selling him so cheaply, was led away to become the prisoner of Parliament at Holmby House in Northamptonshire. The first phase of the fighting was over.

After the defeat at Stow-on-the-Wold, the vanquished Royalist commander, old Sir Jacob Astley, sat down on a drum among his captors and told them: "You have done your work, boys, and may go play, unless you will fall out among yourselves." The words proved prophetic, for the Parliamentarian forces soon found themselves bitterly divided. The members of the Long Parliament regarded themselves as the arbiter of the new society that was to emerge with the ending of the war. But in creating the New Model Army, they had established a fresh power in the land, and one whose views were markedly different from their own. The officers of the New Model Army were more radical in both their religion and their politics; many of them were zealous followers of a variety of independent nonconformist sects, as were some of the ordinary soldiers.

CHRONICLER OF LONDON LIFE

The brilliant son of a London tailor, Samuel Pepys rose to become an important public figure. He was a Member of Parliament and president of the Royal Society, which promoted the sciences. As secretary of the Admiralty, he restored England's power at sea, doubling the strength of the navy and enabling it to compete on equal terms with the fleets of France and the Netherlands. Yet he came to be remembered most for his intimate diary, which provides a vivid, detailed and revealing portrait of social life in London during the 1660s.

Using shorthand for greater privacy, Pepys candidly wrote of his own weaknesses and gave enthusiastic accounts of his dinners, his visits to theatres and concerts and his many sexual adventures. But he also found room to discuss current affairs of state, commenting on corruption among public servants and describing the two terrible disasters that devastated London in the decade: the Great Plague and the Great Fire.

The pestilence – an outbreak of bubonic plague that produced soft black swellings on victims – killed almost 80,000 people in 1665. The fire raged through the city the following year until Charles II gave orders for all buildings in its path to be blown up. In all, some 13,000 houses and 87 churches were consumed. But the disaster provided a unique opportunity for one of Pepys's many friends, the architect Christopher Wren, who supervised the rebuilding of the city and enriched it with 53 churches and a splendid cathedral.

Dressed in an Indian robe hired specially for the occasion, the diarist Samuel Pepys poses for a portrait holding the manuscript of his favourite song, *Beauty Retire*, with words by the poet Sir William Davenant and a tune written by Pepys himself. The painting dates from 1666, when Pepys was 33. On seeing it, he confided to his diary, "I am very well satisfied".

"Lay long, being bitter, cold, frosty day, the frost being now grown old, and the Thames covered with ice."

1st January, 1666

With its flow impeded by the arches of old bridges, the Thames froze in harsh winters, and citizens held Frost Fairs on the ice, as in this late 17th-century painting. But the "bitter cold" of 1665 to 1666 also helped to kill off the Great Plague, spread by fleas on rats during an unusually long, hot summer.

"It being darkish we saw the fire as only one entire arch of fire from this to the other side of the bridge, and in a bow up the hill, for an arch of above a mile long. It made me weep to see it. The churches, houses, and all on fire and flaming at once, and a horrid noise the flames made, and the cracking of houses at their ruin."

2nd September, 1666

The Great Fire of London, depicted here at its height by a Dutch artist who was almost certainly an eyewitness, began in a baker's shop near the River Thames and raged for three days through 160 hectares of timber-framed houses, leaving 200,000 people homeless.

"The people die so, that now it seems they are fain to carry the dead to be buried by daylight, the nights not sufficing to do it in. And my Lord Mayor commands people to be within at 9 at night, all (as they say) that the sick may have liberty to go abroad for ayre."

12th August, 1665

Hand bells such as this one *(right)* were rung as a warning of their approach by the drivers of the "dead-carts" that carried the contagious corpses of plague victims. The bodies were buried in quicklime in huge "plague pits" by ceaseless shifts of often drunken grave-diggers.

In September 1646, without pausing to fully consider the consequences, the pro-Presbyterian majority in Parliament introduced bills which ruled that proponents of certain named sects, including the Unitarians who denied the doctrine of the Trinity, could be put to death; less heretical nonconformists, such as Baptists who merely advocated adult baptism, could be imprisoned for life. In December, they introduced another ruling that no layman should be allowed to preach. The army leaders protested vehemently, but Parliament continued blindly along the road to self-destruction. Eight months later, as a prelude to the sectarian persecutions promised by its ordinances, it ordered the soldiers of the New Model Army to disband or else volunteer for service against the Catholic rebels in Ireland. The troops, already close to mutiny because their pay was badly in arrears, refused to do either and defiantly withdrew to their headquarters at Newmarket, east of Cambridge. As the local Member of Parliament, Oliver Cromwell rode over to try and negotiate a compromise, but once he realized that the men were adamant, he remained among them and took their side.

A few days later, acting on his own initiative, a young officer called George Joyce led 500 troopers to Holmby House, arrested the King and brought him back to Newmarket as a prisoner of the army. When the King asked to see his commission, Joyce simply pointed to the men behind him. "Indeed," said His Majesty, "it is one I can read without spelling."

Cromwell and some of the other officers offered to restore the King to his throne in return for religious toleration and parliamentary control of state appointments. It was the best offer that any of his opponents ever made to him, but Charles refused it, believing now that he could play his enemies off against one another.

For a time it looked as though he might be right. The army bolstered its position by marching on London in order to protect its interests, but its own members were divided in their aspirations. In the autumn, an elected army council met at Putney to determine the next move. Some spokesmen still hoped to reach a constitutional agreement with the King. Others, particularly from the rank and file, wanted to abolish the monarchy and the House of Lords and establish a democracy with votes for all men. And while they debated, the King slipped away to the Isle of Wight and started secret negotiations with the Scots.

Suddenly the weary country found itself at war again. By promising to accept Presbyterianism for three years and to allow parliamentary control of the army for ten, the King managed to forge a strange alliance between forces that had been fighting one another little more than a year previously. As the Scots army crossed the border in the north, Royalists rose in rebellion in Wales and in the south and west of England, and English Presbyterians who had previously fought against the King rallied in response to his promises. Half the navy mutinied in his favour.

The only force that stood against them all was the New Model Army, but it proved more than a match for them. Fairfax routed the Royalists in the south and west. Cromwell suppressed the Welsh and then marched north to defeat the Scots in a running battle at Preston, Wigan and Warrington. When the soldiers returned to London, they were eager for vengeance against the King, who had in their view deceitfully played at negotiating with the army while secretly planning to renew the war. Their leaders also came increasingly to support this point of view.

Angry voices now urged that the King be killed. Yet such a drastic move could not be considered without the support of Parliament; and the great majority of its members, by now more scared of the radical elements in the army than of the poor remnants of royal power, would not contemplate such a deed. The impasse was finally resolved by force. On December 6, 1648, Colonel Thomas Pride at the head of a company of musketeers secluded or arrested 96 members of the Commons. Pride's Purge, as the coup became known, left a rump of about 60 nonconformist Parliamentarians who were prepared to support the army line.

The "Rump Parliament" did the job that the army desired of it. It set up a specially appointed high court of justice that brought the King to London and tried him for treason in Westminster Hall. He was duly found guilty and sentenced to death. The less politicized elements of the nation, who still tended to see the King as God's anointed representative sent to rule his people on earth, reacted with stunned disbelief. Indeed, there were few people in England outside the ranks of the army who did not regard the sentence as a crime. But there was none who could prevent its being carried out.

On January 30, 1649, the King stepped through a window on to a scaffold set up outside the beautiful Banqueting House which Inigo Jones had designed for his father at the royal palace of Whitehall. For all his faults, Charles had never been anything but brave. Since it was a cold day, he had insisted on wearing two shirts so that there would be no shivers that the crowd could mistake for fear. He knelt in prayer, then lay down with his head on the block and stretched out a hand as a signal that he was ready. The axe fell, cutting through the King's neck with a single blow, and the huge crowd groaned as his head was held up to them.

This glazed earthenware bust of King William III was made at Delft in the Netherlands, where William had served as stadholder – military commander – for 16 years before his accession to the English throne. Invited to England by Protestants discontented with the rule of the Catholic James II, William took power after a bloodless coup that ended in James's flight to France. He was to rule jointly with his wife Mary, daughter of the deposed monarch, until her death in 1694, and then on his own for a further eight years. For William, the price of the throne was acceptance of the Bill of Rights, a document that limited royal power and upheld the role of Parliament in the government of the land.

The widespread revulsion at the execution of the King gave momentum to the last phase of the fighting. The Irish Catholic Royalists, who were still undefeated, transferred their allegiance to the King's 19-year-old heir, Prince Charles. And the Scots agreed to provide the young Charles with an army in return for the promise of a Presbyterian England. But the New Model Army had now reached the height of its power, and in the last campaigns it was Cromwell who led it.

After returning from Ireland, where he had broken the resistance with ruthless and unforgettable brutality, he marched north to defeat the Scots at the Battle of Dunbar. When Prince Charles invaded England at the head of a second Scots army, collecting Royalist reinforcements as he advanced, Cromwell annihilated them at the Battle of Worcester. For six weeks after the battle the young prince evaded Cromwell's troopers, hiding in an oak tree, disguising himself as a woodcutter and passing through their ranks dressed as a lady's maid, until at last he found a boat at Brighton on the south coast and sailed away to France and safety.

The Battle of Worcester, on August 24, 1651, secured the rule of the new government within the boundaries of Great Britain, and by the middle of the following year it was secure beyond the seas as well. A squadron of Royalist ships under the command of Prince Rupert had been driven into the Mediterranean, and the Royalist colonies of Barbados, Virginia and Maryland had submitted. In the years that followed, the commercial interests in Parliament led England into a fierce naval war with the Dutch, whose merchant ships were carrying much of the trade between England and her colonies in Asia, Africa and America. They passed Navigation Acts which ruled that all such trade must be carried in ships built and manned by Englishmen; and in enforcing these acts, English warships asserted their control over the Channel and proved a match for what was then the most powerful and professional navy in the world. As a result, England's reputation rose in Europe to a level unknown since the days of the Tudors.

At home it was a very different story. The triumph of the New Model Army was not the triumph of democracy. After the execution of the King, the House of Lords was abolished and England was declared a Commonwealth. But antagonism grew between the Rump Parliament and the army, which disliked the many lawyers among Parliament's members, criticized the Dutch war and wanted radical religious and constitutional reforms. On April 20, 1653, Cromwell forcibly dissolved Parliament and locked the doors of its debating chamber. Soon afterwards a new Parliament purged of all those opposed to Cromwell declared him Lord Protector, and it was not long before he was ruling England as little less than a military dictator. It was not a position that he wanted; when his supporters offered to make him King, he refused. Yet, as he said himself, "No man climbs so high as he who does not know where he is going".

By the time Cromwell died in 1658, the English had had their fill of Puritan austerity. Old animosities rose again, and on a new tide of Royalism the throne was offered to Prince Charles – on no conditions other than a general amnesty, religious toleration and payment of the army's arrears. On May 29, 1660, King Charles II entered London to a delirious welcome from its citizens. Soon afterwards Prince Rupert returned as well and spent the rest of his life in England, becoming a vice admiral and the first governor of the Hudson's Bay Company in North America.

Under the rule of Charles II, the cultural life of the kingdom found new energy to fill the void left by the Puritans. The theatre was revived. The architects who had travelled with the King in Europe began to build fine new classical houses. And guided by the advice of his first minister, Lord Clarendon, the King maintained a statesmanlike, if not always cordial, relationship with his Parliament.

But the restoration of Charles II was not the end of the conflict between King and Parliament. Although Charles had many children, he left no legitimate heir, and he was succeeded by his brother James, who had become a Roman Catholic. James II promoted fellow Catholics to high office in both the state and the army; when his subjects protested, he simply emulated his father and invoked the royal prerogative. Within a couple of years, Members of Parliament were again plotting to overthrow their king. In secret negotiations they offered the throne jointly to James's daughter Mary and her Dutch husband, Prince William of Orange.

On November 5, 1688, at the start of what became known as the Glorious Revolution, William landed in England. James, knowing that he was without support, fled across the Channel to France. Six months later, William and Mary were jointly crowned. But the English Parliament laid down terms for its support. The price of their accession was the Bill of Rights, which barred Catholics from the throne, abolished the royal power to suspend laws and to levy money by "pretence of prerogative", made standing armies illegal in time of peace, and insisted that there should be frequent Parliaments and free elections.

The restoration of Charles II had re-established the balance of power between monarchy and Parliament. With the Bill of Rights, the Glorious Revolution tipped the scales in favour of Parliament. The struggle and the excesses were over. A constitutional monarchy had been created. At last, the basic liberties that English men and women had crossed the Atlantic to establish in a new world had been planted just as firmly in the blood-stained soil of the kingdom that they left behind.

Throughout Europe, the 17th century saw government concentrated in the hands of rulers with almost despotic powers. This centralizing tendency found theoretical expression in the doctrine of absolutism – the belief that sovereignty was vested exclusively in a nation-state's ruler, who was not obliged to share his authority with any other person or body.

Although he was subject to no agency of the state, the new style of monarch appeared in the political thought of the time as a defender of individual rights and liberties. Theorists argued that the unconditional power of a king, exercised from a central seat of government, was an advance upon the warring influences of regional nobles and magistrates. Centralized rule brought greater efficiency and control, and when these led to economic and military successes, they provided apparent justification for the system.

Such was the case in 17th-century France, where absolutism reached its most developed form. The nation's young king, Louis XIV, became for all Europe the apotheosis of the absolute monarch. He came to the throne in 1643 when he was only four years old, but it was not until the death of his adviser Cardinal Mazarin in 1661 that he established the personal control over every aspect of government that became central to his view of kingship. During his long reign – he died in 1715 – he embodied an entire era of political development. He believed that "the profession of king is great, noble, a fount of delight. It is through and for work that one reigns." His advice to a new king was, "God who made you king will give you the necessary guidance".

In 1662 Louis adopted the sun *(above)* as his personal symbol, citing "the unique quality of the radiance . . . the light it imparts to other stars . . . the good it does in every place". By then he had already made the decision to build a palace that would be a worthy setting for his conception of royal majesty. The court that he created at Versailles was to be France's seat of government for more than a century; in its halls and gardens was played out day by day, as though on a public stage, a living tableau of kingly power.

AT THE COURT OF THE SUN KING

A SETTING FOR SUPREME POWER

Louis XIV's huge palace at Versailles, 20 kilometres southwest of Paris, had its origins in a hunting lodge built by the King's father from 1624 on. Successive stages of enlargement and remodelling spread over 60 years transformed the complex from a country retreat for the pleasure-loving young king and his circle into the administrative nerve centre of the realm and a symbolic monument to Europe's supreme monarch.

The scale of the building was colossal – in the 1680s it was reported that 36,000 bricklayers were at work daily on the palace – and the cost, though never precisely divulged, was astronomical. By the mid-1670s the King was spending long periods at Versailles, accompanied by courtiers and some government ministers, and in 1682 the court with all its staff and functions was transferred there from Paris.

Grandeur, rather than comfort or convenience, was the guiding principle. The palace, explicitly conceived as a formal setting for the art of kingship, abounded with allegorical statuary and symbolic references, but there were many complaints about the unhealthy air, the cramped living quarters, and the vast grounds that were muddy in winter and scorching in summer.

Beneath the extravagant show lay hardheaded political expediency. The removal of the court from Paris underlined the King's Olympian superiority to all external influences. The courtiers who vied with each other for a place at his side and beggared themselves to keep up with court life remained constantly under Louis' eye, and had neither the time nor the money to challenge his position.

Versailles served also as an international showcase that other monarchs came to marvel at and went home to imitate. Its glass, tapestries, marble and lace, all produced locally, firmly established France as the arbiter of European taste.

Clad in his coronation robes, Louis XIV gazes from a portrait by Hyacinth Rigaud. The King's physical grace was well noted; he was an accomplished dancer whose "least gesture, his walk, his bearing" was, in Saint-Simon's words, "all seemly, noble . . . and withal very natural".

A long column of outriders stream into Versailles' circular forecourt as the King and Queen arrive at the palace buildings in separate coaches. Painted by Pierre Patel, the scene shows the palace in 1668 when the original lodge – the central block between the projecting wings – was still clearly discernible among the grandiose additions.

Louise de la Vallière

Mme de Montespan

Mme de Maintenon

The first of Louis' three official mistresses was an officer's daughter, Louise de la Vallière, who shared the King's equestrian skill. She was succeeded by Mme de Montespan; intelligent and ambitious, she kept the court lively and witty. The 48-year-old Mme de Maintenon became his morganatic wife after Queen Marie-Thérèse died in 1683.

An allegorical painting by Jean Nocret represents Louis as the Greek god Apollo, and his family as fellow divinities. Portrayed as the earth mother Cybele, the King's mother, Anne of Austria, is shown seated at centre even though she had died in 1666, three years before the painting was completed. To her right, the King's brother, "Monsieur", and his wife are shown as Pluto and Flora. Queen Marie-Thérèse, sitting on the King's left hand, represents Juno, queen of the gods.

OLYMPIAN ACTORS IN THE ROYAL PLAY

The world Louis created at Versailles was peopled with courtiers, civil servants, government officials, chamberlains, cooks, huntsmen, maids, governesses – all the inhabitants of a small city. After 1682, there were said to be 10,000 people resident in the palace, with perhaps 50,000 other attendants and servants accommodated in the vicinity.

But the main players to whom all eyes turned were the King and and his circle. The court, ruled by Louis' favour and patronage, was full of intrigue; even the King's own family jockeyed for position. Louis' brother, known as "Monsieur", was one of the most important members of the inner circle. Monsieur's wife, called "Madame", and Louis' cousin, "Mademoiselle", also ranked high in the order of precedence. Louis' queen was his cousin Marie-Thérèse of Spain, by whom he had six children, only one of whom – the Dauphin – lived to adulthood. In addition, certain other women favoured by Louis were accorded much honour as the King's official mistresses. Two of his three principal favourites *(above left)* gave him other children who were ennobled to become important members of the court, and were eventually legitimized.

In spite of the exclusivity and privilege of the court, it was easy for the public to witness the spectacle provided by the King's daily life. It was a fashionable outing for Parisians to drive to Versailles to see the royal party as they dined on the interminable courses of a meal that had been carried from the kitchens almost a kilometre away.

THE DAILY PAGEANT OF COURT LIFE

In the early days of Versailles, the newly enlarged palace was the scene of fêtes of fantastic extravagance; but after the court had migrated to the palace and Louis had entered middle age, the round of pleasure and diversion which courtiers fought so hard to enter took on a clockwork regularity. The Duc de Saint-Simon remarked that given a timepiece and an almanac, it would be possible to work out exactly what Louis was doing at any moment of the day.

The life of the court and all its attendants revolved completely around the King and his timetable. Louis was a man of tremendous vigour who devoted eight or nine hours a day to matters of state, regularly rode and hunted, ate with phenomenal appetite – and exacted similar efforts from all the courtiers who swarmed round him. His sister-in-law Elizabeth-Charlotte sent a friend a description of a typical day at court: "We hunted all morning, got back about 3 o'clock in the afternoon, changed, went up to gamble until 7 o'clock, then to the play, which never ended before 10.30, then on to supper and afterwards to the ball until 3 o'clock in the morning . . . So you see how much time I had for writing."

The card players in this engraving of 1695 include Louis' daughter – the Duchess of Bourbon – and his mistress Mme de Montespan with her husband *(seated on the left)*. At the evening receptions held every Monday, Wednesday and Friday in the suite of rooms known as the Grand Appartement, gambling for high stakes was *de rigueur*.

Playing an early form of billiards, Louis XIV, resplendent in a plumed hat, lines up a shot. His fellow-players include his brother "Monsieur" *(far left)* and other grandees of the court.

In a painting by Claude-Guy Hallé, Louis welcomes the Doge of Genoa in Versailles' Hall of Mirrors on a state visit made in 1685.

the focus of courtiers' attention, as this painting by Pierre-Denis Martin indicates. Behind him rise all the grand effects of the Versailles landscape, including the fountains of the Basin of Apollo – the pivotal point of the perspectives laid out by André Le Nôtre.

A late 17th-century painting shows a jostling crowd of richly dressed courtiers – men, women and children – surrounding the young king as he rides past the Grotto of Thetis, a folly in the grounds of Versailles. Louis' love of hunting and the open air lasted all his life – even in his later days when his growing piety led him to pull down the grotto and build a chapel in its place.

THE RISE OF THE DUTCH REPUBLIC

5

On the face of it, there was nothing very remarkable in the sight of four heavily laden cargo ships as they moved through the Zuider Zee and into the teeming port of Amsterdam. The city, in that year of 1599, drew its wealth and sustenance, as it had for generations past, from seaborne trade. The tall brick warehouses that lined the network of canals were crammed with all the goods of Europe: grain and fish, woollens and wine. The harbour was always full of traffic – a dense, floating forest of masts and rigging.

But on the day in July when these particular vessels came home, Amsterdam celebrated with a fervour more commonly reserved for victory in war. Church bells pealed out a message of triumph and thanksgiving that echoed even in the marshy wastes beyond the town. Welcomed with pomp and ceremony, the ships' commanders and their commercial backers were regaled with a lavish official banquet. Meanwhile, the more lowly members of the crew prepared to spend their wages in the town's notorious taverns and brothels.

As the city fathers rehearsed their laudatory speeches, the lightermen at the docks set to and began to unload the precious cargo, releasing its powerful aromas into the already pungent harbour air. The sacks that emerged from the depths of the ships' bellies were crammed full of cloves and nutmegs from the East Indies, the fabled islands of spices on the far side of the world. The small, dark pellets might as well have been rubies: counting-house clerks calculated that the expedition's financial backers would reap a clear 400 per cent profit on their investment from the vessels that had come home and their four sister ships still awaited. "As long as Holland has been Holland," marvelled one contemporary chronicler, "such richly laden ships have never been seen."

But the safe return of the Far Lands Company fleet represented far more than a fat harvest for a handful of investors. For a community that lived by trade, this first successful foray to the distant islands of the East Indies was a significant turning point; a promise of untold riches, and a mark of heaven's favour. Such a positive sign of hope could not have come at a better time to a country that was engaged in a prolonged and bitter struggle for survival.

For the Dutch were still in the process of becoming a nation. The merchants and mariners of Amsterdam, the peat cutters, cheesemakers and market gardeners of the rural hinterlands, the North Sea fishermen and the bargees on the River Rhine, lived within a loose confederation of towns and provinces that had been brought together for the sake of someone else's political convenience. Calvinists and dissenting Protestants rubbed shoulders with Catholics and people with little or no religious affiliation among a population of some 1.5 million. If they were united now, it was only because they were fighting for their freedom against a common foe.

In a mid-17th-century portrait by Pieter de Hooch, a soberly clad Dutch family exudes calm prosperity from the security of its well-swept courtyard in the city of Delft. Middle-class merchants were the backbone of the Dutch Republic which, after winning independence from the Habsburg rulers of Spain in the early years of the 17th century, rapidly became the world's most dynamic trading nation.

Early in the 16th century, the shifting fortunes and strategic marriages of Europe's ruling dynasties had brought the Netherlands — 17 low-lying, French or Dutch-speaking provinces on or near the shores of the North Sea — under Spanish domination. By the latter part of the century, the provinces had built up a stock of rankling resentments: religious persecution and economic exploitation by inept or tyrannical governors had led to a number of bloody revolts. Unilaterally, the Dutch-speaking people of the northern Netherlands declared their independence, committing themselves to a war that would not finally end until 1648.

Meanwhile, as always, the Dutch contended with another enemy, one even more intractable than Spain: their own precarious geography. Lying at sea level — or, in places, below it — they battled constantly with the aid of dykes to hold back the menacing waters of the North Sea.

A land too waterlogged to feed its own population, a people with little common history, professing different — and mutually hostile — forms of Christian faith, a war of independence dragging on for generations: put together, the elements did not constitute a promising beginning. But, within a few decades, both the sea and the Spanish would be beaten back, and the Dutch would rise with astonishing speed to become the most important commercial power in Europe. Their wealth would excite the envy of the world, and their domination of European and overseas trade would infuriate their neighbours. And they would achieve all this without a prince

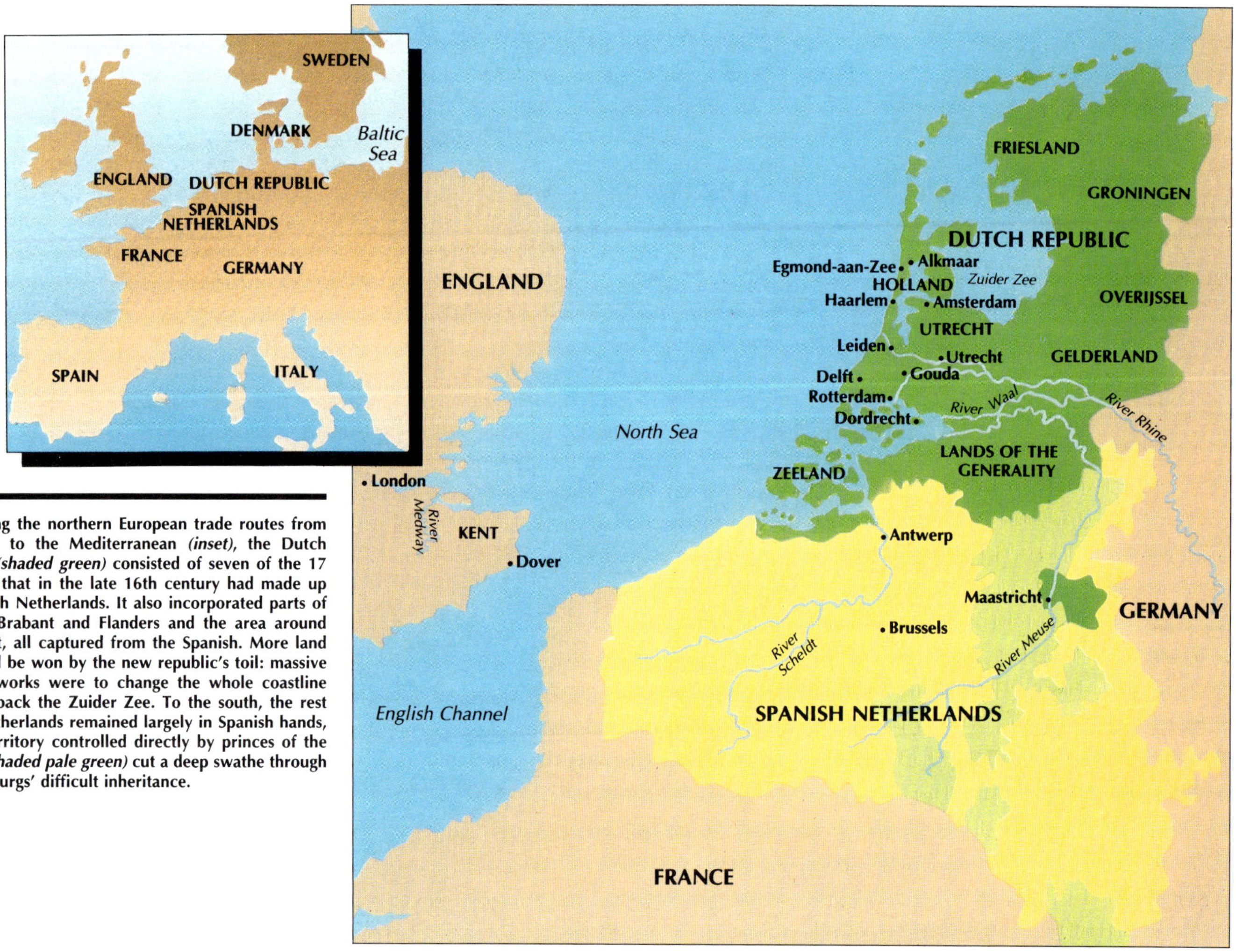

Dominating the northern European trade routes from the Baltic to the Mediterranean *(inset)*, the Dutch Republic *(shaded green)* consisted of seven of the 17 provinces that in the late 16th century had made up the Spanish Netherlands. It also incorporated parts of northern Brabant and Flanders and the area around Maastricht, all captured from the Spanish. More land still would be won by the new republic's toil: massive drainage works were to change the whole coastline and trim back the Zuider Zee. To the south, the rest of the Netherlands remained largely in Spanish hands, though territory controlled directly by princes of the Church *(shaded pale green)* cut a deep swathe through the Habsburgs' difficult inheritance.

to rule them. In an age of autocratic, empire-building monarchies, this was a disturbing phenomenon: an autonomous republic, with more sovereignty lodged in its constituent towns and provinces than in any centralized organs of state.

In 1548 Charles V, ruler of Austria, Spain, Burgundy and a multitude of other, smaller territories scattered across Europe, had made the 17 provinces into a single administrative unit within his Habsburg empire. Under Charles, the provinces enjoyed considerable autonomy. The towns, such as Amsterdam and the much larger port city of Antwerp in the south, were controlled by networks of wealthy mercantile families, jealously guarding their municipal rights and privileges. In some rural districts, the local nobility dominated public life. But each of the 17 provinces had its own chamber of representatives – the States; these bodies, in turn, sent deputies to a central forum, the States General in Brussels, which the Habsburgs had made their northern capital.

In 1556, Charles abdicated from power, and in the ensuing division of his domains the Netherlands fell to his son Philip II, the king of Spain. Philip tried to impose his will upon his distant provinces without worrying unduly if his actions violated their traditional liberties. He sought to control their domestic policies, intervened in the appointment of their bishops, and reorganized the Catholic Inquisition set up by Charles V to persecute the Calvinist Protestants, whose heretical beliefs were gaining ground throughout the north. Still worse, he imposed new and burdensome taxes in an effort to replenish an exchequer drained by foreign wars.

Roused in equal part by matters of God and mammon, the Netherlands rebelled against their Spanish overlord, and the battle for Dutch independence began. At their head, the rebels boasted a leader of outstanding ability. William the Silent, prince of Orange, was a Protestant nobleman with large estates in Germany and the principality of Orange in southern France, in addition to his extensive estates in various parts of the Low Countries. Against all odds, he forged an alliance among the divergent, often mutually hostile groups, winning the support of rural nobles, urban patricians, middle-class merchants and the populace at large. His support was strongest in the north, where Calvinism had made the greatest gains. In 1579, under his leadership, the seven northern provinces solemnly bound themselves together in the Union of Utrecht. Two years later, these united provinces unilaterally declared their independence from Spain.

A stalemate ensued. Philip's shaky finances were depleted by the war effort. With his ill-paid and ill-fed army in a state of near-constant mutiny, he never succeeded in stamping out the rebel forces – although his agents did eventually manage to assassinate Prince William in 1584. Meanwhile the Orangists made a little headway against Spain, but lacked the financial and military aid from Europe's other Protestant countries that they needed to consolidate their gains.

Soon after William's death, Elizabeth of England, fearful that her old Spanish enemy might regain control across the Channel, decided that the time had come to intervene on behalf of the rebels. The Dutch now had at least one powerful ally.

In 1588, the Spanish Armada, sweeping up the Channel to invade England, was destroyed by the joint efforts of the English, the Dutch and the weather. Neither Spain's exchequer, nor its self-esteem, recovered from the blow. Subsequently, Philip directed his attentions elsewhere, to battles over the succession to the French throne. By 1598 he was dead, and the Spanish were finally driven out

WINNING FARMLAND FROM THE SEA

"God created the world," went the saying, "but the Dutchman created Holland." Since at least the 15th century, the needs of a growing population had been met by a system of drainage that won land from the sea for farming use. The reclaimed areas, called polders, provided both grazing and cropland, as the 1590 painting below shows.

By the 17th century, the Dutch had become the world's greatest hydraulic engineers, using windmills *(inset)* to reclaim up to 1,800 hectares annually. For drainage, an expanse of shallow water was enclosed by a dyke, and a ring canal was built around it. Then the windmills pumped the water up to the canal, from which it ran off into the sea. A stepped array of mills, each one passing its output to the next, could drain a sheet of water that was 4.5 metres deep.

But the sea could always return. Despite careful maintenance, the web of dykes sometimes failed, and the steady progress of the engineers was punctuated by occasional disastrous floods.

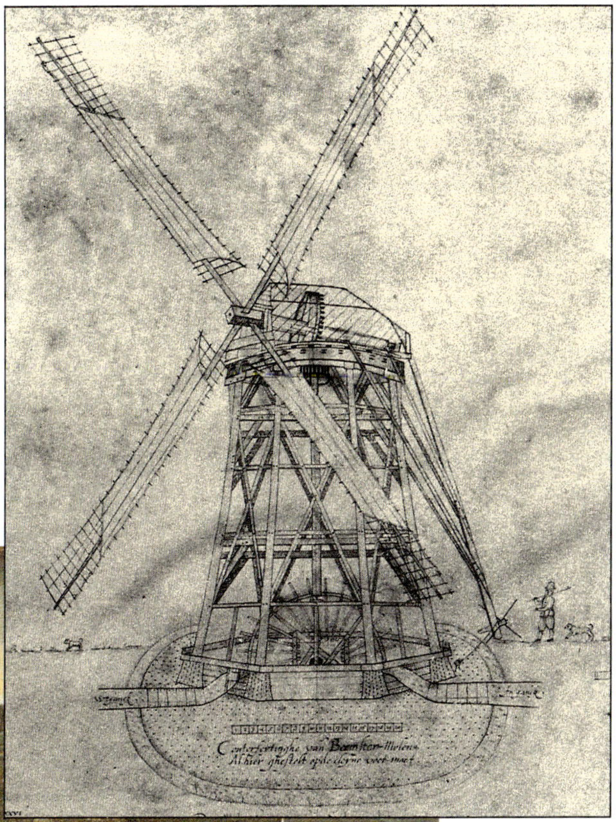

of their last strongholds in the northern Netherlands. Devastating plagues and famines in Spain itself made it impossible for Philip's heir to sustain anything more than a defensive war from his remaining fastnesses in the southern provinces. Even so, it was not until the year 1609 that Spain eventually proved willing to sign a truce. Twelve years later hostilities were renewed. Spain finally gave formal recognition to the independence of the seven northern provinces in 1648 by the Treaty of Westphalia. (The southern provinces, approximating geographically to modern-day Belgium, were to remain in Habsburg hands as the Spanish – later the Austrian – Netherlands until 1794.)

Though not blessed by Spanish recognition, the United Provinces functioned as an independent political entity almost from the time of the Union of Utrecht in 1579. The fledgling state was a republic, with no single apex of power. By the terms of the union, each province governed its own internal affairs through the provincial States, while sending delegates – as they had done under the Spanish crown – to a central States General to debate matters concerning the collective interests of the union. Within this assembly, the patricians and burghers of Holland – the richest and most populous province – generally spoke with the strongest voice.

The provinces appointed a military leader, the stadholder, inevitably a member of the princely house of Orange or its allied family of Nassau. The post had been established during the early years of revolt, when William of Orange held the office. The stadholder's noble birth ensured him the military training and knightly prestige required for the job, but his aristocratic lineage conferred no superior status. Sovereignty remained firmly in the hands of the provincial States.

Cooperation between the civil power and the stadholderate was vital, if not always easily achieved. After the death of William of Orange, his son, Maurice of Nassau, was named stadholder for Holland and Zeeland. His civil counterpart was Johan van Oldenbarnevelt, chief advocate of Holland in the States General and, by extension, the leading minister of the Republic. Their initial collaboration, in the last years of combat against Spain and early days of independence, was fruitful: Maurice's military skills kept the Spanish at bay, while Oldenbarnevelt, a consummate politician, forged the policies that placed the union on a firm foundation and negotiated with friendly foreign governments.

But tensions between the two leaders were never far from the surface. Oldenbarnevelt represented the oligarchy of wealthy Holland burghers, who saw no need for any higher sovereign power; Prince Maurice was closer to the Dutch nobility, some of whom hoped that the new state might yet become a monarchy under an Orange ruler. Yet he was also a hero to the common people, whose own royalist inclinations – if any – lay in their resentment of the patricians who ran the towns, controlled the magistrates and enjoyed the lion's share of the wealth.

Maurice had not been in favour of the 1609 truce with Spain; he would have preferred to fight until the enemy was forced from the southern provinces too, and the whole of the Netherlands was free. He had the support of the most zealously orthodox Calvinist clergymen, who now saw the conflict as a holy war against a Papist foe. But Oldenbarnevelt, with the pragmatism of his constituency, supported the truce: it was time to resume amassing wealth through trade.

It was religion that proved Oldenbarnevelt's undoing. With the struggle for survival against Rome won, internal schisms threatened the young Reformed church. Two tendencies were at war within Dutch Calvinism, divided over, among other issues, whether an individual's sins could keep him or her out of heaven. According to strict Calvinist doctrine, the number and names of God's Elect had been set down at the world's beginning, so personal morality could make no difference.

Oldenbarnevelt's faction, the Arminians, representing a more liberal school, placed higher value on individual thought and action. They favoured a policy of greater religious tolerance, arguing against the zealots who would have liked to see Papists, Jews and members of dissident Protestant sects purged from the land. Their credo was: "In essentials unity, in doubtful matters liberty, in all things charity"; a doctrine despised by extreme Calvinists, certain of their own monopoly on truth.

Matters came to a head in 1618. One winter's morning, five life-size snowmen representing Oldenbarnevelt and four leading fellow liberals appeared on a street in The Hague. Gangs of urchins began pelting them with stones and snowballs, chanting biblically, "An Arminian is a plague on the land; his house is a nest of salamanders! Arminians to the gallows!" Soon after, riots erupted in many towns. Oldenbarnevelt, on behalf of the States of Holland, passed an order allowing communities within the province to muster special militias to restore order. The States General, dominated by anti-Arminians and under the sway of Maurice, ordered all the troops thus raised to be disbanded. Oldenbarnevelt himself was accused of flouting the expressed will of the States General, taken prisoner and, following a rigged trial, beheaded as a traitor. Other prominent Arminians, including some of Holland's leading scholars and teachers, were purged, jailed or exiled.

Oldenbarnevelt's execution, however, was only a temporary setback for the advocates of religious tolerance. Without a strong, centralized state able to enforce censorship, there was neither the collective will nor the political machinery to curb the circulation of dissident ideas. Individual municipalities had their own, more or less liberal, rules on the freedom of the press; what printers in one town feared to touch, their counterparts in the next province would often happily publish.

Liberty from legislated religious orthodoxy was a rare luxury in Europe of that age. In other countries, to belong to a Church that was not the state Church was to suffer some loss of civil rights, if not persecution. Thanks to its religious tolerance, the Dutch Republic enjoyed a climate of intellectual freedom unequalled in Europe. The French philosopher René Descartes spent 30 years in Holland, producing his great work, *The Discourse on Method,* and other major texts. Others came in search of a haven. The political thinker John Locke, forced out of England for his dangerous ideas, passed his time of exile in Holland; and the philosopher Baruch Spinoza, excommunicated by his Jewish brethren for denying that the Bible was God's word, praised Amsterdam for its liberality: "In this flourishing state, this city without a peer, men of every race and sect live in the greatest harmony."

The energies the Dutch saved from strife and bigotry they expended on the pursuit of wealth. The most prosperous areas of the young republic were the three westward-facing coastal provinces, where the inhabitants lived by fishing and

A towering silver saltcellar and a precisely engraved wine beaker commemorate Dutch victories in the long war with Spain. The Spanish renewed their efforts to win back the lost provinces in 1621, after a 12-year truce; early successes against a disunited foe included the capture of the southern fortress of Breda. But the Dutch rallied under a new leader, Prince Frederick Henry. He captured 's Hertogenbosch in 1629, subsequently presenting the saltcellar to one of his officers as a reward for courage during the siege. The Prince went on to take the fortress-city of Maastricht before eventually regaining Breda itself in a campaign recorded on the beaker.

maritime trade. Holland, by far the richest and most populous, embraced most of the great towns: Amsterdam, Rotterdam, Delft, Gouda, Leiden and Haarlem all lay within a compass of 50 kilometres. Friesland, to its north, handled a substantial slice of the flourishing Baltic trade and a still higher proportion of the Norwegian timber business. To the south was Zeeland, a flat expanse of marshes and islands lying in the waters where the well-trafficked trade routes from Europe's heart – the rivers Rhine, Meuse and Scheldt – flowed into the North Sea.

For the Hollanders and Zeelanders, the sea was, in equal measure, enemy and friend. For centuries, they had built dykes and other defences to hold back its waters. The Dutch had become experts in the technologies of drainage, canal building and land reclamation; between 1590 and 1640 their efforts won them 80,000 new hectares of agricultural land. Even when the rich alluvial soil of this recovered ground brought forth its crops, the Dutch were not completely self-sufficient in food. They had long ago learnt that what their land could not provide must be brought in from the sea. Massive quantities of grain were imported from the Baltic countries, and every year, from June to December, the boats went out from Holland and Zeeland on an enterprise known as "the great fishery", to sweep up the shoals of herring moving down from the Baltic and into the North Sea.

The Dutch fleet operated with prodigious efficiency. Their specially designed vessels, the herring buses, were large enough to house a crew throughout the six-month season, and to permit the fish to be salted and packed on board. Instead of returning to harbour, the buses relied on a fleet of smaller service boats to bring out fresh provisions and take away the barrelled catches. At home, the industry was backed up by other trades: shipwrights, chandlers, warehousemen, rope and sail makers, coopers and brokers.

The business brought in foreign earnings too, for the oil-rich herring, salted to preserve it, was a prized source of protein – not least in the Catholic countries, where the eating of meat was banned on many fast days. The silver fish became almost a form of currency. Herring sent to France and Germany bought luxury goods; those shipped to the Baltic lands came back as grain.

The buses formed only part of a fleet that was the envy of seamen elsewhere in Europe. The Dutch shipwrights also devised the finest cargo vessels of the age: the capacious *fluyten*, which were cheap to build – in the shipyards, mass-production techniques and the use of cranes and wind-powered sawmills kept labour costs down – and inexpensive to run. Equipped with simple rigging and fitted with winches and tackles for loading cargo, they needed fewer crewmen than other craft: 10 sailors on a *fluyt* did the work of 30 on an English vessel of the same size. Low wage costs and cheap provisioning meant that Dutch shipowners could undercut competitors' freight charges by up to 50 per cent. It made financial sense for foreign merchants to buy or charter Dutch ships rather than use their own.

The fountainhead of Dutch mercantile activity was Amsterdam. The city had always been in the vanguard of the Baltic trade, but its spectacular growth at the start of the 17th century came, in effect, from the spoils of war. Its major competitor, the port of Antwerp, suffered badly during the revolt, losing much of its trade to Amsterdam, which at the same time benefited from the hordes of southern refugees who migrated into the northern towns. Some were Calvinists, drawn northwards on religious grounds; others saw a chance to improve their fortunes in a land that had freed itself from Spain. They came from all sectors of society, bringing commercial acumen, capital, energy, intelligence and a host of marketable talents.

Amsterdam, as befitted its new importance, became the processing centre for the most valuable raw material of all: money. In 1609, the year of the truce with Spain, the city's financiers set up an exchange bank to help Dutch merchants do business with one another. The same year also saw the completion of the Bourse, whose colonnades and stone-built cloisters sheltered the representatives of every financial interest group. In the shadow of one particular column, the Baltic grain merchants gathered; near another, investors in the young East India trade exchanged news of their voyages. It was a frenetic marketplace, raucous with the sounds of bidding, where deals were done, shares traded, and partners found for joint ventures.

The Dutch had long preferred collective financial effort to the derring-do of the lone entrepreneur. To pool resources and dilute the risks, investors formed consortia for every maritime project. The pioneering East Indian spice fleet of 1599 was the fruit of one such joint enterprise. Cloves and nutmegs were native to the Moluccas – a handful of tiny islands northeast of Java – and in the 16th century grew nowhere else. For centuries, these spices had reached Europe via a chain of merchants who each undertook part of the journey. Untold wealth awaited any trader who could eliminate all the middlemen. That was the aim of nine of Amsterdam's wealthiest merchant princes, who had come together for a series of secret meetings in an obscure wine shop to draw up plans for the Far Lands Company.

In March 1602, three years after their successful first expedition, the Far Lands directors formed an even larger consortium, the United East India Company. Its aim was to eliminate wasteful competition between Dutch venturers and pool their resources to establish a monopoly of overseas trade in spices and in every other commodity. As well as edging out the Portuguese and English, already active in the Orient, they planned to beat native Asian traders on their own ground.

The East India Company did not expect to achieve this simply by offering better terms and trade goods. With the blessing of the nation's political masters, its employees were empowered to wage war, conclude peace treaties, build forts and recruit civil, military and naval personnel, all bound by an oath of loyalty to the company itself. As the company's governor in the East Indies, Jan Pieterszoon Coen, said, "We cannot carry on trade without war, nor war without trade."

The first to feel the brunt of such policies were the Portuguese, who had been established in the East Indies for a century, but whose grip on these territories was

This model of a Dutch *fluyt*, which is anglicised as "flyboat", was constructed for the future owner of a full-size vessel. Broad-beamed and robustly seaworthy, such ships were Europe's finest vessels for carrying bulky goods. Holland's advanced shipyards used wind-powered sawmills and standardized parts to build the craft cheaply as well as soundly; ingeniously designed winch-operated rigging kept manning levels low. Unlike rival merchantmen, weighed down by defensive armament, the flyboats carried no cannon: if protection was needed, they sailed in convoys escorted by warships. The extra cargo space thus provided allowed their owners to undercut rivals' freight charges, giving the Dutch an unchallenged ascendancy over the European bulk transport trade.

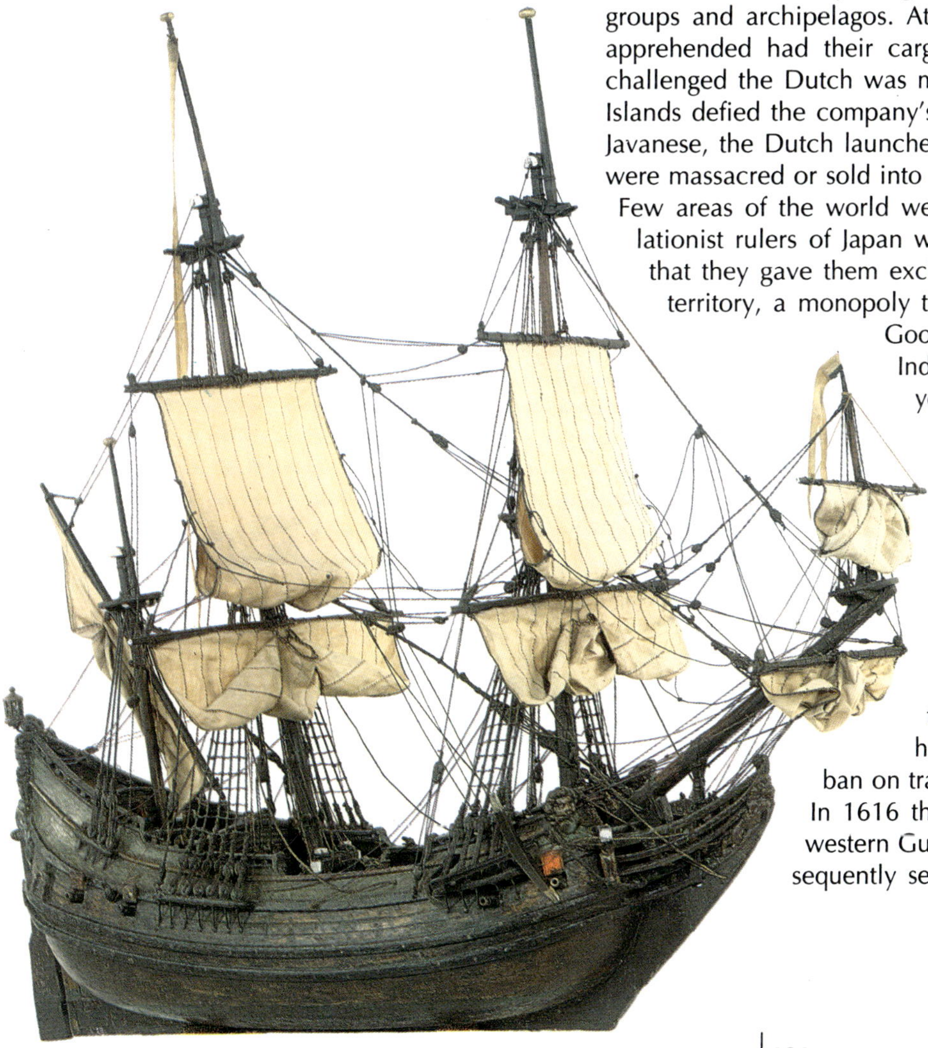

now weakening. Their energies were sapped by struggles at home, and their seamanship was inferior to that of their Dutch rivals. When the two nations' armed merchantmen clashed in maritime battles, the Netherlanders carried the day.

Where the Portuguese were dispatched with relative ease, England presented a greater problem. For a time, the English and Dutch East India companies tried to work together. But this policy, forged in London and Amsterdam, did not please Jan Pieterszoon Coen out in Batavia, his company's newly established trading base on the island of Java. With every outward show of cooperation, he proposed hugely ambitious collaborative projects, well knowing that they required greater financial outlays than the English would be prepared to provide. When such ploys failed, he ordered a series of attacks on the English fleet, capturing several ships. For the English, the final provocation came in 1623, when one of Coen's subordinates arrested eight of their men on the island of Amboina, tortured them, and then executed them on trumped-up charges. The Anglo-Dutch partnership was over.

Apart from eradicating all of their European competitors, the company was also determined to prevent any large-scale native enterprise from undermining its trade monopoly. Total control of the East Indies was impossible; thousands of islands lay scattered across an area that spanned some 4,500 kilometres from east to west, and another 2,000 north to south. But Coen and his colleagues found strategic points where men and ships might be stationed to block access to whole island groups and archipelagos. At the very least, unauthorized vessels that were apprehended had their cargoes confiscated. Often the fate of those who challenged the Dutch was more severe: when the inhabitants of the Banda Islands defied the company's demands that they cease supplying rice to the Javanese, the Dutch launched a surprise attack in which 15,000 Bandanese were massacred or sold into slavery.

Few areas of the world were left untouched by Dutch voyagers. The isolationist rulers of Japan were so impressed with the yellow-haired aliens that they gave them exclusive rights to maintain a trading post on their territory, a monopoly that would continue until 1853. At the Cape of Good Hope, a settlement grew up to service the East Indian ships with fresh provisions. Within a few years, the independent-minded colonists, already known as Boers, were pushing out into the hinterland in search of fresh pastures. And a North American colony, New Amsterdam, was established on Manhattan Island in the year 1611. Some of the settlers prospered as farmers, cultivating the fertile shores of the river named after the English explorer, Henry Hudson. Others made a comfortable living as smugglers, through supplying cut-price goods to the neighbouring English colonies, whose inhabitants gladly ignored their mother country's ban on trade with any merchants but her own.

In 1616 the Dutch won a foothold in South America, in western Guyana. The Dutch West India Company was subsequently set up to challenge the dominance of Spain and

Portugal in the Caribbean. The company bought slaves in West Africa, and sold them, in defiance of Spain's attempts at monopoly, to her labour-hungry American colonists. As well as supporting this venture, the company gave funds to privateers who raided Spanish settlements and hijacked their cargo ships. The greatest boost to the company's morale, and to its coffers, was Admiral Piet Heyn's capture, in 1628, of the Spanish treasure fleet laden with silver from the Mexican mines. The booty was valued at 11 million guilders, enough to pay two thirds of the yearly costs of the Dutch army, by then enmeshed again in war with Spain.

While Piet Heyn and his men harried Spanish ships, many of their countrymen were content to do business with the enemy. During the 80 years of official or undeclared hostilities, Dutch merchants continued to trade, discreetly or overtly, with the Spanish. Not everyone approved. But when the stadholder remonstrated with one such entrepreneur, the merchant retorted that he would happily sail his ships into hell and risk singeing their timbers if he saw some profit in it.

By the middle of the century, the young republic's commercial supremacy was firmly established. Dutch merchants were at work from Siberia to the Cape of Good Hope. Closer to home, 13 times as many Dutch ships as English ones passed through the Baltic Sound, carrying three quarters of the Baltic countries' grain and timber, as well as half the metal exported from Swedish mines. No consumer in western Europe could be untouched by the activities of the Dutch. In a wealthy household in London or Paris, a visitor might be received in a room covered with Flemish tapestries, offered West Indian sugar in a Chinese porcelain bowl, invited to light a pipe of North American tobacco, and tempted with a goblet of Peruvian silver filled with German wine: all provided by Dutch traders and sailors.

According to some observers, among them the Englishman William Temple, these delights were for export only. "They are the great masters of the Indian spices and of the Persian silks, but wear plain woollen, and feed upon their own fish and roots . . . they furnish infinite luxury, which they never practise, and traffic in pleasures, which they never taste."

Temple's assertion was only partly true. The Calvinist burghers of Holland and Zeeland may have had a reputation for thrift and plain living, but they stopped far short of asceticism. They reserved the enjoyment of their enhanced incomes for the privacy of their homes. Even families of moderate means had cabinets to display crockery, and deep chests or ornately carved cupboards to hold the household linen, the quantity and quality of which served as a yardstick of prosperity.

The laundering of all this clothing and napery formed part of a national obsession with domestic cleanliness. Dutch housewives believed that the dirt of the world should never be allowed to cross the threshold or to sully the sacred hearth. In a poem by Pieter van Godewijk, a Dordrecht schoolmaster, a magistrate's daughter declares: "My brush is my sword; my broom my weapon."

The interiors of their carefully tended houses — tranquil chambers illuminated by a shaft of sunlight from a tall window; halls of polished tiles, lit by the gleam of brass and copper; neat back yards,

A 1665 painting shows the Dutch East India Company's trading station on the Hooghly River in Bengal, its well-defended warehouses laid out with geometric precision. The depot was a key link in the network of bases that made up Holland's eastern trading empire. Through it, ships streamed to and from the Moluccas, Batavia — present-day Jakarta — and as far eastwards as China and Japan, returning with lucrative cargoes of spices and fine textiles. By the end of the century, the Dutch controlled substantial territories in Ceylon and southern India as well as much of Indonesia.

paved in brick, leading to narrow, walled gardens — were objects of pride, and as such were minutely recorded in the paintings that prosperous burghers purchased to adorn their walls. Not that the love of pictures was restricted to the well-to-do. An English traveller arriving in 1640 marvelled that "blacksmiths, cobblers, etc. will have some picture or other by their forge and in their stall. Such is the general notion, inclination and delight that these country natives have to painting".

The art of painting flourished, nurtured by an enthusiastic public in love with colour, realistic detail and mirror images of their own lives. Every town of any size had its community of professional artists, women as well as men, who were viewed as ordinary tradespeople, much like carpenters or tilers. They strove to meet the huge demand for paintings of every kind, from rural landscapes and naval battles through still lives and Biblical narratives to lowlife scenes in taverns and gambling dens. These last were often the cheapest, produced for the lower end of the market, but even the most elegant and ambitious works were relatively inexpensive.

While private individuals and public institutions alike built up collections, many paintings were sold for export. Dutch merchants in the East Indian trading posts ordered pictures for their overseas residences. Native princes purchased them for their palaces. As the reputation of Dutch artists spread, gentlemen of taste in England, France and Scotland obtained works through agents or gathered them on their travels. Perspicacious Dutch collectors realized that something the rest of the world wanted so badly was likely to be a good investment; although great artists continued to die in poverty, the price of their pictures gradually went up.

One reason was the lack of alternative investment opportunities in a cramped and crowded country. The English diarist John Evelyn, touring the Republic, noted that "The reason of this store of pictures and their cheapness proceeds from want of land to employ their stock, so that it is an ordinary thing to find a common farmer lay out two or three thousand pounds in this commodity."

Evelyn's assessment perhaps underestimated the aesthetic sense of the Dutch burghers, most of whom also found time to enjoy the life of the mind. The pleasures of intellectual disputation became a sociable pursuit in local literary societies known as chambers of rhetoric. These associations, which held poetry competitions and organized amateur dramatics and formal debates, flourished throughout the Republic. Each devised its own rituals and regalia, usually choosing a plant or flower for its

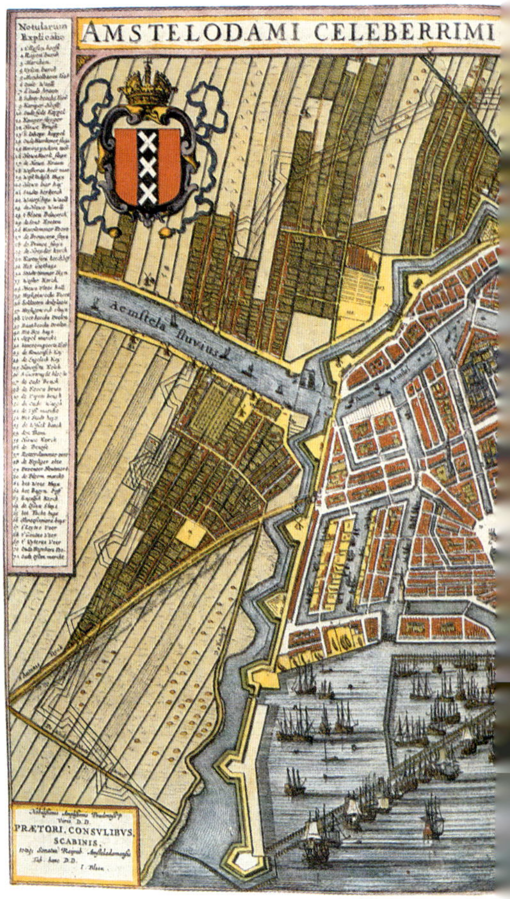

name. Leiden boasted three — the Palm Tree, the White Columbine and the Orange Lily; Alkmaar was home to the Green Laurel; Amsterdammers attended the White Lavender and the Eglantine. Chambers usually met on Sundays, after church, and members encouraged the muse with rounds of beer or wine. House rules varied, but most societies required their meetings to be conducted entirely in verse — even orders for drinks had to be composed in rhyme.

Burghers of a less literary bent found comradeship in recreational clubs and trade associations. Musical societies offered concerts and communal singing; local militias became more social than strategic in their importance. And every convocation of like-minded extroverts provided an excuse for gargantuan feasts at regular intervals. One society of Amsterdam merchants, the Guild of St. Martin, organized a banquet that lasted for two full days.

In the midst of this good living, the poor were not forgotten. Charity was a public duty, and was conducted — in the manner of many commercial enterprises — as a cooperative venture. Boards of male and female patricians supervised the almshouses, the orphanages and other institutions, which were supported by municipal funds and private bequests. Local magistrates or voluntary groups, including the chambers of rhetoric, sponsored vast public lotteries with a range of dazzling prizes to raise money for worthy causes. Items such as gold chains, silver tableware and lace petticoats were raffled off to help build a new home for aged paupers in Haarlem, or raise funds for destitute widows in the flood-battered fishing village of Egmond-aan-Zee. Ticket sales could rise into the hundreds of thousands, and potential players with little money bartered goods instead: sacks of peat, wheels of cheese, wine, textiles and pictures were all grist to the lotteries' mill.

Whatever the hopes of its more enlightened inhabitants, the Republic still fell far short of Utopia. Large sectors of the population enjoyed no share of the new-found prosperity. In Friesland and the remote rural province of Overijssel, a small coterie of noble families forming about one per cent of the population held nearly one half of the region's wealth. In the more affluent mercantile provinces of Holland and Zeeland, beggars still wandered the streets and workmen and artisans struggled to feed their families. All over the Republic, bad harvests and bouts of inflation could bring less favoured districts to the brink of famine, while an economy dependent on foreign trade was vulnerable to any sign of trouble in the world outside.

Nor was the state free from political turbulence. By the middle of the century, relations between the urban patricians of Holland and the House of Orange had deteriorated. In 1647, William II of Orange, grandson of William the Silent, quarrelled with the States of Holland over their refusal to allow him to launch yet another military action against Spain. They were ready for an end to the war that drained their finances and hindered their trade, and wished to see the stadholder's expensive army — with its preponderance of foreign mercenaries — reduced to a modest domestic defence force.

The balance of power between States and stadholder, between provincial States and States General, remained delicate. When William took office, tensions came to a head. He had acquired considerable support in the other six provinces; Holland alone stood against him. In 1650, the States of Holland defied William by dismissing some of the troops stationed in the province and paid for out of its funds. Angry at this interference with his rights as supreme military commander, William, with

As depicted in this 1649 map, the swelling city of Amsterdam had grown by the mid-17th century into a metropolis of 150,000 people. It was already outgrowing its moated fortifications, where windmills posted on the breezy ramparts ground the citizens' corn; a new fortress line (outlined on the left) was being planned to cope with further expansion. With over 1,000 ocean-going ships claiming it as their home port, Amsterdam boasted the world's busiest harbour, from which a network of canals carried goods to every corner of the city. With their series of locks and dams, these waterways also helped protect Amsterdam from flooding: on average, the city stood more than three metres below sea level.

the uneasy consent of the States General, arrested six Holland deputies for treason and sent 10,000 troops to mount a surprise attack on Amsterdam.

But the soldiers got lost in a night fog in the marshlands near the city. They were spotted by a courier carrying post from Hamburg, who raised the alarm in Amsterdam that some foreign army was on the way. At dawn, when the Orange forces arrived at the city walls, they found the gates barred against them. Both sides were equally surprised. The officers were puzzled that their midnight manoeuvres had been noticed, the Amsterdammers astonished that the invaders were Dutch.

Within a few days, the two parties reached a fragile compromise. The Amsterdam authorities agreed to dismiss the most militant anti-Orangists from the city government; in return, William saw to it that the six imprisoned deputies were released without trial. The States General resolved that decisions on collective concerns should henceforth be made through unanimous agreement by all seven provinces. It then sought to negotiate troop reductions with William, insisting that the foreign mercenaries should be the first to go.

For a few weeks, there was a standoff. William continued to make warlike noises against Spain, and there were rumours that he was plotting with the French to stage some sort of coup. The whole republic seemed to be holding its breath, waiting for something to happen, when fate intervened. The 23-year-old William caught a virulent strain of smallpox, and within weeks was dead. His widow, daughter of the late king of England, Charles I, gave birth a few months afterwards to a son.

The States General had made no provision for a successor. The result was a 22-year interregnum, known by some as the "stadholderless period" and by others as the time of the "true freedom". During this interval, Holland's political leader, the grand pensionary, became the most powerful figure in the Republic. Supreme military command was vested in the hands of the States General itself, whose members appointed a field marshal or other chief officer for the duration of hostilities.

Inevitably, the need for mobilization did arise. In 1651 the English Parliament made a direct attack on Dutch commerce by passing a Navigation Act that had the effect of banning the Dutch from carrying goods from any country other than their own to England or England's colonies. The Dutch sent representatives to bargain with the English, but while the two parties met at the negotiating table, their naval commanders, the Republic's Admiral Tromp and England's Admiral Blake, were also receiving instructions for war.

Blake was charged with harrying the Republic's vital Baltic trade. He was also instructed to seize the Dutch East Indiamen returning from the Orient, and encouraged to disrupt the herring fishery along the English and Scottish coasts and confiscate all captured buses and their catches. Tromp's orders were to defeat the English while defending all this vulnerable traffic. He chafed at the assignment. "I should wish to be so fortunate," he complained to the States General, "as to have only one of the two duties, to seek out the enemy or to give convoy: for to do both is attended by great difficulties." His civilian superiors wanted him to give priority to the protection of trade, shipping and property. He wanted to take the offensive. Why settle for survival, he asked, when the nation could enjoy total victory?

The Dutch had more ships and better sailors, and the English coast was vulnerable to bombardment and blockade. The English – with better warships and greater fire power – set up their own blockade, though their men grew mutinous inside the cramped vessels patrolling the Republic's shores. Admiral Tromp died in

AN ORDERED DOMESTIC WORLD

As befitted a mercantile republic, 17th-century Holland bestowed the great wealth its trade had won not on lavish palaces for kings and aristocrats but on middle-class traders' homes. The guilders spent on these buildings were not always immediately obvious: town houses were generally narrow, especially in Amsterdam where everyone wanted to live in a home with a canal frontage, and where by law no house could be more than eight metres wide. But to compensate for this width restriction, wealthier merchants frequently built their dwellings up to 50 metres deep, decorated them with moneyed taste and packed them with the fine furnishings shown overleaf.

Dirt was banished both indoors and out: housefronts, steps and even the streets themselves were scrubbed to a state of cleanliness that amazed foreign visitors, accustomed to the general squalor and filth of most towns of the day. The streets were so clean, marvelled one Englishman on a visit, that people "even seem to take pleasure in walking them".

Protected from the winds of Holland's polder landscape by wooden walls and high well-trimmed hedges, a Dutch merchant's country villa near Haarlem boasts a carefully organized garden crammed with fruit trees and ornamental shrubs. As this contemporary painting shows, a private canal provided drainage and access by boat to a river.

This painting shows a typical morning scene: a maid helps to dress her mistress before tidying the room. Behind the four-poster bed – probably the most expensive item of furniture in the house – lies the toilet, with the close-stool – a wooden frame enclosing a chamber-pot.

In a detail from Vermeer's *Girl with a Wineglass*, a Turkish rug serves as a tablecloth, while a lute rests on a fine silk cushion on a leather-backed chair. Oriental carpets were often too delicate, and too highly valued, to be consigned to the floor.

Oriental carpets, imported from the Ottoman Empire and Persia, were luxury goods that only the wealthy could afford.

Brass chandeliers were exported to much of Europe from the Netherlands. They were hung low to allow for easy lighting.

Mirrors became larger and more decorative in the 17th century as a direct result of the introduction of plate glass.

Another Vermeer detail illustrates the 17th-century fashion for displaying family coats of arms in stained glass. Problems with sheet-glass manufacture meant that windows had to be assembled from many small panes, but Dutch artisans often managed to turn the drawback into an advantage by the quality of their workmanship.

In Emanuel de Witte's *Interior with a Woman at a Spinet*, the mistress of a prosperous Dutch household finds time for music practice while her husband remains comfortably in bed. Framed by twin doorways, a maidservant performs the daily ritual of most Dutch housewives: sweeping up.

The spinet was still a novelty; many people found the opportunity it offered for making music at home almost magical.

the attempt to break the blockade, and the first Anglo-Dutch war ended with little real satisfaction for either side, although the English were, nominally, the victors.

By the 1660s, the two sides were at war again. The English made no secret of their purpose. "What we want," said the Duke of Albemarle, who commanded the English fleet, "is more of the trade the Dutch now have." But this time the Republic's morale was better, and its naval strategies more clearly mapped. Clashes were not restricted to domestic waters; the two sides fought in the East and West Indies, up and down the coasts of the Americas, and off West Africa.

In a bold stroke, Admiral de Ruyter led a Dutch attack force up the River Medway, whose estuary cuts deep into the English county of Kent. Breaking the chain barrier that had been drawn across the waterway, his men-of-war pounced on the fleet that lay at anchor there. Some ships they burnt; others were taken as prizes, among them the English flagship, the *Royal Charles*. With this booty in tow, and the English gaping in outrage, the invaders sailed safely home. In July 1667, the two nations met to make peace, this time on the Republic's terms.

With the fighting scarcely over at sea, the United Provinces were shaken by dramas that threatened their status as a republic. Throughout the 1650s and 1660s, political continuity and stability had been provided by the grand pensionary of Holland, Johan de Witt. With formidable persuasive powers and political acumen, de Witt put the Republic's financial house in order, strengthened and reorganized the navy to bring victory in the second English war, and directed foreign and domestic policy-making with a skill and style not seen since the days of Oldenbarnevelt. He also made enemies, especially among the Orangists, who hoped for the day when young William III would take his late father's place as stadholder.

Within the States General, de Witt and his supporters expressed the view that the Republic was surviving very well without a stadholder, and that the nation's debt to William the Silent and his Orange heirs had now been paid in full: they no longer deserved that exalted post as a matter of right. Nevertheless, when the States General took charge of the Prince's education, de Witt agreed to instruct him in the arts of statecraft. As the grandson of one English king and the nephew of another, the youth was acutely conscious of his own royal blood. But he developed considerable respect for his republican tutor, and later claimed that de Witt had taught him more about the world than all his other instructors.

Neighbouring states watched the debate over the stadholderate with interest, for the Dutch were now important players on the chessboard of European power politics. England's Charles II, lately restored to the throne taken from his father, hoped that his country's war with the Dutch would undermine their republican government, opening the way for his Orange nephew to rule as a prince.

The French king, Louis XIV, was anxious to prevent the Orangists from taking power, fearing that any thaw in relations between the Dutch and the English would inevitably pose a threat to France. Meanwhile, he was engaged in his own war against Spain, and in May 1667 marched his armies into the Spanish Netherlands. The Dutch and the English, sensing that France was now more dangerous to each of them than either was to the other, hastily concluded a peace treaty and formed a triple alliance, with Sweden, to force an end to the Franco-Spanish war.

To break up this pact, Louis began to pay court to Charles II. He suggested that it would be to England's financial and political advantage to join him in a campaign against the Dutch. In 1670, the two monarchs signed the Treaty of Dover, resolving to remove de Witt, to destroy the Dutch Republic and replace it with a puppet monarchy, ruled by William under the joint control of Charles and Louis.

Despite strong personal ties between the English king and the young prince of Orange, William knew better than to trust his uncle; he was not willing to purchase a crown by sacrificing Dutch sovereignty. He was also a devout Protestant, and the heir to a princely house that had long been the standard-bearer for the Protestant cause; his English uncle was revealing himself as far too Papist in his preferences for William's liking, and Louis was, above all else, a staunchly Catholic king.

Two years after the Treaty of Dover, the crisis came to a head. With their enemies breathing down their necks, the Dutch could no longer do without a military leader. William was named captain-general and joined forces with his old tutor to build up the army, which was quickly accomplished; for 20 years, de Witt had kept the nation's finances on a healthy footing, so there were sufficient funds, or good sources of credit, to organize the necessary troops, weapons and supplies.

In April, France declared war. Two months later, its army marched along the fringes of the Spanish Netherlands, through the German Rhineland, and entered the United Provinces from the east. The troops forced their way halfway across the country, and were west of Utrecht when the Dutch opened the dykes and flooded the low-lying polder lands to keep the invaders from advancing farther.

Instead of uniting in the face of a common enemy, the Dutch now began fighting among themselves. Riots broke out in towns throughout the Republic; witnesses observed that the mobs appeared to include numbers of respectable citizens as well as the rougher elements more usually associated with public disorder. Possibly outside agitators were behind some of the outbursts; rumour certainly had it so.

De Witt, passing along an Amsterdam street, was attacked by four unknown, but apparently well-dressed, young men. They left him half dead, bleeding from wounds that took many weeks to heal. While he lay recovering from his injuries, the States General hastily sent emissaries to Louis XIV, encamped in Utrecht province, offering sizable financial and territorial concessions in return for peace. Louis, enjoying the advantage, bided his time and refused to negotiate.

The Orangists insisted that the Republic could no longer fend off its enemies without a strong leader at the helm, and demanded that William be appointed to a restored and more powerful stadholderate. Shortly after he took up his post, a scandal erupted which showed William in an unattractive light.

Johan de Witt's brother Cornelius, a magistrate and senior member of the government of the province of Holland, was accused of conspiring to assassinate the Prince. The charges were false, brought by a barber-surgeon of dubious reputation who had once been tried by Cornelius on a charge of rape. Even under torture, Cornelius would not admit to a crime of which he was innocent. But his brother's powerful Orangist enemies saw their opportunity, and persuaded or coerced the judges to ensure an unfair trial. During these proceedings, the Grand Pensionary, recovered from his wounds, resigned from public office.

Despite the best efforts of Cornelius de Witt's opponents, the court was unable to find him guilty of conspiracy. Nevertheless, the judges stripped him of all his public offices and declared him banished for life from the province of Holland.

The day the trial ended, a message reached Johan de Witt to the effect that his brother wished him to escort him home from the prison in which he was being held. When Johan de Witt reached the jail, he found it surrounded by an angry crowd, with troops of cavalry struggling to keep order. Shortly after he had entered the building the soldiers disappeared, called to the outskirts of the city to quell a supposed peasant riot that in fact turned out to be a hoax. Meanwhile the de Witt brothers found themselves besieged inside the prison. An appeal to William to send troops to restore order proved fruitless; the Stadholder declared that, between French invaders and public strife elsewhere, he had no soldiers to spare.

Late in the afternoon, the mob broke into the prison, dragged out the de Witts, slaughtered them, and hung their bodies upside down from the public gallows. The attackers reportedly included prominent Orangist citizens and members of the civil guard. When these local worthies left the scene, the populace fell upon the corpses and tore them to pieces. It was later whispered that parts of the bodies were auctioned off to the highest bidders, cooked and eaten in an orgy of vengeance.

In the towns of Holland, the crowds went wild. "King Mob," remarked one pamphleteer, "plays boss." Many in the poorer sectors of the population had loathed the de Witts as representatives of the clique of urban patricians who in their view ran the nation for their own advantage. The rioters demanded a purge of republican magistrates and local officials. William, although no more a populist than de Witt had been, exploited this fever of Orangist enthusiasm. He restored calm, refilled public offices with his own loyal supporters and left them to manage domestic affairs while he pursued his own highest priority: the war against France.

The Stadholder launched a bold attack against Louis. In the dead of winter, when hostilities were usually suspended, he led an army through the Rhineland to launch a surprise assault on the main French arsenal at Bonn. Caught off balance, the French began to lose ground. The Dutch

Tulipmania

In the 1630s tulips seemed to be the ideal commodity to Holland's adventurous investors: the flowers, a recent import from Turkey, were fashionable in European courts, horticulturists were vying to create new varieties, and the bulbs fetched high prices. The result was a speculative frenzy in which tulips, and tulip futures, were traded on credit for spiralling prices. At the height of the boom, flowerbeds were guarded by armed men and an entire house in Haarlem was swapped for just three tulip bulbs.

In a rising market, it seemed that nobody could lose. But when prices finally reached a level at which no more buyers could be found, the bubble burst and thousands found themselves ruinously in debt – fair game for satirical artists like Crispijn van de Pas the Younger, who portrayed the goddess Flora's triumphal car as a ship of fools *(right).*

struggle gradually expanded into a general European war. The English eventually dropped out, and the French, though slower to give up the fight, finally signed a treaty with William in 1678, returning all captured Dutch territory and agreeing to drop the restrictive tariffs they had imposed to hinder the Republic's foreign trade.

During the war, the Prince had strengthened his ties with the English crown by marrying his cousin Mary, daughter of the Duke of York and second after her father in line to the throne. The wedding made Mary a far more popular figure in Britain than her father the Duke, whose Catholic faith alarmed his future subjects. When in 1685 the Duke succeeded to the throne as King James II, William found himself under pressure from English Protestants to cross the Channel and intervene. In 1688, backed by a Dutch army and carried by a Dutch fleet, he responded to the invitation. James II fled the kingdom, and William and Mary were proclaimed joint monarchs in his place. The Orangists were elated: their prince had now taken his rightful place among the crowned heads of Europe, even if on a foreign throne.

Within the Republic, he would continue to be stadholder, officially the servant of the States General but capable of wielding considerable power. Yet with fresh demands now being made upon his energies elsewhere, the States General and its leaders were generally left free to manage their own affairs.

It would be more than a century before the stadholderate became a monarchy but, in the eyes of its inhabitants, the golden age of the Dutch Republic seemed to be drawing to a close. The economy, although reasonably stable, had ceased to grow. Crippling taxation was sending skilled craftsmen and entrepreneurs out in search of more congenial environments; the other European nations were becoming more self-sufficient, and less dependent on Dutch traders; and such was the Republic's new-found importance that it could not avoid being sucked into Europe's political upheavals, which grew ever more disruptive. The 18th century would see her involved in prolonged wars over the succession to the Spanish and Austrian thrones, invaded once more by the French, and at loggerheads once again with England.

If the poor suffered under the high tax burden, the patricians, at least, still had money to spend. Yet the old days, when merchants ploughed profits back into new ventures and lived comfortably but with a certain simplicity, were over. Those who could afford to purchase land built themselves suburban or rural estates and lived off their investments, far away from the warehouses full of Baltic timber or salt herring that had made their first fortunes.

Observers lamented that the Dutch were giving up the virtues that had brought them success. Some blamed the French for sapping Dutch vitality by encouraging a lamentable vogue for extravagant fashions. Certainly, the befrilled and periwigged burghers of the United Provinces no longer looked much like their republican grandparents, clad in no-nonsense Puritan black. The Dutch, as they themselves realized, were becoming much like other Western nations.

But if the Dutch were being transformed into conventional Europeans, then they could reflect with some satisfaction that they too had played their part in changing Europe. For they had supplied the world not only with such material goods as butter, cheese and herrings, but also with enlightened values and ideas: they demonstrated that it was possible to be tolerant as well as pious, charitable as well as rich, visionary as well as hard-headed. They also showed that a self-governing, secular, republican state might not only survive, but flourish beyond all expectations.

NEWCOMERS TO THE NEW WORLD

6

There was nothing spectacular about the low strip of land on the horizon, scarcely distinguishable from the surface of the sea. For the devout passengers on board the little ship, however, this first glimpse of the New World represented an answer to prayer and a vision of the future. Sixty-seven days of sickness and fear, of close confinement in a malodorous and heaving prison, made the prospect of any solid land seem irresistible. On November 11, 1620, the *Mayflower* cast anchor where God had directed her, sheltered from Atlantic storms by the sandy northern hook of Cape Cod. For 102 English men, women and children, the long ordeal was over. In the words of William Bradford, their young chronicler and their future leader, "they were not a little joyful".

On dry land, according to Bradford, the new colonists relished the luxury of exercising their aching limbs at last. The men explored the forests along the shore for food, water and signs of habitation; the women washed the party's clothes in a brackish pool near the beach, while the children – amazed by the space suddenly available to them – scrambled over the grassy dunes and raced along the flat sands.

More thoughtful members of the party realized that the immediate future promised nothing but hardship. Winter was nearly upon them, "and they that know the winters of that country, know them to be sharp and violent," observed Bradford. They had no shelter except the cramped and fetid ship and no provisions except the dwindling supplies that they had brought with them. "What could they see but a hideous and desolate wilderness?" asked Bradford, confronting their situation with stoic objectivity. But not in their worst imaginings could Bradford and his companions have envisaged the horrors of the ensuing winter. Over the next few months, disease and malnutrition took the lives of nearly half of the colonists.

Throughout these misfortunes, battling to gain a foothold on the edge of the unwelcoming continent, they began to build the village they called New Plymouth. That this frail settlement survived and eventually flourished was a tribute to the faith, courage and common sense of the Pilgrims, as they became known. "It pleased the Lord to give the plantation peace," Bradford humbly wrote home after five years of incessant struggle. Just a decade later, Bradford's Pilgrims would also be able to survey the smoke rising from the kitchen fires of several neighbouring communities that had sprung up in the area around Plymouth. New England's "desolate wilderness" was in rapid retreat.

The New World was hardly new to Europe by 1620. For more than a century pamphlets, ballads, histories and plays had acquainted poor and rich alike with the vast land lying to the west of the Atlantic Ocean. In the course of the 16th century the Spanish had firmly entrenched themselves in the old Aztec lands of Mexico,

An engraving by the Flemish artist Theodore de Bry shows the English explorer Captain Bartholomew Gosnold making a landfall in 1602 on the island of Martha's Vineyard off the New England coast. Working in Europe from written accounts, de Bry got many details wrong; Gosnold had a single ship, and the native inhabitants shown greeting him are portrayed fancifully. Nonetheless, Gosnold did trade successfully for skins with the Indians who met him, and returned with such glowing reports of the area that further exploration was assured. Four years later, Gosnold commanded one of the boats that brought settlers to Jamestown, Virginia, 700 kilometres to the south – the first permanent English outpost in America.

In the first decades of the 17th century, most of the maritime nations of Europe, including Sweden, Holland, France and Britain, laid claim to parts of eastern North America. But by the end of the century, the French and British were the dominant powers; the Spanish, who had made many pioneering journeys overland and were established in New Mexico, were confined on the east coast to the Florida peninsula. The pattern of English and French settlement — shaded respectively green and yellow on the map — reflects the different priorities of the colonists. The English were primarily farmers drawn to the fertile lands of New England, Virginia and Pennsylvania. The French were more interested in the fur trade, which took them far inland along the country's great waterways.

and had colonized much of the continent to the south, while conceding Brazil to the Portuguese. North America, however, had been relatively neglected.

It was not for lack of effort by Iberian explorers. Their expeditions had ranged far and wide across and around the continent. In the 1520s the Portuguese, who had already explored Newfoundland and Labrador, attempted a settlement on Cape Breton Island in Nova Scotia — the first by Europeans in North America since Viking days. The Spanish visited the St. Lawrence River in 1525, and briefly established colonies in the Carolinas. By sea, they travelled up the Pacific coast, perhaps as far as the southern boundary of modern Oregon. By land, an expedition from Mexico reached Arizona, encountered the Grand Canyon and found the Great Plains to the east of the Rocky Mountains. Another expedition marched from Florida in 1539 into what are now Arkansas and Oklahoma. But the distances involved were vast, the costs were huge, and the rewards seemed slight; there was no sign that North

America boasted the vast resources of silver that had lured Europeans to the lands farther south. In addition, the native peoples were hostile. Consequently, Spanish interest in the lands to the north declined. San Juan and Santa Fe, two struggling settlements in what is now New Mexico, remained Spain's solitary 17th-century outposts in the southwest. St. Augustine, established on the Florida coast in 1565, represented Spanish influence in the east of the continent.

Explorers from other nations also had little immediate luck. In northern Europe the New World was at first viewed primarily as an inhospitable obstacle between Europe and Asia. John Cabot, an Italian mariner who led English expeditions across the North Atlantic in the late 1600s, was convinced that Japan lay just beyond Newfoundland. He even carried a letter – never to be delivered – from Henry VII to the Great Khan of China. What Cabot did discover were vast breeding grounds of cod in the shallow seas between Newfoundland and Nova Scotia – fish could be scooped from the water with a basket, he claimed. But cod lacked the glamour of gold and spices, and Cabot never lived to appreciate the importance of this finding.

Sailing farther into the same waters 40 years later, the French explorer Jacques Cartier was charged by King Francis I "to discover certain islands and lands where it is said a great quantity of gold and other precious things are to be found". In this commission Cartier failed. The gold he triumphantly brought back to France turned out to be iron pyrites, the diamonds worthless quartz. But he sailed deep into the Gulf of St. Lawrence, discovering furs and forests in what he described as "as goodly and pleasant a country as possibly can be wished for".

As this first century of exploration wore on, it became clear that furs and forests were what North America had principally to offer. Trees covered the entire Atlantic coastal plain, creating a near-continuous carpet of foliage 20 metres or more above the ground from the Gulf of St. Lawrence to the Gulf of Mexico. Hickory, oak, basswood, cherry and other hardwoods comprised the southern temperate forests. White pine and hemlock mixed with beech, maple and birch in northern regions. This did not represent instant wealth, but to the business-minded European it soon suggested a vast repository of masts, spars and planks. Here too was one of the world's great breeding grounds for animals whose pelts had commercial value: bear, deer, otter, marten and – most important of all – the beaver (*see page 146*).

To the great disappointment of French and English explorers, however, there was no sign that the native peoples – the very name given to them, Indians, perpetuated the Asian error – had developed rich civilizations of the kind that Spain had so profitably exploited in the south. In all of North America there may have been about 10 million indigenous inhabitants when European exploration began. Those along the east coast, living in loosely associated tribes, belonged mainly to the Algonquian or the Iroquois language groups. Although they cultivated crops, employing remarkably sophisticated agricultural techniques, they were still stone-age people, whose small copper ornaments held no allure for acquisitive Europeans.

With no easy pickings to lure them, England and France were in no haste to establish settlements. When they did try later in the century, the first experiments were conspicuous failures. An attempt by French Protestants – Huguenots – to settle near the banks of the St. Johns River in Florida ended in their brutal massacre by an expeditionary force sent from Spain to drive them out. On Roanoke Island off the coast of present-day North Carolina, where Sir Walter Raleigh established a colony that he named Virginia in honour of England's virgin queen, Elizabeth I,

Most revealing of all White's drawings were his portraits. The series on the right shows an Indian decorated with body paint for hunting or feasting; a "flyer" or shaman; and an elder dressed for winter in a deerskin mantle. The tattoos adorning the women below probably indicate their status as wives of chiefs or counsellors.

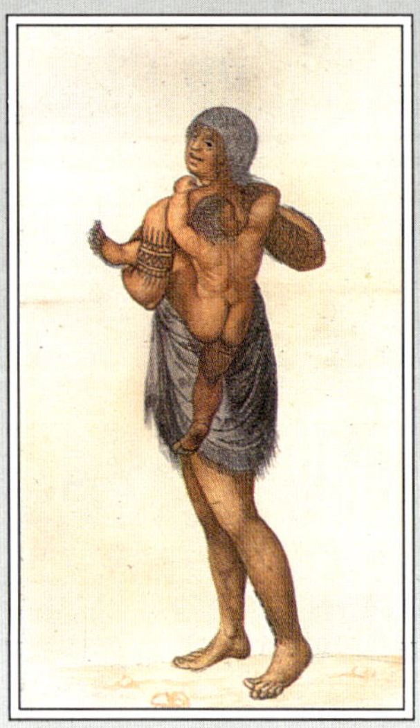

One of White's drawings shows an Indian man and woman sharing a meal of hominy – maize kernels swollen by soaking and boiling. Maize was the staple crop, planted in three sowings. After the late September harvest, most Indians left the villages to fish, hunt and trap, or to gather fruit, berries or nuts.

FIRST GLIMPSES OF INDIAN LIFE

Thousands of years before Europeans discovered North America, Palaeolithic immigrants from Asia had colonized the land. By the time the first white settlers arrived, the peoples they called Indians numbered as many as 10 million, divided into dozens of different language groups and hundreds of tribal entities.

Unlike the Aztecs or Incas, the North American Indians did not establish urban cultures. Whether farmers or hunters, they lived within their available resources, adapting their livelihoods to the contours of nature and expressing a deep reverence for the land and its wildlife.

Among the first Indians to be met by European settlers were an Algonquian-speaking group who lived by fishing, hunting and slash-and-burn farming in what is now North Carolina and the most southerly part of Virginia. A glimpse of these people at the time of contact is provided in the works of John White, official artist on a series of colonial ventures promoted by the English courtier Sir Walter Raleigh between 1584 and 1590.

White's rendering of the Indian village of Pomeioc shows houses of bent and tied poles covered with matting or bark. Such settlements, scattered along the coast and rivers, contained as many as 200 inhabitants each. Some were undefended; others, including Pomeioc, were protected by a palisade.

more than 100 English men and women simply disappeared. The fate of the colony is still one of the enigmas of North American history.

The episode did not discourage other would-be settlers, although it was not until the early 17th century that the first such venture took root. In 1620, when William Bradford contemplated the isolation of New England, he was not alone in North America. Some 750 kilometres southwest of Plymouth, around the settlement of Jamestown and along the rich river valleys of Virginia, fellow Englishmen had already cut back the forests and begun cultivating tobacco, the cash crop that was to make the fortune of the southern colonies. Far to the north, in a wilderness sterner than New England, French fur traders and priests were bargaining for beaver pelts and human souls in what is now Nova Scotia and the Gulf of St. Lawrence.

"There were never Englishmen left in a foreign country in such misery as we were in the new discovered Virginia," wrote George Percy, a survivor of Jamestown's first tragic summer of 1607. During its early years, starvation, disease and warfare constantly threatened England's first permanent settlement in the New World.

The establishment of a colony in Virginia made good sense to English statesmen and merchants at the dawn of the 17th century. This huge territory stretched from present-day North Carolina to northern Maine. It was claimed by both Spain and France, but England argued that there was no possession without occupation. A settlement on the fertile shores of Chesapeake Bay would serve as a defiant notice to Spain, while maintaining a safe distance from aggressive Spanish colonies.

To the London businessmen who backed the venture, Jamestown made good sense too. Many still believed that the American continent was merely a narrow strip of land dividing the Atlantic Ocean from all the riches of Asia. A colony in Virginia would be a useful trading station. Besides, there was the prospect of gold and silver in the great Indian kingdoms that optimists still hoped to find in the forests of North America. More realistically, English merchants had by now begun to appreciate the value of the fish, furs and timber. Buoyed up by the expectations of an attractive return, they formed a joint-stock company, an association of shareholders who agreed to fund the new colony for a share of the profits. Many in the Virginia Company would rue the day that they had invested in Jamestown.

It was not difficult finding volunteers for the Jamestown expedition. Young Englishmen had read with great excitement the colourful accounts of 16th-century voyages compiled by the geographer Richard Hakluyt, or Thomas Harriot's *A briefe and true report of the new found land of Virginia*, which described the New World's natural wonders. North America seemed to offer adventure with the chance of a good living.

The long and stormy passage, which lasted more than four months, may have drained some of the adventurers' high spirits. But few could resist the beauties of Virginia in April. Here were broad rivers meandering through woodland and meadows to the sea. "I was almost ravished at the sight thereof," wrote

Samuel de Champlain, explorer and champion of French settlement in Canada, is shown in armour at the centre of a battle between rival Indian tribes in 1609. The previous year Champlain, with the help of friendly Indians, had founded Quebec as a mart for the Indian-French fur trade. Eager to expand the commerce into hostile Indian territory, he and three armed companions joined a Huron war party in a raid against their enemies, the Iroquois. Panic-stricken by the unaccustomed gunfire, which killed three of their number, the Iroquois fled. The incident greatly increased French prestige among the Hurons and their allies, but made bitter enemies of the Iroquois, who later supported the British in their struggle against the colonists of New France.

George Percy, who also marvelled at strawberries that were four times the size of those in England – and much tastier – as well as the mussels and oysters which lay on the beach "as thick as stones".

There followed a succession of tragic mistakes. The first was to establish their settlement – named after King James I – on a marshy, mosquito-infested peninsula in the James River. The brackish water was scarcely drinkable, and the highest ground only three metres above the level of the river. Then there was endless bickering and fatal idleness. Few of the young gentlemen of Jamestown had anticipated blistering their hands with agricultural labour, and even fewer had any useful skills. The result was that insufficient land was cultivated that first spring for an adequate harvest. By midsummer the stores of salt beef, cheese and hardtack had come to an end. Even in this season of plenty the settlers began to starve.

All through that summer and autumn the Jamestown settlers died. Malaria and intermittent warfare with Indians – principally the Paspaheghs, on whose hunting grounds they had settled – accounted for a few, but "for the most part, they died of mere famine," wrote George Percy. "In the mornings their bodies trailed out of their cabins like dogs to be buried." Of the 104 settlers living in June, all but 38 had died by the following January. Those who survived were saved by their wits, their strength, and life-saving handouts of food from the Indians.

Yet more tragedies ensued as further shiploads of unskilled and unprepared English gentlemen – along with a few women – disembarked at Jamestown. In vain did John Smith, the colony's leader, entreat the parent company to send carpenters, gardeners, fishermen, blacksmiths and "diggers up of trees". In August 1609, some 400 ill and hungry new arrivals precipitated a crisis known as "the starving time". Cannibalism became a way of life; one man, it was asserted, killed, salted and ate his wife. Only 60 remained alive the following spring.

In the end it was a simple weed that preserved the colony in Virginia; *nicotiana tabacum.* Although King James himself had condemned the habit as "harmful to the brains and dangerous to the lungs", smoking tobacco had become a popular pastime in Europe by the early 17th century. The variety native to Virginia and smoked by the Indians was "poor and weak and of a bitter taste", according to one contemporary. In 1612, however, an enterprising settler named John Rolfe introduced the esteemed and expensive West Indian plant. Within two years, his experiments at growing and curing this variety proved so successful that the fortunes of the colony were transformed. Suddenly everyone was cultivating tobacco on every available patch of land, even in the streets of Jamestown itself.

The discovery of a successful cash crop imposed a new way of life upon Virginia. Because tobacco could be grown most economically on large estates, prosperous Englishmen were tempted now to try their hands at this lucrative profession. Their plantations soon extended beyond the immediate vicinity of Jamestown, reaching inland along the shores of the James River. From private riverside quays, English captains collected valuable shipments of cured Virginia tobacco.

Most work in the fields and tobacco warehouses was done by indentured servants, immigrant English contracted to work for from three to seven years for the master who "purchased" them. When his contract expired, a servant was theoretically rewarded with seeds, tools and often land; in reality, few were so lucky. Recruited mainly from the homeless and unemployed of the Old World, some had virtually been kidnapped by agents – or "spirits", as they were called – who made

Portrayed here in Elizabethan dress, Matoaka – better known by her pet name of Pocahontas or "little wanton" – was the daughter of Powhatan, leader of a powerful Indian confederation in Virginia. In 1608, aged about 13, she interceded for the life of Captain John Smith, who had come to ask her father's help for the starving Jamestown colony. Abducted by the English in 1612, she converted to Christianity, took the baptismal name Rebecca, and married John Rolfe, who is credited with turning the fortunes of the colony by planting its first crop of tobacco. With her husband, she came to England in 1616; the following year, she contracted smallpox and died. Five years later her father's successor, alarmed by the expansion of the Jamestown colony, led a massacre of 347 settlers. From then on, the colonists' goal was the extermination of the Indians.

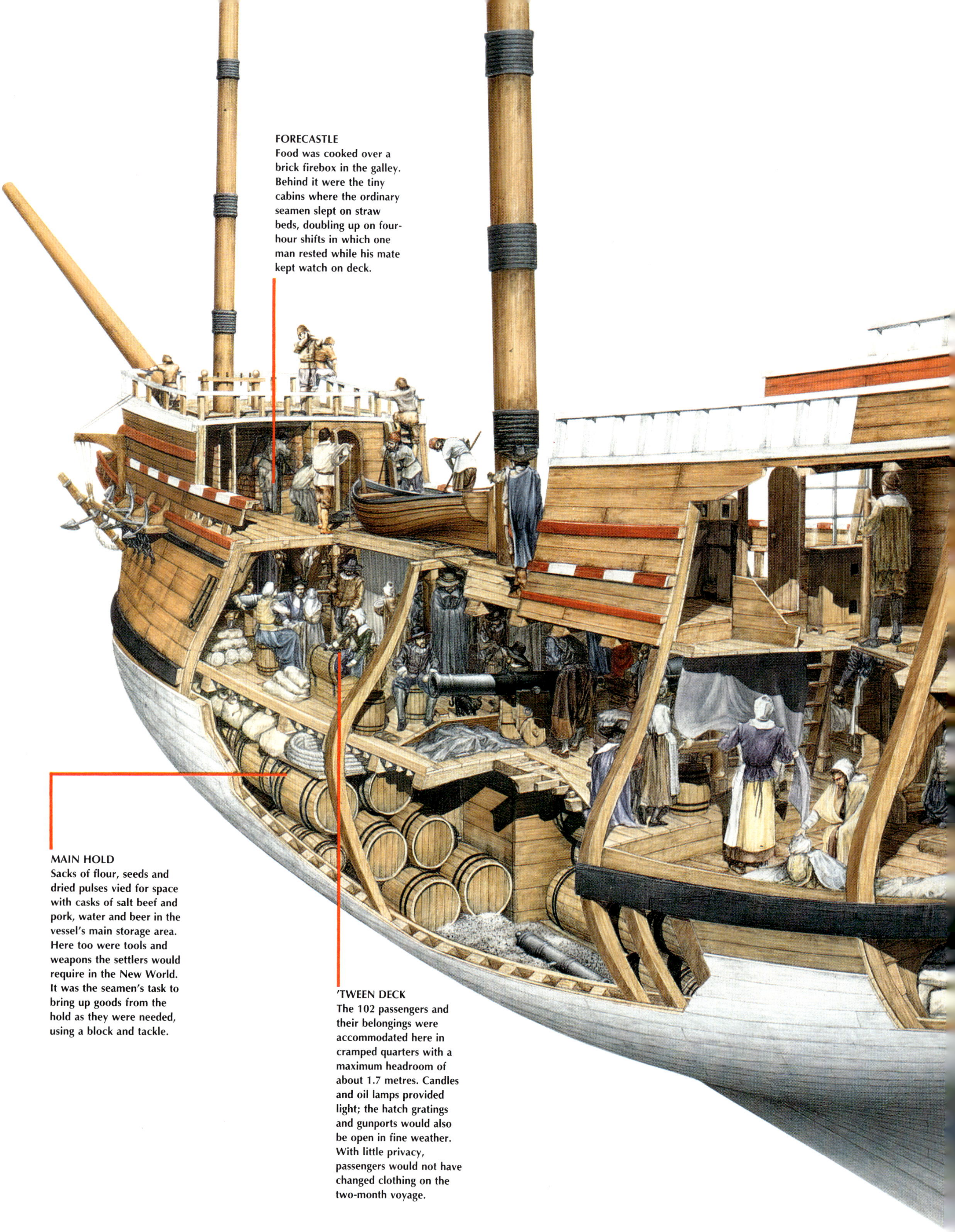
FORECASTLE
Food was cooked over a brick firebox in the galley. Behind it were the tiny cabins where the ordinary seamen slept on straw beds, doubling up on four-hour shifts in which one man rested while his mate kept watch on deck.
MAIN HOLD
Sacks of flour, seeds and dried pulses vied for space with casks of salt beef and pork, water and beer in the vessel's main storage area. Here too were tools and weapons the settlers would require in the New World. It was the seamen's task to bring up goods from the hold as they were needed, using a block and tackle.
'TWEEN DECK
The 102 passengers and their belongings were accommodated here in cramped quarters with a maximum headroom of about 1.7 metres. Candles and oil lamps provided light; the hatch gratings and gunports would also be open in fine weather. With little privacy, passengers would not have changed clothing on the two-month voyage.

CRAMPED QUARTERS FOR THE PILGRIMS

When the *Mayflower* left England on September 6, 1620, carrying Puritan settlers to the New World, it was the third time the ship had set sail for America. The Pilgrims on board had intended to travel in two boats, but twice leaks in the smaller vessel, the *Speedwell*, forced both ships to return. Demoralized, some 20 Pilgrims abandoned the enterprise, leaving 102 men, women and children to brave the perils of the Atlantic crossing.

With a crew of 25, the *Mayflower* was a three-masted merchantman about 32 metres long. Since about 1609 she had probably been engaged in the wine trade between France and England, in consequence of which she was known as a "sweet ship", her bilges being free from the residues of noisome cargos.

Even so, shipboard life for the passengers was extremely uncomfortable and insanitary. With only about one square metre of space each below deck, some chose to sleep on deck in the ship's boat. There were no toilet facilities on board; for cooking, the crew had access to a galley on deck, but the Pilgrims had to make do with braziers.

As a result of her late departure, the *Mayflower* soon ran into fierce storms that opened her deck seams and soaked the passengers' sleeping quarters. During one severe gale a main beam cracked. In another, a young Pilgrim was swept overboard but managed to grab a rope and was hauled back to safety.

a handsome profit from this trade in human souls. Women too were illegally press-ganged, or "spirited away", to provide breeding-mates for the men.

Both sexes found themselves subjected to conditions that were tantamount to slavery. Their movements were restricted; those who ran away were subjected to corporal or even capital punishment. They could be sold like slaves and flogged senseless for even minor misdemeanours. Some of the men escaped to become pirates; others ran off to live among the Indians, assuming Indian dress and ways. A few – perhaps two out of ten – were fortunate; at the end of their term of service they might manage through hard work to become craftsmen or farmers.

Against others, the odds were even more heavily stacked. In 1619 a tragic social revolution began with the arrival of 20 slaves on a Dutch privateer. By then African slavery was well established in South America and the sugar plantations of the West Indies. At first, however, blacks in Virginia were employed on the same terms as white indentured servants. Only later were the Africans denied all rights. By the early 1700s, black slaves made up about 20 per cent of Maryland's population.

In addition, there was vigorous Indian slaving in the south. In the Carolinas the settlers provided local tribes with weapons and drink, and encouraged tribal wars. Prisoners taken in the fighting, which reached as far south as Spanish Florida by the turn of the century, were enslaved for service in Carolina itself – there were 1,400 such Indians in the capital, Charleston, in 1708 – or shipped to the West Indies,

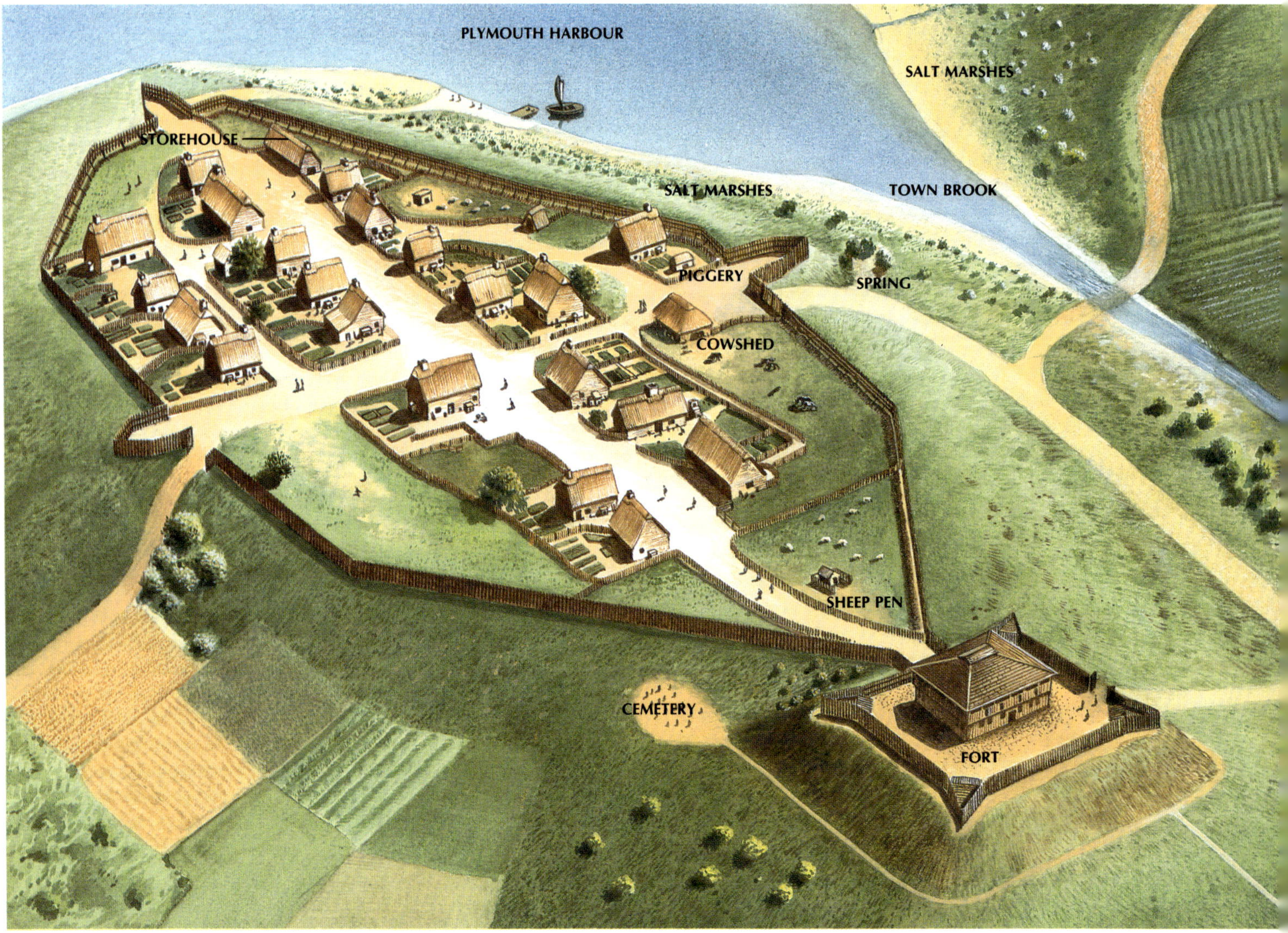

New York or New England. Slavery was by no means restricted to the south. It was a Boston schoolmistress at the end of the century who complained that Connecticut farmers were too indulgent to their slaves, "permitting them to sit at table and eat with them . . . and into the dish goes the black hoof as freely as the white hand".

Virginia's new economy needed a fresh political order as well as a reliable workforce. Initially ruled by a local council appointed in London, the colony found itself under martial law supervised by an absolute governor after Jamestown's first two disastrous seasons. In 1619, a new era began with the convening of Virginia's – and America's – first elected assembly. The House of Burgesses made laws on nearly all aspects of life, from farming to churchgoing. When James I dissolved the Virginia Company in 1624 and established royal control, he permitted the House to continue as a lower legislative assembly. This early example of self-government was an important marker on the road to America's political independence.

The demise of the Virginia Company followed hard on the heels of a nearly fatal disaster for the colony: the Indian uprising of 1622. The Jamestown colonists had unwittingly settled among a powerful confederacy of about 30 Indian tribes under a chief known as Powhatan. At first relations were edgy; skirmishes alternated with periods of cooperation. Peace seemed assured, however, when John Rolfe, the man who revolutionized Virginia's agriculture, married Powhatan's witty and beautiful daughter, Pocahontas. At the age of about 13, this remarkable woman reputedly saved the life of the colonist's leader, John Smith – then her father's prisoner – by throwing herself between him and his intended executioner. As Mistress Rolfe she travelled to London, astonishing the English court with her queenly bearing.

The untimely death of Pocahontas in 1617, followed by her father's demise a year later, released pent-up resentments among the Indians, on whose lands the colonists were increasingly encroaching. The Indians laid careful plans for a surprise attack. Right up to the last minute, the assailants mixed casually and amicably with the settlers. But then, on Good Friday, 1622, in the words of Smith's *General History of Virginia*, "they came unarmed into our houses with deer, turkeys, fish, fruit and other provisions to sell us; yea, in some places sat down at breakfast with our people, whom immediately with their own tools they slew most barbarously". Three hundred and forty-seven English men, women and children were killed that morning, nearly one third of the colony's total population.

Had the Indians pressed home their advantage, they might have driven the immigrants off the continent. Instead they returned to their villages, satisfied that they had subdued the white man's appetite for expansion. This gave the settlers time to launch a ferocious campaign of reprisals, systematically destroying Indian villages and crops. For nearly a decade the wars continued. It was better, claimed Virginia's Governor, Sir Francis Wyatt, "to have no heathen among us, who are at best but thorns in our sides, than to be at peace and league with them". His policies were vigorously pursued. By mid-century the Indians had withdrawn to the edge of the retreating forests, and the coastal farmers had lost virtually all contact with the people who until so recently had been in sole possession of their lands.

Unlike the English of Virginia, North America's French pioneers quickly proved themselves skilful at dealing with the Indians. According to its charter of 1627, New France extended from Florida to the Arctic Circle. In its early days, however, most of its citizens lived within the boundaries of modern-day eastern Canada: the

The settlement of Plymouth established by the *Mayflower* Pilgrims on the Massachusetts coast in December 1620 had become, within seven years of their landfall, a self-sufficient community of over 200 souls. Its wooden houses lined a road leading to a two-storey building that served both as a fort and as a meeting house. The community's trim prosperity had not been easily attained. In the first winter, half the emigrants died of disease or exposure. The colonists would not have survived without help from local Indians, who taught them how to plant and fertilize maize. But the settlers remained on their guard against attack, and after 1622, when they received news of an Indian massacre in Virginia, they enclosed the plantation with a palisade more than 800 metres long.

An 18th-century engraving shows a beaver pool dammed with trees felled by the animals themselves. The sketch also reveals the ways in which the Indians hunted beavers — with traps, guns, bows and arrows, trained dogs and, in winter, with nets spread over holes cut in the ice around the beavers' "kennels" or lodges.

A FORTUNE IN FUR

Of all the animals sought by hunters in the forests of the New World, none offered richer rewards than the beaver, shown second from the top, between an otter and two species of seal, in the 17th-century drawing below. The creatures' smooth, dense pelts, which had long attracted Indian hunters, found a ready market in Europe and relieved the continent of over-reliance on unpredictable Russian suppliers. "Beaver" hats soon became the height of gentlemanly fashion, while fur muffs and tippets (shoulder capes) were popular items of female attire. Seeking to exploit the demand, French and British traders ventured ever deeper into the interior in search of new sources of fur, and it was this quest more than any other activity that opened up the North American wilderness.

maritime provinces, the Gulf of St. Lawrence and the forests of Ontario. The first French settlement was at Port Royal in Acadia, now Nova Scotia. Although this war-torn outpost changed hands five times between the French and English during the course of the century, it had little more than symbolic value. More central to the development of New France was Quebec on the St. Lawrence River, founded in 1608 by the remarkable Samuel de Champlain.

In Champlain, New France found a tireless and many-faceted champion. Soldier, sailor, author, explorer, fur trader and governor, "he bore the whole burden of administration on his own shoulders," according to a contemporary. Champlain himself explained his achievements as arising from "the desire I have always entertained of making new discoveries in New France for the welfare, advantage and the glory of the French name, as well as of bringing these poor people to the knowledge of God". The "poor people" were, of course, the Indians. No one was more influential in establishing the course of French-Indian relations than Champlain.

Although he was committed to establishing a successful colony in New France, Champlain was also convinced that by exploring farther along the waterways of Canada he could, as he put it, "open the road to China". In this endeavour, he enlisted the help of Indian nations along the St. Lawrence and Ottawa rivers, promising in return to assist them in their war against the dreaded Iroquois, based in what is now upstate New York. In 1609, accompanied by only one other Frenchman, Champlain set out by canoe with a war party of 60 Huron and Algonquin braves. On the banks of the long lake (now called Champlain) that is the northern border of New York State and Vermont, they came upon a party of 200 Iroquois. With a single shot of his arquebus, Champlain killed two Iroquois chiefs. Terrified by this unfamiliar weapon, the warriors fled in wild panic. This easy victory gained Champlain the undying gratitude of his Indian allies. But he had made a dangerous enemy in the Iroquois, whose frequent raids and subsequent alliance with the New England English proved a constant menace to New France.

Champlain never discovered a route to the East Indies, but many of his countrymen found riches enough in the forests of New France. Friendly Indians sailed down the tributaries of the St. Lawrence, their canoes laden with furs accumulated during the long winter trapping season; these were exchanged for axes, scalping knives, guns, blankets and shoes. The annual spring fair at Montreal, founded in 1642 by priests and fur traders, was an important business occasion – and a riotous celebration until the Bishop of New France forbade providing alcohol to Indians, except, he wisely allowed, "in long, fatiguing and extraordinary voyages."

Not all Frenchmen were content to wait for the furs to come to them. A breed of lawless young trappers, known as *coureurs de bois*, took to the wilds, becoming as adept at tracking on snowshoes and shooting rapids in birchbark canoes as the Indians among whom they lived. Their familiarity with Indian languages and society made them invaluable sources of information in times of war.

Perhaps the most remarkable immigrants to New France were the Jesuits. These tough, intellectual clerics first arrived at Quebec in 1626 and began converting the Indians – not in the relative comfort of a white settlement, but in the villages of the Indians themselves. Some were horrified by their strange companions; cannibalism, torture, incest, polygamy and uncontrollable vermin were more than they had bargained for. "It is enough to say that they were altogether savage," wrote one missionary; "from morning until night they have no other thought than to fill their stomachs." Many, however, developed a sympathetic relationship with their new parishioners. "There are Indians as there are Frenchmen," wrote an appreciative Ursuline nun, "but generally speaking they are more devout than the French."

A very different kind of society was taking shape on the coast between New France and Virginia. The men and women of New England, as the area north of the Hudson River became known, had not come to the New World to convert the savages or to discover gold. Their aim was freedom of worship. These were the Puritans, English Protestants who insisted on simplicity, or "purity", of worship, and who believed that religion should be stripped of all popish ritual and bishops denied their lordly role in church administration. Their intellectual, moral and political convictions were to exert a profound influence on the future of America.

Some extreme Puritans, the *Mayflower* pilgrims of 1620 among them, sought complete independence from the Anglican church, and were consequently known as separatists. A majority of the later arrivals, however, were prepared to pledge loyalty to the English church and state.

Such was the case with a fresh wave of English settlers who arrived 10 years after the *Mayflower*, bringing a royal charter to establish a colony named Massachusetts Bay. Although the newcomers did not call themselves separatists, the colony they established was politically and religiously the most headstrong in the New World. Despite the hardships that attended its foundation – 200 settlers died of disease during the first winter – the progress made by Massachusetts was astonishing. Twenty thousand immigrants arrived over the colony's first 10 years. Many were

Sketched in the 1650s, this view of New Amsterdam was only completed after 1664, when the city was captured by the English, who renamed it New York. In the centre lies the little wharf where passengers and goods landed; behind it stand a weighing beam and a crane. The large building in the background to the left was the fort, which contained a church as well as a barracks and a jail. New Amsterdam had been founded in the 1620s as a Dutch centre for the fur trade. The city soon prospered, exporting more than 7,000 beaver pelts to Holland in a single cargo in 1626 – together with the news that the people of New Netherland had bought the island of Manhattan from the Indians for 60 guilders, about three months' wage for a craftsman. With the loss of the city Dutch colonization in North America came to an end.

highly educated or skilled; all were single-mindedly dedicated to establishing a pure society. Communities quickly sprang up along the bay shore or on the banks of the Charles River, including Boston, spiritual and financial heart of the colony.

Commercially these hard-working Englishmen did not put a foot wrong. The immigrants were far wealthier than the impoverished idealists on the *Mayflower*; in addition, they came in groups from clearly defined areas of England, East Anglia in particular, so the makings of a social structure were soon in place. Within five years of their arrival the Puritans were exporting locally grown wheat to the West Indies. But it quickly became apparent that agriculture was not an easy way to prosper. A man took 60 days, it was said, to clear one New England acre of the great glacial boulders that studded his fields; and the following year a fresh crop of rock, heaved up by the winter's frost, would have arisen from the earth.

The Puritans of Boston turned instead to the sea, where the codfish provided a reliable source of revenue. (It was later to become the symbol of Massachusetts.) The sea also became the high road to wealth for New England's shrewd merchants. By the latter part of the century, Boston had come to dominate North American trade, carrying New England fish and timber, Virginian tobacco and West Indian sugar to Europe, then distributing English manufactured goods to the East Coast colonies on their return journeys. The success of Massachusetts Bay as a centre of trade would soon aggravate London merchants and influence English policy.

Financial success was, however, not the main concern of Massachusetts Bay. The Church was the centre of colonial life. The Puritans' outspoken aim was to create a new Zion, a society in which laws, where possible, were derived from the Bible. "We shall be as a city upon a hill, the eyes of all the people are upon us," Massachusetts' first governor, John Winthrop, claimed in 1630.

In their efforts to establish a godly state, the Puritans enjoyed complete freedom. Like early Jamestown, Massachusetts Bay was financed by a joint-stock company, but while the Virginia Company had ruled from London, Massachusetts Bay moved its entire governing council to the colony in New England, well away from the prying eyes of the English church and state.

Religious freedom for the Puritan settlers meant freedom from the Church of England, by no means freedom of conscience for the individual living within the new colony. Although Puritan ministers did not hold political office, the council of religious elders became increasingly influential as interpreters of law. The result was theocracy, a government dominated by the Church. Sunday was rigidly observed; in the Boston area all work, play and travel stopped at six o'clock on Saturday evening. Churches doubled as political meeting-houses; those not attending risked a fine, and only Church members – a select group of males who were considered suitable by the clergy to receive communion – were permitted to vote. "If people shall be governors, who shall be governed?" asked one Puritan divine in defence of such limited suffrage.

Laws became ever more severe. In an attempt to stamp out "the hideous clamour for liberty of conscience", political or religious dissent was promptly stifled. Some offences were minor. A wilful settler named Ursula Cole was sentenced to pay a fine or be whipped for saying "she had as lief hear a cat meow as Mr. Shephard preach". Those perceived as heretics, however, met with severe punishment. Few suffered more than the Quakers, members of a radical religious movement founded in England in the mid-17th century. By teaching that God could communicate directly to the common man, these eccentric outsiders threatened to undermine the authority of the Puritan leaders. Exile was the mildest punishment a Quaker could expect. If he came back to the colony he would lose an ear; a second return would cost the other ear. If he were foolish enough to appear yet again, the authorities would bore a hole in his tongue with a red-hot iron. This law was subsequently simplified: a Quaker returning from exile would be hanged. Several in fact lost their lives before popular resentment forced the repeal of this cruel ordinance.

The most remarkable opponent of the regime was Roger Williams. Although an orthodox Puritan in most doctrinal matters, this distinguished preacher dared to contend that church and state should be separated and that the colony's land was held illegally because it had not been purchased from the Indians. Exiled in the dead of winter for these subversive opinions, he established Providence, later the capital of Rhode Island. This tiny colony, presided over by Williams, became a haven for all the quarrelsome misfits of New England. Rogues' Island, its opponents mockingly called it; but Rhode Island remained the one place in North America where those of any belief – or none at all – could officially make their home.

Other colonists left Massachusetts Bay for more worldly reasons, lured by the rich farmlands of the Connecticut River valley. Connecticut became self-governing in 1639, later absorbing the independent colony of New Haven.

Despite its self-righteous elders and official intolerance, Massachusetts was not the grey, cheerless society it was later painted. The Puritans wore bright colours, enjoyed sports and were far from teetotal. There were taverns in Boston where a man could drink, smoke and gossip. "Drink is in itself a good creature of God," wrote Increase Mather, a pillar of Boston's church. The Puritans also had a devout respect for education, and established Harvard College in 1636 as a theological institution. Harvard Commencement Day was an annual holiday in Massachusetts, starting with sermons and ending with celebrations. Harvard was, according to Increase's son, Cotton, "the best thing that ever New England thought upon".

During the early years, the Puritans of New England had been more kindly disposed towards the Indians than Christians of differing views. Indeed, the Plymouth Pilgrims had cultivated excellent relations with the local Wampanoag tribe under its chief Massasoit. Towards the end of their first, starving winter, an English-speaking Indian named Squanto had descended on Plymouth like a gift from God and taught the Pilgrims to fish, farm and hunt. The joyous first Thanksgiving of 1621 – a three-day harvest celebration of food and friendship to which Massasoit brought 90 men – was a genuine and spontaneous expression of racial harmony.

Relations soon turned sour. In the 1630s, when feuding broke out in Connecticut between settlers and the Pequot Indians, there was no question where the immigrants' loyalty lay. Surrounding the Pequots in their fort at Mystic, the Puritans showed no quarter. "In a little more than one hour, five or six hundred of these barbarians were dismissed from a world that was burdened with them," wrote the Boston divine, Cotton Mather. To confront the Indian menace more effectively, in 1643 Massachusetts Bay, Connecticut, Plymouth and New Haven formed the New England Confederation, the first such alliance of colonies.

While New England and Virginia were developing their characteristic societies 750 kilometres apart, other communities sprang up along the bays and rivers in between. One of the most promising experiments was undertaken by Cecilius Calvert, Lord Baltimore, whose family had been granted by Charles I about four million hectares of land north of the Potomac River. For this Baltimore promised to pay the King two Indian arrows per year plus one fifth of any gold and silver discovered.

The new colony was ideally situated. The climate was neither too hot nor too cold for Englishmen, game abounded and the forests were free of undergrowth. "Even the peas in those parts grow 10 inches [25 centimetres] long in 10 days," marvelled one contemporary. What is more, the Indians greeted the newcomers enthusiastically, offering them every assistance.

The idyll was short-lived. A Roman Catholic, Calvert intended the new colony, which he called Maryland, to serve as a haven for his persecuted coreligionists. From the beginning, he insisted that there be religious toleration between Catholics and Protestants. Early on, however, conflicts arose between the proprietors of Maryland's great plantations – mainly Catholics – and their Puritan tenants, who soon constituted a majority of the population. Economically the colony prospered, but Lord Baltimore's dream of religious harmony collapsed into political bickering and occasional civil disorder. Even the Act Concerning Religion of 1649, which was conceived by Lord Baltimore as a law to ensure toleration, was corrupted by

An engraving depicting the forced departure of prostitutes to New France is captioned: "The sad embarkation of Parisian ladies of joy in December, 1687, and their farewell to the apothecaries and surgeons as well as to their lovers." The scene is probably intended to be satirical, for some of the ladies have surnames that signify good birth – suggesting that they did not really go to America, but perhaps had morals that classed them as fit for such. Nevertheless, the French government did transport prostitutes and criminals in an attempt to populate the empty spaces of the New World. Many died during the passage or soon after, and by the end of the century the population of New France was still no more than 10,000, compared to about 250,000 in the English colonies.

bigotry. A paragraph insisted upon by strict Puritans declared that anyone denying the divinity of Christ or even making "reproachful speeches" concerning the Holy Trinity was to be punished with death.

Greater tolerance existed in the colony of New Netherland, founded by the Dutch West India Company, which monopolized Dutch trade in the New World. The Dutch built trading posts along the Atlantic coast and up the Hudson and Connecticut rivers, frequently clashing with Indians and English settlers in their efforts to acquire furs, timber and other natural resources. In 1655 they annexed New Sweden, Scandinavia's only colony, which later became the state of Delaware. Yet New Netherland had problems of its own. It had difficulty in attracting settlers, not least since few could be tempted to leave their rich and tolerant mother country to start afresh in a hostile land. It therefore had to draw in such peoples as it could, which meant that it lacked the social cohesiveness of its English neighbours.

The main settlement was New Amsterdam, at the southern tip of Manhattan Island, named after the Indian tribe from whom it had been purchased in 1626. The town that grew up was a secular, cosmopolitan place. Drunkenness was a perpetual problem and a law had to be enacted prohibiting playing golf in the streets. The city was run autocratically by its peg-legged governor, Peter Stuyvesant, who ruled the colony for 17 years; but even he was unable to subdue this unruly community. "Shut your eyes," wrote the West India Company directors to Stuyvesant, "allow everyone to have his own belief as long as he behaves quietly and legally."

England remained the nation with the greatest stake in North America, and by mid-century its rulers were realizing that unless they tightened the reins on their semi-independent colonies, they might lose control entirely. Once the trauma of the English Civil War had ended, first Oliver Cromwell as Lord Protector of the Commonwealth and then the restored Charles II tried to limit the economic and political freedoms that the New World had begun to take for granted.

During the years of confusion and war in England, colonial merchants had relied on ships of other countries, particularly the Netherlands, to transport their goods. To end this practice, England enacted two Navigation Acts aimed at debarring the Dutch and other foreign competitors from sharing in the colonial trade.

An early casualty of the acts was New Netherland. In 1664, four English warships anchored off Manhattan Island and demanded the surrender of New Amsterdam. Peter Stuyvesant stood on the parapet of the fort, a gunner with a lighted match by his side, prepared to answer with cannonfire. But Stuyvesant's senior advisers talked him out of defending his colony; there was a small Dutch militia, but of the town's 1,500 or so inhabitants, only 250 were capable of bearing arms, and many flatly refused to do so. The English marched in unopposed and claimed New Amsterdam in the name of King Charles's brother James, Duke of York. That same day, Captain Richard Nicolls informed New England of the successful action, signing his letter "from New York". With the fall of New Amsterdam, the entire colony of New Netherland likewise changed its name and passed into English hands.

The transition from New Amsterdam to New York was remarkably peaceful. It remained a worldly, tolerant, untidy town, quite willing and able to absorb Scots, Huguenots, Catholics, Quakers, Anabaptists and Jews, who made it one of the New World's major centres of trade. The governor had absolute power; not until the end of the century did a representative assembly give the ordinary New Yorkers a say in

THE LIMNERS' HONEST ART

Sturdy and plain of faith, the Puritans of New England had a correspondingly unvarnished attitude to art. Their painters were themselves plain, ordinary folk – usually craftsmen for whom portraiture was a sideline of their work as sign or coach painters. These predominantly anonymous artists, called limners, worked in a medieval convention, making no more than a rudimentary attempt at three-dimensional representation, and usually setting their subjects against a simple background. But as is apparent from the examples of their portraits reproduced here, they recorded their compatriots with unsparing realism, for they believed that the smallest details of life were an expression of God's will.

The earliest surviving portrait, dated 1664, is of a Mrs Elizabeth Eggington *(centre)*. Wealth and social standing is conveyed in the painting of John Freake, a Boston merchant and attorney *(top)*, whose anonymous portraitist also painted his relative, Elizabeth *(below, right)*, shown tenderly holding her baby. There is no tenderness, however, in the self-portrait of Captain Thomas Smith *(below, left)*, whose stern outlook is summed up in the first two lines of the paper in his hand: "Why should I the world be minding therein a World of Evils Finding".

running his city. But the governor was under instructions from England to tolerate people of all religions, "provided they give no disturbance to the public". So relaxed was the atmosphere of New York that Peter Stuyvesant himself remained in the colony, retiring to his Manhattan farm, where he died in 1672.

In the English colonies, the Navigation Acts were regarded with hostility and widely flouted. Angered by such insubordination, England began to investigate the administration of her colonies, and in nearly all cases found it wanting. King Charles had need of money, and the colonies seemed to offer a source of revenue not dependent on the constant supervision of the English parliament. The result was increased interference in colonial affairs, with agents from London trying to ensure that governors enforced the law. In Virginia, a one-crop colony where the governor was a royal appointee, it was easy enough to insist on obedience. Massachusetts, however, remained rebelliously independent for much of the century.

So consistent was Massachusetts Bay's flouting of the Navigation Acts, and so worrying the tales of discrimination and persecution told of the colony, that in 1676 King Charles sent a special agent named Edward Randolph to investigate its affairs. Randolph, an orthodox royalist, wrote a damning report, asserting that Massachusetts was not only openly trading with other states, but had established its own customs office which was pocketing all the revenue from foreign trade.

England's solution was to revoke the charter of the colony. In 1686 Charles's successor, the Catholic James II, incorporated it into the newly created Dominion of New England. This huge new colony, which stretched from Maine to the Hudson River, was intended to strengthen the colonies in face of the threat from the French to the north, with whom the settlers found themselves increasingly in conflict.

The man appointed to govern the dominion, Sir Edmund Andros, was a royal placeman whose policies seemed calculated to antagonize the elders of Massachusetts Bay. Legislation was no longer initiated by a representative assembly; taxation was imposed arbitrarily. Worse, churches were used for Anglican services. Andros even permitted the erection of a maypole on Boston common, and encouraged the celebration of Christmas, regarded as a pagan festivity by the devout Puritans.

It seemed as if God himself had raised his hand against this profane administration when, in 1688, William of Orange — a devout Protestant — overthrew James

The Fairest Dealer

Of all the English colonies in North America, Pennsylvania had the most enlightened policy towards the Indians and, in consequence, saw the least warfare. The colony was founded in 1682 by William Penn, son of a wealthy admiral, who was granted the territory in lieu of a debt owed by the Crown to his father. A convert to Quakerism, imprisoned in England several times for preaching the virtues of religious tolerance and pacifism, Penn considered his colony a "Holy Experiment" and established it with high idealism, treating the Indians fairly, acknowledging their title to the land and trying to protect them in their dealings with settlers and traders.

Power was concentrated in the governor and his council, but liberty of conscience was guaranteed, and in an age when the death penalty was meted out to petty thieves, Penn made only murder and treason capital crimes. He was also a shrewd promoter, writing glowing reports of the colony that helped attract 9,000 settlers within three years of its founding.

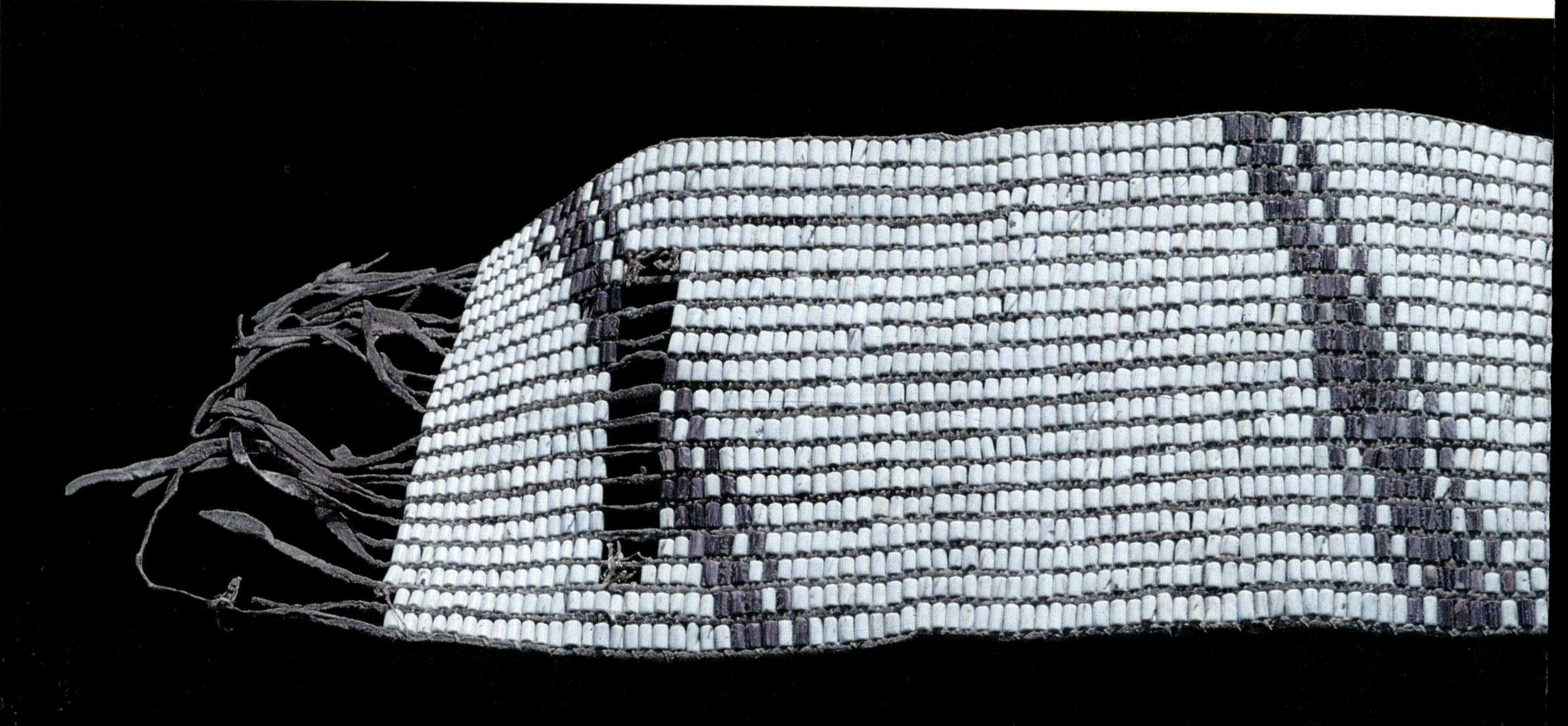

to become king of England. The jubliant Puritans imprisoned Andros and shipped him home to London. The Dominion of New England was dissolved.

A fresh charter was devised for Massachusetts Bay, with Plymouth and Maine now part of the colony. This document was carefully drafted to prevent a repetition of previous abuses. Suffrage would be determined by ownership of property, not by church membership. But 60 years of theocracy were not to die with the signing of a charter. One last spasm of religious violence rocked the colony to its core.

In 1691 the daughter and niece of the minister of Salem, a village north of Boston on Massachusetts Bay, suffered recurring hysterical fits. The girls claimed to have been visited by spectral forms of local women, who urged them to sign a pact with the devil; their torments, it seemed, resulted from the devil's anger at their refusal to collaborate. Before long other young, unmarried women confessed to similar visitations. Those they named were accused of witchcraft and arrested.

By the time the governor, Sir William Phips, set up a court of inquiry into the matter, more than 100 people – mostly women aged between 40 and 60 – had been imprisoned. After a summer of trials, during which evidence often could not be heard above the howling of the possessed, 19 were found guilty and hanged. One man who refused to answer charges was crushed to death with stones; two dogs were also executed. The district became gripped by collective hysteria, and few were safe from accusation. Only when rumours began that the governor's own wife was in league with the devil did the authorities bring the trials to an abrupt end. The frenzy soon ebbed, but the Salem witch trials had offered a frightening glimpse of the fear and suspicion simmering under the surface of New England life.

The last substantial area of the North American coast not colonized by Europeans lay between Virginia and Spanish Florida. In 1670, with Spain no longer strong enough to resist, King Charles II awarded this region to eight of his court favourites. The new colony, known as Carolina in honour of the King, comprised a northern and southern territory. It was run along undemocratic lines, with the proprietors appointing a governor and half of his governing council. French Huguenots were among the early settlers; English immigrants came largely from the other American colonies. Charles Town (now Charleston) soon became a prosperous centre for the export of rice, the staple crop of southern Carolina's marshy coastal plantations.

The Delaware Indians commemorated their 1682 treaty with William Penn – shown below in a portrait sketched by Francis Place in about 1698 – in wampum belts made from seashells acquired by trade with coastal tribes. In the example below, a hatted white man and an Indian clasp hands in friendship; territorial information is given in the diagonal stripes on each side.

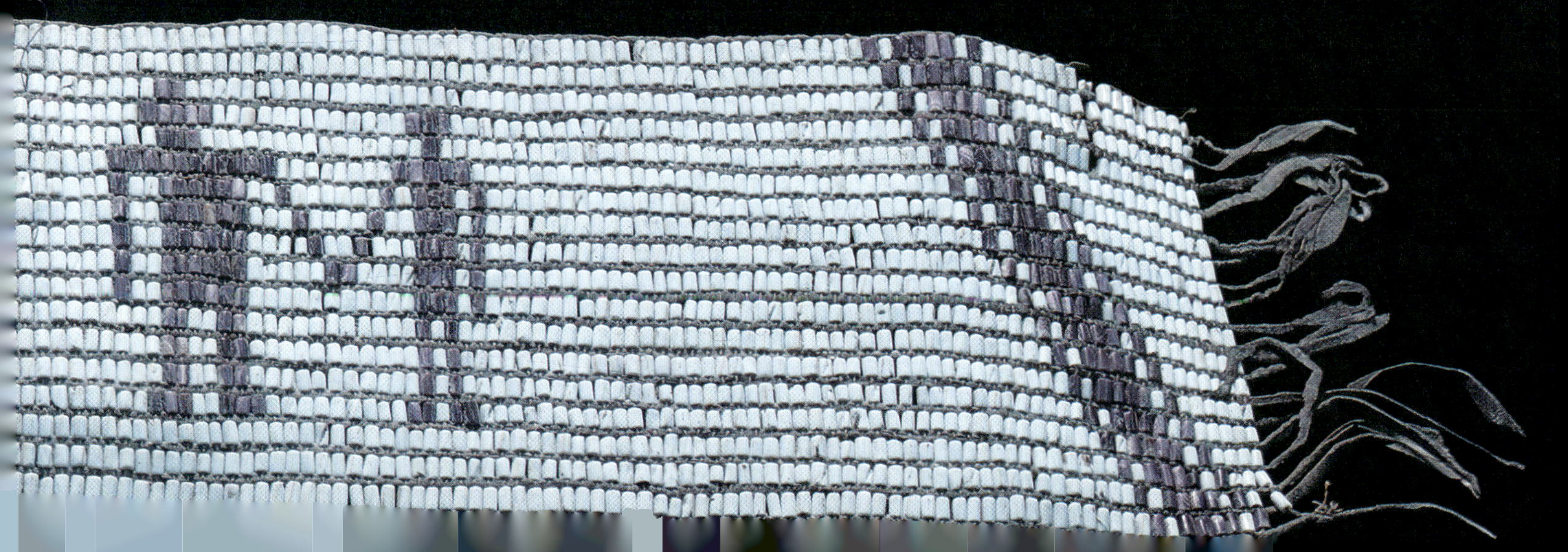

The colony was not entirely peaceful. Threats from Spain had been anticipated. What came as a surprise, however, was to discover that the deer-hunting lands on the western frontier were contested not so much with Indians as with the French.

"We have turned our eyes to New France," announced King Louis XIV in 1663, "where to our regret, we see few inhabitants established . . . and these are in daily danger from the Iroquois." The Sun King had reason for concern. Between 1641 and 1653 the Iroquois had waged two ruinous campaigns against the French. Generally regarded as the fiercest, best organized Indian people north of Mexico, they had decimated the Hurons, France's loyal allies in trade and war. "I would make this paper blush and my listeners would shudder," wrote one Jesuit, declining to describe the tortures inflicted upon his Christian charges by the Iroquois.

With New France on the brink of destruction, Louis and his chief minister Jean Baptiste Colbert reorganized the huge colony. They abolished the Company of New France and the old order under which a small number of aristocratic landowners sublet their holdings to peasant farmers. A governor acting as head of state, a bishop and an officer called an intendant, in charge of civil affairs, now took their place, but ultimate authority lay with Louis and Colbert. They encouraged new colonists, especially artisans, and urged women to emigrate as wives for the soldiers. These policies proved effective. Between 1665 and 1690 the population of New France increased from 3,000 to 15,000. Security also improved after a successful winter campaign against the Iroquois. The Indians vanished on their snowshoes into the forests, leaving the pursuing French to lay waste the territory.

Still searching for the great river that would carry them westwards to the Pacific Ocean, the French found instead the greatest river of North America flowing south to the Gulf of Mexico. Jacques Marquette, a Jesuit priest, and Louis Joliet were the first to explore the Mississippi, followed by Robert de La Salle, who descended the river to its mouth. On the basis of this voyage, de la Salle claimed the entire Mississippi valley for France, naming it Louisiana after the King. A series of forts, from Detroit to Biloxi, sought to establish French rights to this vast territory.

But New France remained a beleaguered colony. The last two decades of the century were blighted by almost continual war with England. There had long been battles over possession of Newfoundland and Acadia. To these were added conflicts over fur trading in the Hudson Bay region, as well as over the Carolina deer trade in the south. Meanwhile, the savage dispute over the hinterland of northern New York and New England continued to drain the resources of both nations.

By the latter part of the century, a new order was taking shape in North America as the populous and aggressive English colonies expanded. All along the coast the Indians had been pushed back from their traditional lands. In many regions political weakness, together with European diseases to which they had no natural immunity, left them powerless to offer any organized resistance.

Such was not the case in New England. After the Pequot War of 1637, the Puritans had shown increased interest in the Indians, largely due to the efforts of John Eliot. A fervent missionary, he translated the Bible into Algonquian – it became *Up-Biblum God* – and established two Indian churches, where more than 1,000 "praying Indians" could worship. There was even a college at Harvard for Indians.

The great majority of Indians, however, were not interested in the white man's religion, and resented the loss of their hunting grounds to the settlers. The peace came abruptly to an end in 1675, when Massasoit's son Metacom, known to the English as King Philip, led an alliance of the tribes living in the region from Maine to Rhode Island in a remarkably well-coordinated campaign. "I am resolved not to see the day when I have no country," Metacom said to an English friend.

In the summer of that year, Metacom's braves launched a series of lightning raids on English villages and homesteads. At first these guerrilla attacks were successful, pushing the colonists back to within 30 kilometres of Boston by that winter. But English firepower and manpower — the settlers outnumbered the Indians by four to one — inevitably prevailed. By the following summer the Indians were running out of food and ammunition and had begun to surrender. The fight may have gone out of Metacom as well, for his wife and child were captured and sold as slaves to Bermuda. He died at the hands of an Indian in the service of the settlers. His head was carried to Plymouth and impaled there on the walls of the blockhouse.

King Philip's War, as it became known, severely tested the colony. One in 16 of the male settlers died. Of 90 Puritan towns, 52 had been attacked and 12 totally destroyed. The colonial frontier was pushed back some 65 kilometres. The war was even more disastrous for the coastal Indians. Most withdrew westwards. Those who remained were either forced to accept Christianity and live in "praying villages" or to work as tenant farmers, a sight that Metacom, happily, never lived to see.

Meanwhile, Indian trouble had broken out in Virginia, where settlers in the hilly frontier country known as the Piedmont persuaded themselves that they were to be the victims of an all-out assault. Led by a fiery and charismatic aristocrat named Nathaniel Bacon, the up-country Virginians marched on Jamestown. "I come for a commission against the heathen who daily, inhumanly murder us and spill our brethren's blood," announced Bacon to the assembled burgesses. Having obtained

By the time this view of Harvard was engraved in 1725, the college had been in existence for 89 years, making it the oldest in America. Named after a benefactor who endowed the institution, it was founded to provide a Puritan education and especially to prepare young men for the ministry. In order to gain admission for the three-year course, students had to be able to read, write and speak Latin in verse and prose, and to demonstrate a familiarity with Greek nouns and verbs. When classes began in 1638, there was only one master in a single frame house. Old Harvard, the college building to the left of the quadrangle, was built in 1674, and Stoughton College opposite was opened in 1689. By the end of the century, Harvard's educational regimen had become too liberal for some other New Englanders, who responded by founding a college of their own, now Yale University.

his commission by the threat of force, Bacon launched a ruthless campaign against the Indians. Then, outlawed for his rebellious conduct, he turned his anger on the colony's governors. He marched again on Jamestown, burning it to the ground.

For a time it seemed that Bacon might take over the colony, but before he could engage the governor's troops, he was struck down by "the bloody flux", probably dysentery, and died. The revolt collapsed, to the relief of the rich coastal tobacco farmers who had considered him, in the words of a Royal Commission set up to investigate the rising, "of a most imperious and dangerous hidden pride of heart".

Bacon's Rebellion had little effect on Virginian society, which remained divided between rich and poor. The only real beneficiary of the conflict was Charles II, who took advantage of the situation to replace the governor and tighten royal control. There were losers too: the rebel leaders were hanged for their part in the rising, and the Indians of the Piedmont retreated into the wilderness, a broken power.

A happier story was provided by the last colony to be established during this first century of settlement. The idealism of its founder illuminated the early history of America. William Penn was the son of an admiral with close connections to the court of Charles II. Early in his life, the young man enraged his father by becoming a Quaker at a time when many members of the sect were being persecuted for their beliefs. Young Penn himself served terms in both Newgate jail and the Tower of London. "My prison shall be my grave ere I budge a jot," he wrote, "for I owe obedience of my conscience to no mortal man."

It was presumably with a sense of relief that King Charles found a way of ridding England of this troublesome aristocrat. Money he had borrowed from Penn's father had accumulated to the tune of £16,000 by 1680. The King wrote off the debt by granting the younger Penn absolute proprietorship over a large tract of land north of Maryland, to which the King's brother James added the territory of Delaware.

The colony of Pennsylvania, established in 1682, was conceived by Penn on the highest of principles. "I went thither to lay the foundation of a free colony for all mankind," he wrote. Its chief settlement of Philadelphia – meaning city of brotherly love – was spaciously laid out in a formal grid of streets with large lots for each house, conforming to Penn's instructions "that it may be a green country town, which will never be burnt and always be wholesome". By the turn of the century it numbered at least 5,000 inhabitants – as many as New York.

Although Pennsylvania's colonists – among them many Germans – chafed under Penn's paternalistic rule and their relatively limited representation in government, the colony prospered. It came to serve as a model in its relations with the Indians, with whom Penn made several treaties of amity, promising mutual tolerance and respect for property. "I am very sensible of unkindness and injustice that hath been too much exercised toward you by the people of these parts of the world," wrote Penn to the Indians; "but I am not such a man." He lived up to his word.

William Penn's "holy experiment" was the last piece to fall into place in the jigsaw of settlements that made up 17th-century North America. By the year 1700, some 250,000 settlers owing allegiance to the rulers of England inhabited a string of colonies stretching from Canada to the Carolinas. Ranged against them in growing hostility were the 10,000 inhabitants of New France. The conflict was only to be resolved in 1763, in favour of the English. But soon after that triumph, the king of England would find himself facing the wrath of his own rebellious colonists – an outcome few could have foreseen in the pioneering days of the 17th century.

ELUCIDATING THE LAWS OF NATURE

"The new philosophy calls all in doubt." So wrote the English poet John Donne in 1611, lamenting that a fresh world-view that he had seen gaining ground in his lifetime left "all in pieces, all coherence gone". Old certainties had indeed been challenged in the previous century, and by no-one more disturbingly than the Polish divine Nicolaus Copernicus, who had argued that the Sun, not the Earth, was the centre of the universe.

In the decades following Donne's complaint students were to push onwards with the investigation of the natural world, showing ever greater concern for direct observation and making use of experimentation in a more systematic way than their learned forebears had done. In their quest to discover the fundamental laws governing the behaviour of objects and substances, they would develop a view of a world ruled by natural forces rather than by the direct supervision of God. Yet although their discoveries fundamentally changed the way in which people viewed the universe, these seekers were generally far from revolutionary in their intentions. Most of them believed that if Nature resembled a machine, it was nonetheless one that had been created by God, and in the intricate regularity of its workings they saw a reflection of divine perfection.

Alongside the scientific work itself, a number of new methodologies evolved that emphasized objective investigation. The English philosopher Francis Bacon advocated induction, an intellectual method whereby systematic, controlled observation and experimentation establishes the facts, which are then used as a basis for determining general principles. In contrast, the French philosopher René Descartes championed deduction – logical, stepwise argument from fundamental principles. These two approaches were to dominate Western scientific thought in the centuries to come.

A NEW VIEW OF THE HEAVENS

Ottavio Leoni's crayon portrait of Galileo dates from 1624, when the scientist was in Rome arguing for the papacy's acceptance of the Copernican theory. In 1632 he published a book comparing the Copernican with the traditional view of the universe. Urban VIII's initial approval turned to hostility when the work seemed to mock his own opinions, and Galileo was put under house arrest.

Astronomy, the study of the heavens, places the Earth in a cosmic context. The radical advances made by 16th and 17th-century astronomers forced a change in the way people regarded the world and themselves, and were greeted by many with suspicion and hostility.

Previously, Christians had accepted the view handed down by ancient astronomers that the Earth lay at rest at the centre of the universe. The heavenly bodies moved round it in orbits that were either circles or combinations of circles. This picture was first challenged in modern times by Nicolaus Copernicus in his treatise *On the Revolutions of the Heavenly Spheres* (1543), which put down in print the theory he had held for at least 30 years that "the centre of the Earth is not the centre of the universe . . . All orbits encircle the Sun."

The astronomer Johannes Kepler (1571-1630) confirmed and refined Copernicus' sun-centred theory. He derived more accurate laws for planetary motion, and his Rudolphine Tables – named after his patron, the Emperor Rudolph II – predicted with unprecedented accuracy the positions of the planets. Galileo Galilei (1564-1642) – a scientist of great versatility who also established central principles of motion and mechanics – was the first to demonstrate the astronomical use of the telescope in his book *The Starry Messenger*, which was published in 1610.

One of about 100 telescopes made by Galileo, this instrument conformed to the basic design of a tube *(inset)* with a convex lens at one end directing light through a concave lens near the eye to create an enlarged image. With it Galileo could make out craters on the Moon.

An engraving by Jacob van Heyden shows Johannes Kepler when he was working as imperial mathematician in 1620. Kepler initially intended to enter the Church, but an aptitude for mathematics led him to a career in astronomy. Combining aesthetic sensibility with a deeply religious view of creation, he believed that the universe had been made in accordance with a harmonious design.

The solar system, shown as it was known in the 17th century (not to scale), was described by Kepler's three laws of planetary motion as a self-contained system of planets moved by force from the Sun. His third law, set forth in his *Harmony of the World* of 1619, described how the size of orbits is systematically related to their "periods" – the length of time the planets take to complete them.

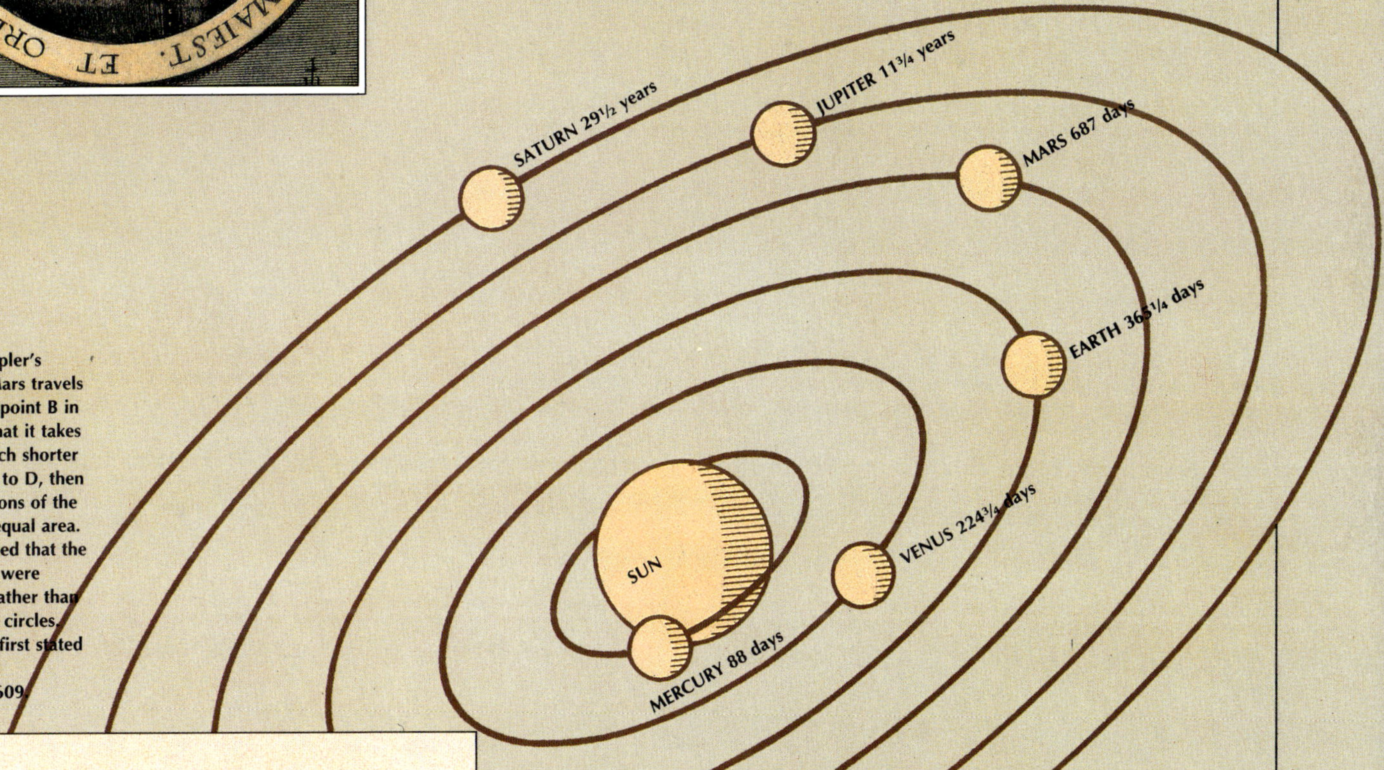

According to Kepler's second law, if Mars travels from point A to point B in the same time that it takes to cover the much shorter distance from C to D, then the shaded sections of the diagram are of equal area. His first law stated that the planetary orbits were simple ellipses rather than combinations of circles. Both laws were first stated in Kepler's *New Astronomy* of 1609.

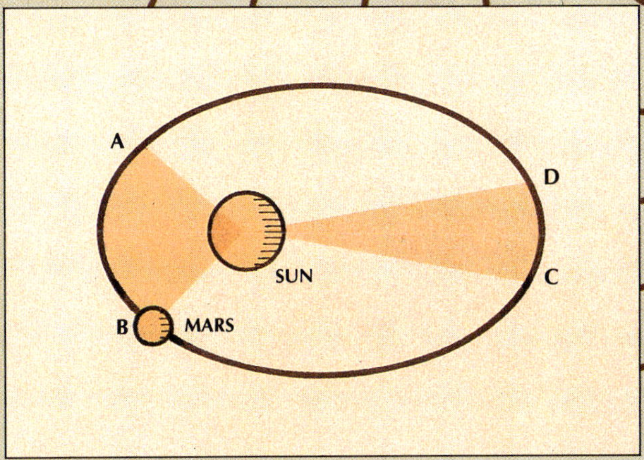

BREAKTHROUGHS IN MEDICINE

For physicians of the early 17th century, the basic principles of medicine had been expounded in the distant past by two Greeks, Aristotle and the second-century-AD writer Galen. A Flemish anatomist, Andreas Vesalius (1514-64), had refined some of Galen's anatomical descriptions, while his Swiss contemporary, Paracelsus, had introduced the idea that disease could be a localized rather than a general disturbance. But it was the English physician William Harvey (1578-1657) who stimulated a surge of fresh physiological ideas by disproving an important element in Galen's description of how the body worked. Veins, the Greek had claimed, carried nutrition derived from food in the intestines to the liver and from there to the rest of the body. The arteries formed an entirely separate system whose function was to transmit blood carrying "natural heat" from the heart and "vital spirit" inhaled from the air.

In his *On the Motion of the Heart* of 1628, Harvey – shown *(right)* in a portrait painted the previous year – recorded the detailed experiments on the exposed hearts and blood vessels of live animals that led him to a different view. The heartbeat, he claimed, corresponds with a constriction of the heart's walls to expel blood, forcing it "from the right [ventricle] into the lungs, and from the left [ventricle] into the aorta whence the pulse of the arteries". He reasoned that the large amounts of blood transferred from veins to arteries required a return flow at some point. The subsequent discovery of capillaries at the extremities of the body by the Italian physiologist Marcello Malpighi provided the missing link between arteries and veins, confirming blood's circulatory passage.

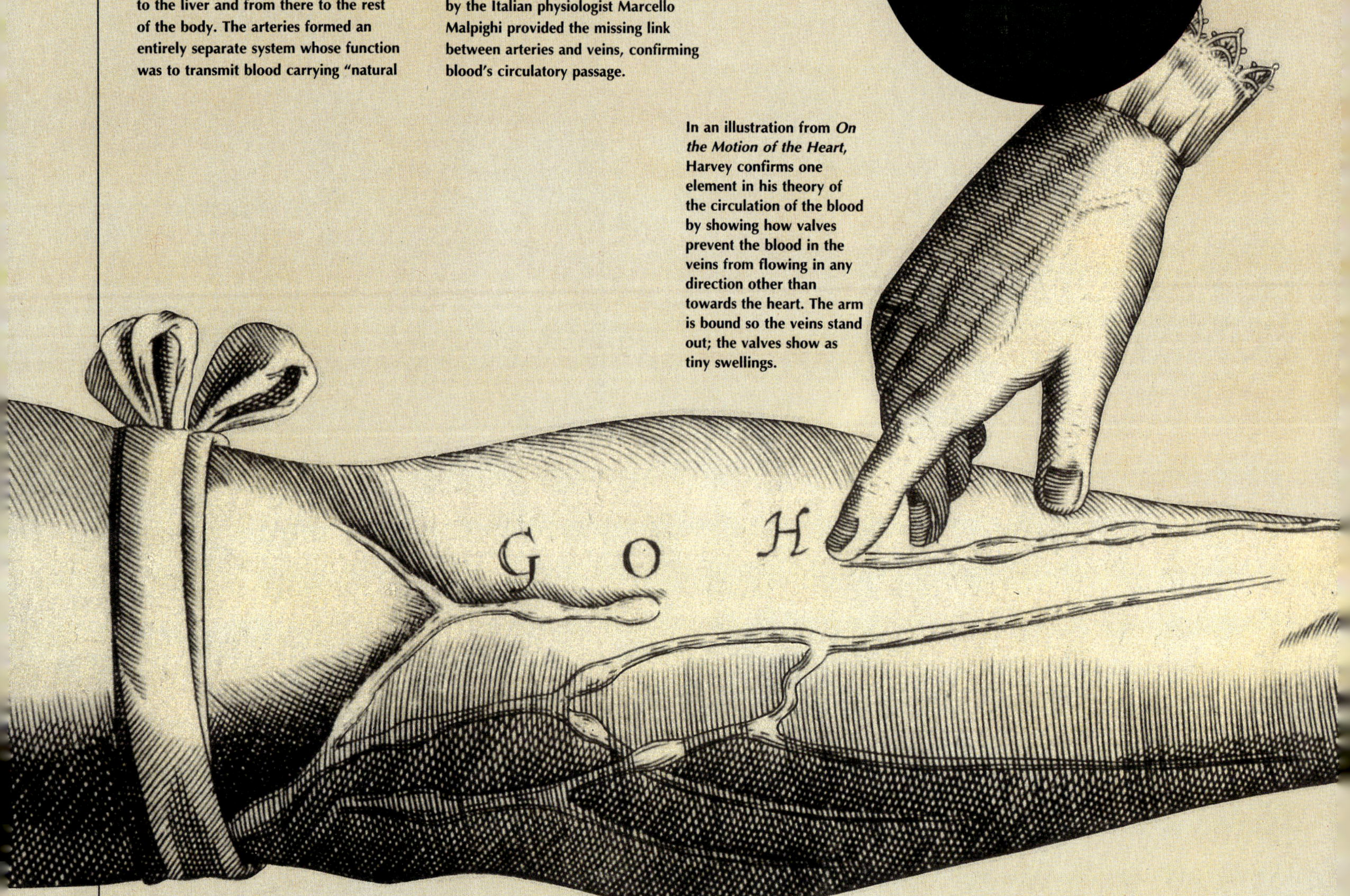

In an illustration from *On the Motion of the Heart,* Harvey confirms one element in his theory of the circulation of the blood by showing how valves prevent the blood in the veins from flowing in any direction other than towards the heart. The arm is bound so the veins stand out; the valves show as tiny swellings.

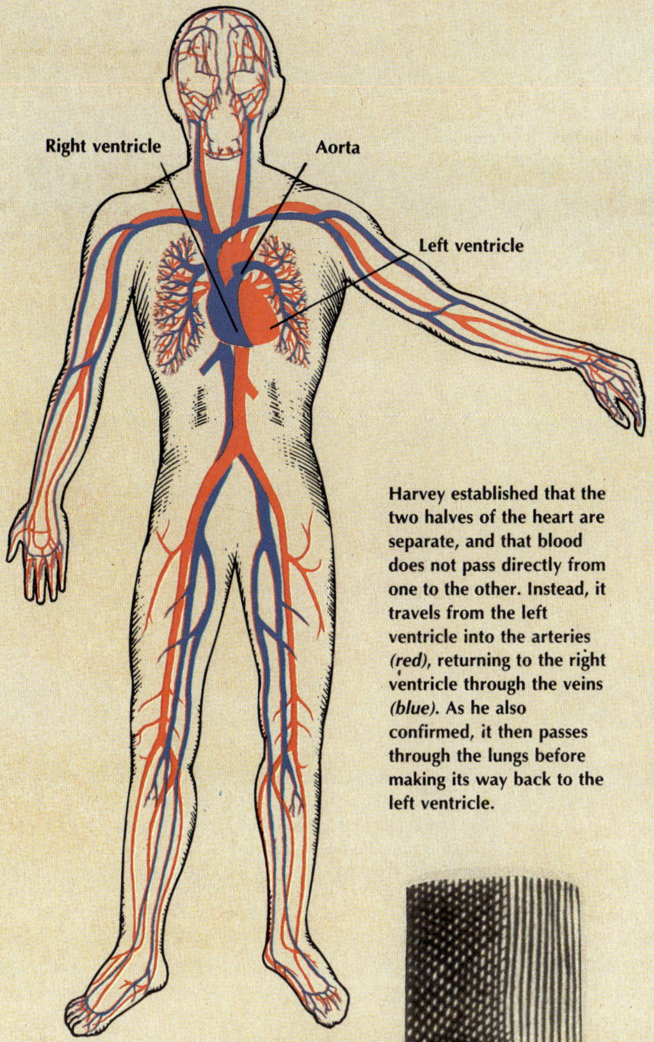

Harvey established that the two halves of the heart are separate, and that blood does not pass directly from one to the other. Instead, it travels from the left ventricle into the arteries *(red)*, returning to the right ventricle through the veins *(blue)*. As he also confirmed, it then passes through the lungs before making its way back to the left ventricle.

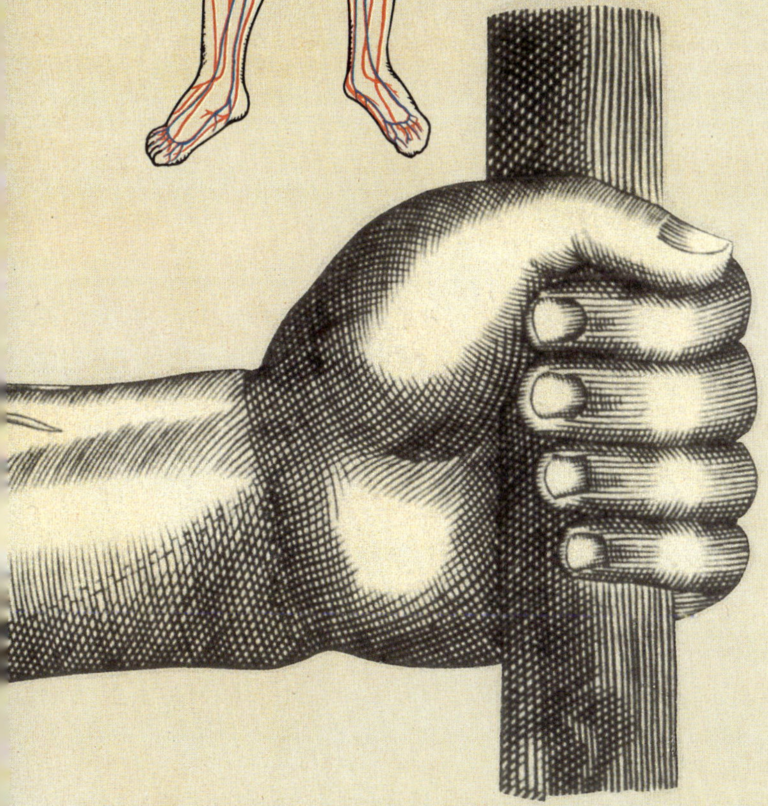

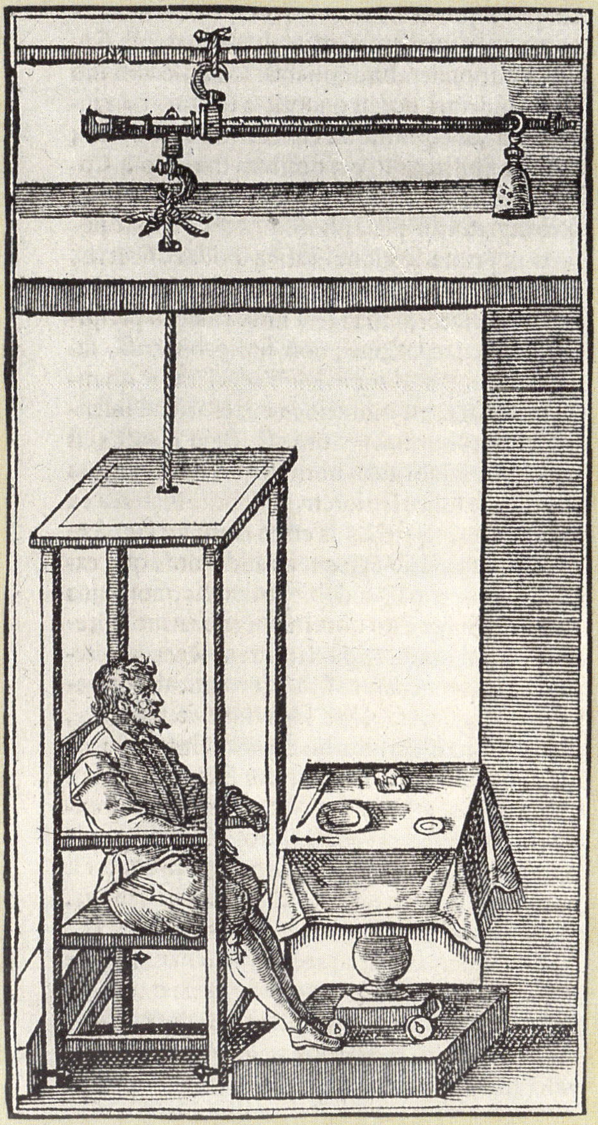

A Patient Pioneer

A pioneer of accurate measurement in medicine, the Italian physician Sanctorius (1561-1636) demonstrates, in this illustration from his book *On Medical Measurement* of 1614, a weighing device used in his study of weight changes in the body following ingestion and excretion. In 30 years of systematic research, during the course of which he invented instruments to measure humidity and body temperature, he conceived that the body loses weight through the skin by a process he termed "insensible perspiration". Believing, mistakenly, that measuring this exudation could be diagnostically useful, he hoped to explore the traditional idea of health as a balance between what the body consumes and what it rejects.

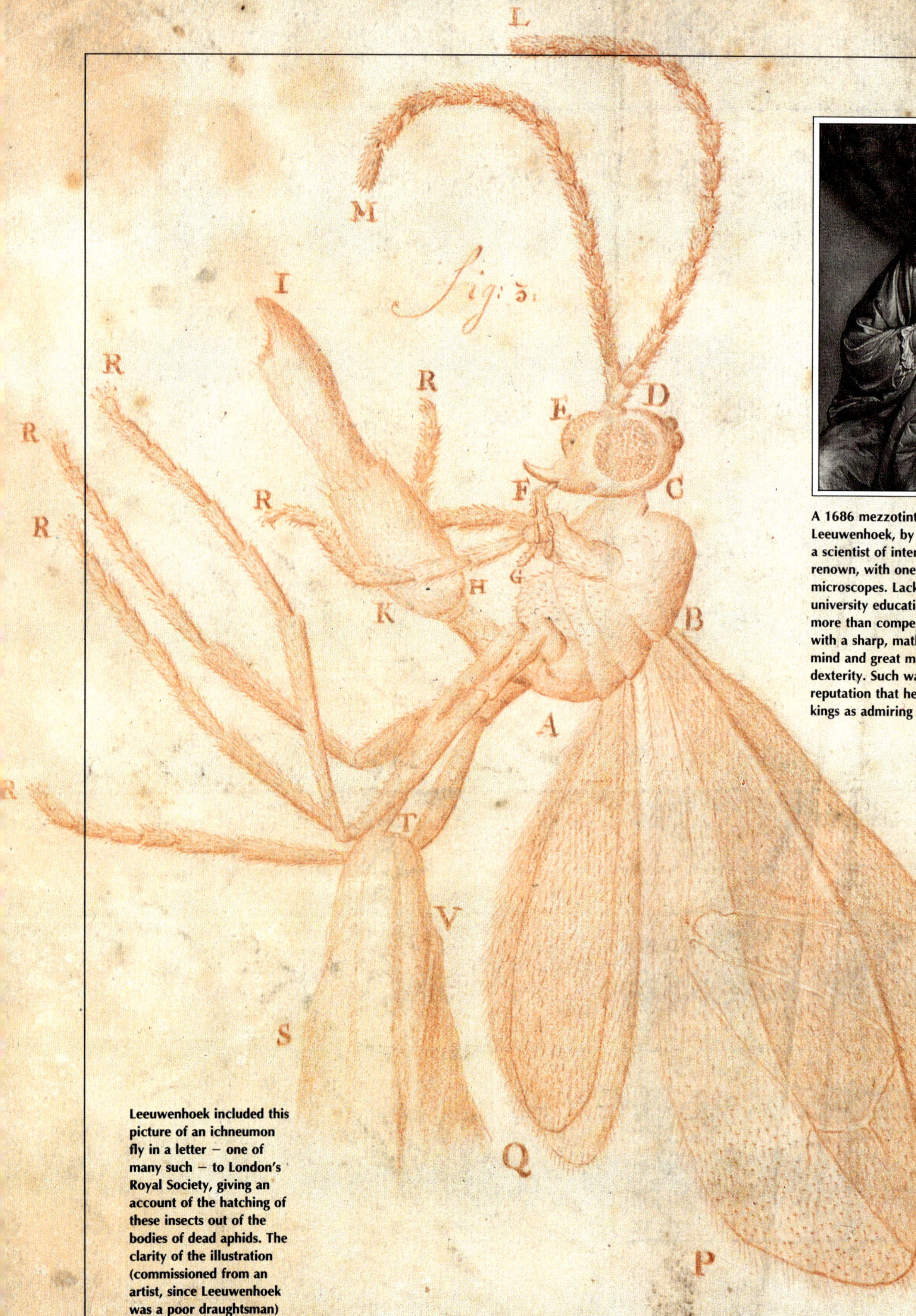

Leeuwenhoek included this picture of an ichneumon fly in a letter – one of many such – to London's Royal Society, giving an account of the hatching of these insects out of the bodies of dead aphids. The clarity of the illustration (commissioned from an artist, since Leeuwenhoek was a poor draughtsman) complements the detail of his verbal description.

A 1686 mezzotint portrays Leeuwenhoek, by that time a scientist of international renown, with one of his microscopes. Lacking a university education, he more than compensated with a sharp, mathematical mind and great manual dexterity. Such was his reputation that he received kings as admiring guests.

EXPLORING A MINIATURE WORLD

Whereas the astronomer used the telescope, the tool of the biologist was the microscope, also invented during the first decade of the 17th century and similarly designed to make visible what was previously invisible.

The microscope's scientific value was only fully realized in the middle of the century, when Malpighi used it to discover capillaries. Then in 1665 Robert Hooke, a founder-member of London's Royal Society, published his superbly illustrated *Micrographia*, the first major work to display the instrument's potential, which revealed the cellular structure of plants.

But it was a Dutch civil servant named Antoni van Leeuwenhoek (1632-1723) who made the most remarkable advances in this field. At the age of 40, he decided to develop the magnifying glasses used by drapers to inspect cloth and in so doing created an instrument powerful enough to discern red blood cells and bacteria. He also invented a high-quality lens-grinding technique, the secret of which he never divulged. True to the rigorous scientific standards then being established in intellectual circles, he presented his observations precisely and in full before attempting any interpretation. His methods revealed the existence of a host of micro-organisms, and allowed him to produce informed theories on the subject of sexual reproduction (he identified sperm) and the transport systems for air and fluids within plants and animals.

A typical Leeuwenhoek microscope, this six-centimetre-long instrument consists of a minute, hand-ground lens clamped between two plates. The specimen was fixed on the pin; its position in relation to the lens could be adjusted by screw threads.

Magnifying Lens Power

Designed by Robert Hooke (1635-1702), this microscope contained a three-lens arrangement (*inset*) as opposed to Leeuwenhoek's single-lens system. Luxuriously finished in gold-embossed leather, it would no doubt have been kept in a library among handsomely bound books. Hooke excelled as an instrument-maker, inventing an efficient air pump, improving clocks and microscopes, and developing a variety of meteorological equipment.

INVESTIGATING THE INVISIBLE

Robert Boyle (1627-91) embodied the spirit of 17th-century scientific enquiry. A pioneer in chemical classification using acid-alkali colour indicators, in the physics of gases and in theories of basic matter, he found in his belief in the orderliness of the universe further evidence for the existence of God.

One of the greatest challenges in the 17th century was the investigation of gases. That air had substance had been shown in the fifth century BC by the Greek philosopher Empedocles: an empty vessel upturned and immersed in water did not fill with the liquid because trapped air resisted the inflow. But further experimentation proved difficult, for air was elusive, invisible and almost intangible. Consequently the Aristotelian view that nature abhors a vacuum and that the effects of a suction pump were created by a mysterious force went unchallenged.

Galileo reopened the question by pumping air into a sealed vessel and weighing it on a balance (the more air pumped in, the heavier the vessel), and Evangelista Torricelli in Rome and Otto von Guericke *(opposite)* in south Germany demonstrated conclusively the existence of air pressure. The first person to formulate a law accurately describing the behaviour of air, however, was the Irishman Robert Boyle, a founder-member of London's Royal Society. To show that even gases could be measured quantitatively, he demonstrated how air, trapped at the end of a sealed tube, would halve its volume in response to doubled pressure, and thus arrived at "Boyle's Law", which states that, for gases, pressure and volume are inversely related.

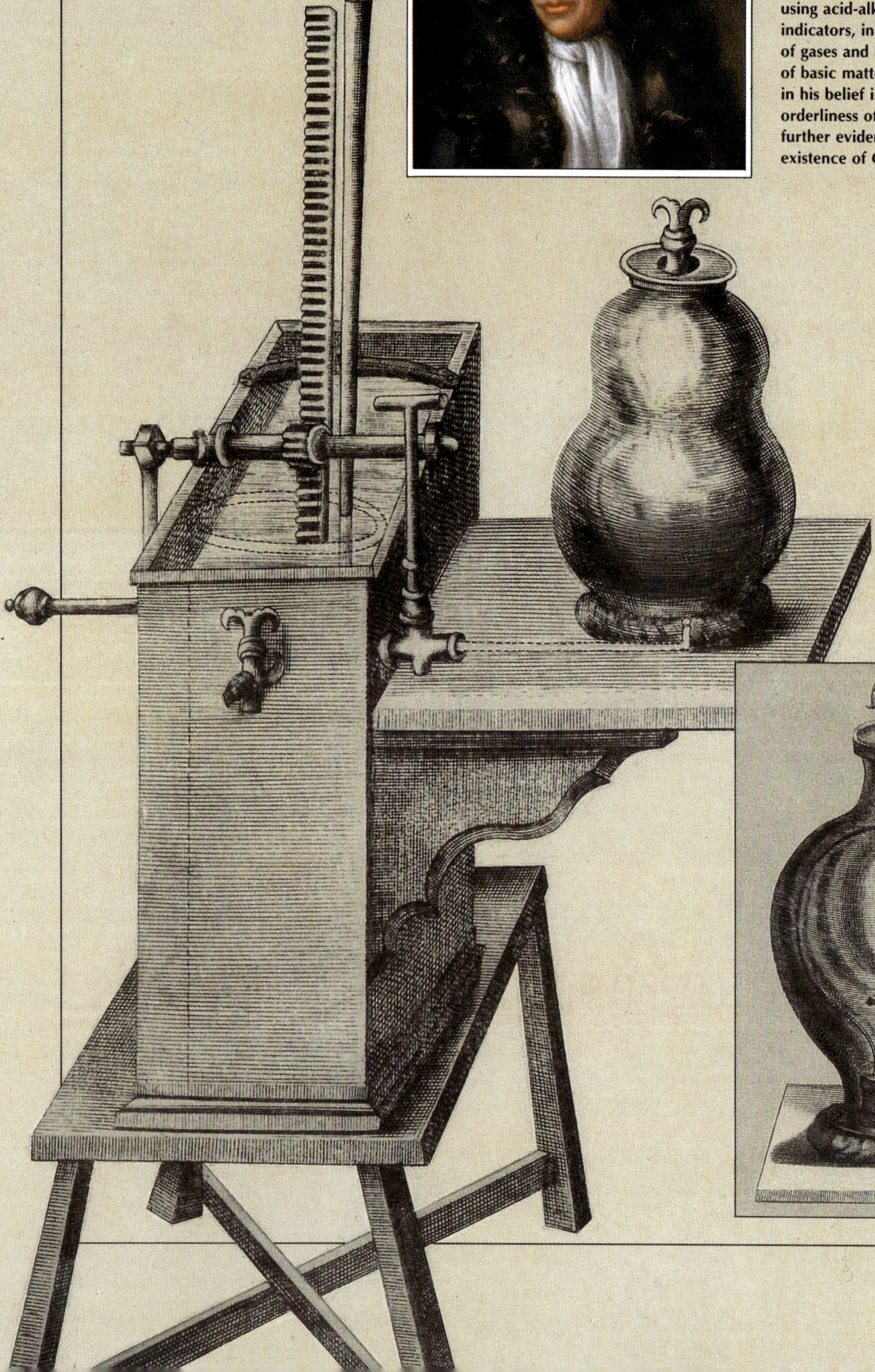

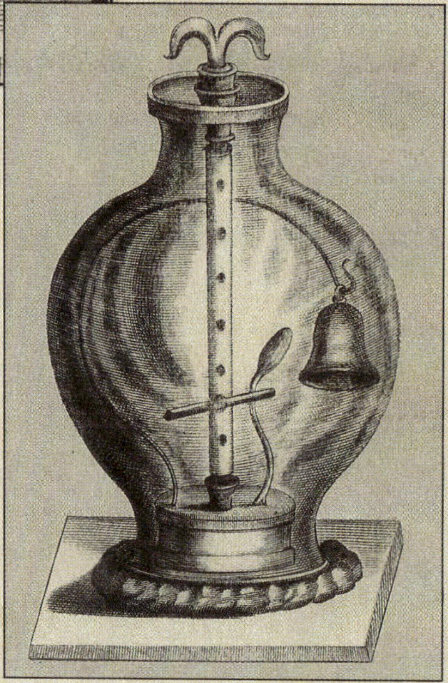

Boyle's 1662 book *New Experiments* describes how a kitten suffocated and a lighted candle was extinguished in the vacuum-jar shown at left when the air was pumped out of it, thus proving air's importance for life and combustion. He also employed a jar containing a bell *(inset)* to investigate the behaviour of air as a sound-conducting medium.

A brilliant pupil of Galileo, Evangelista Torricelli (1608-47), demonstrated that if glass tubes full of mercury were upturned and immersed in bowls or tubs, the mercury was supported at the same height, whatever the shape or size of the tube. This effect was due, he said, to pressure exerted by the "sea of elementary air" in which we are submerged.

A diplomat and mayor of the German town of Magdeburg, Otto von Guericke (1602-86), had sought since his student days to demonstrate the existence of vacuums, thereby disproving Aristotle's theory. In one demonstration, two teams of horses tried unsuccessfully to pull apart two copper hemispheres emptied of air, thereby demonstrating the force of air pressure.

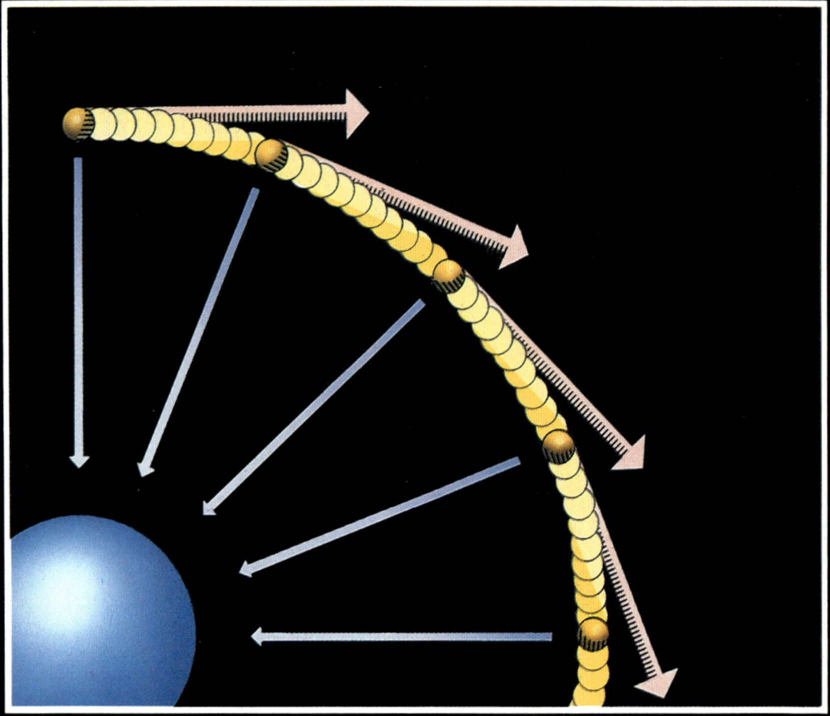

The Moon is diverted from a straight path (*thick arrows*) by the gravitational pull of the Earth (*thin arrows*), resulting in an equilibrium holding the satellite in orbit. A similar explanation for the motion of planets round the sun provided Newton with a cosmic exemplar of the applications of his mathematical law of universal gravitation.

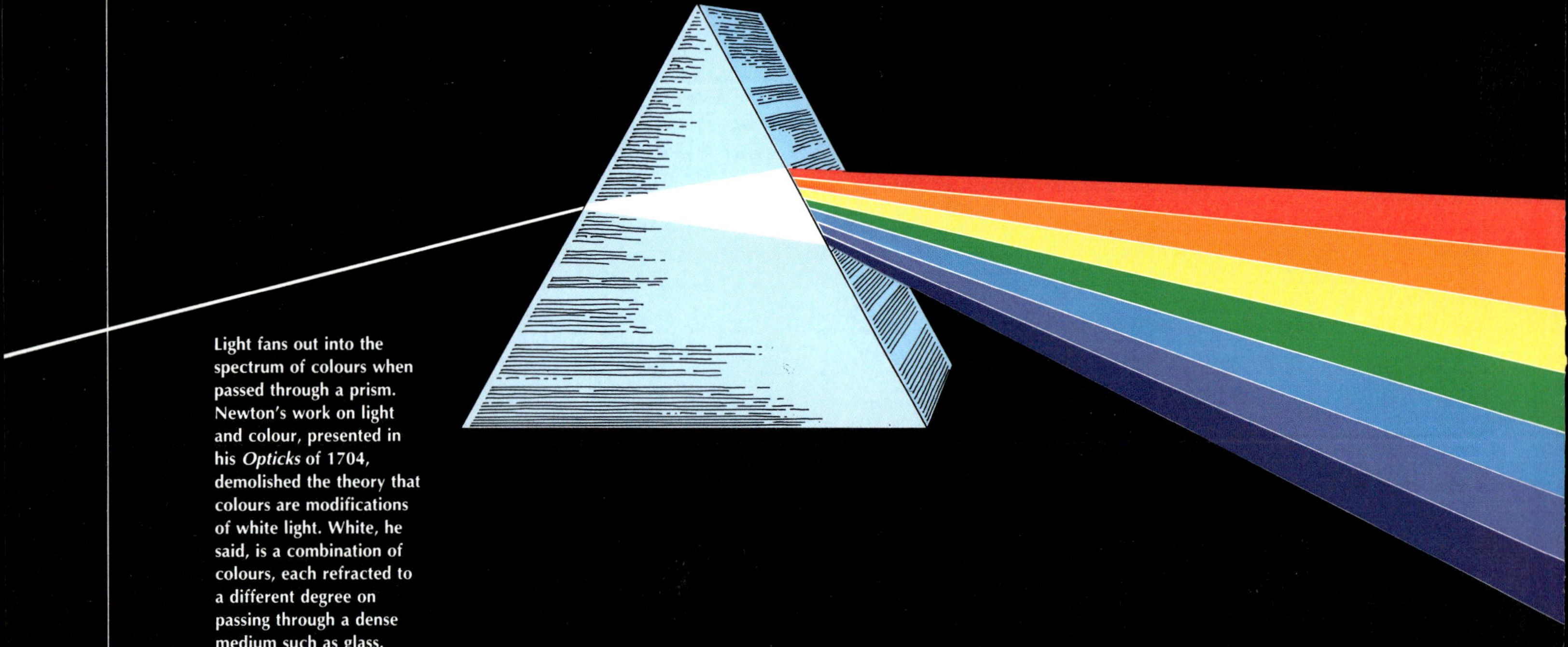

Light fans out into the spectrum of colours when passed through a prism. Newton's work on light and colour, presented in his *Opticks* of 1704, demolished the theory that colours are modifications of white light. White, he said, is a combination of colours, each refracted to a different degree on passing through a dense medium such as glass.

THE FATHER OF MODERN SCIENCE

Isaac Newton (1642-1727) drew together many of the scientific advances of the century into a coherent, universal picture. Unexceptional at school, he blossomed intellectually at Cambridge University, where he was introduced to the work of Descartes and discovered his own gift for mathematics and science.

While still a student he invented the mathematical technique of calculus to analyse movement and change quantitatively. This was followed by work on optics and the reflecting telescope, which in turn gave way to Newton's abiding interest: motion and "force", the cause of change in motion. He dedicated much of his masterpiece, the *Mathematical Principles of Natural Philosophy* of 1687, to exploring the action of forces on bodies. This work contains his three laws of motion, which state that a body continues in a state of rest or of uniform motion in a straight line unless acted on by a force; that a body's acceleration is proportional to, and in the same direction as, the force applied to it; and that to every action there is an equal and opposite reaction.

He also proposed the existence of a universal force of gravity, an attraction exerted by every body in the universe on every other body, and varying with the masses of the bodies and the distances between them. Thus the force drawing an apple to the earth was the same as the one determining the orbits of the planets round the Sun – a unifying principle for the universe.

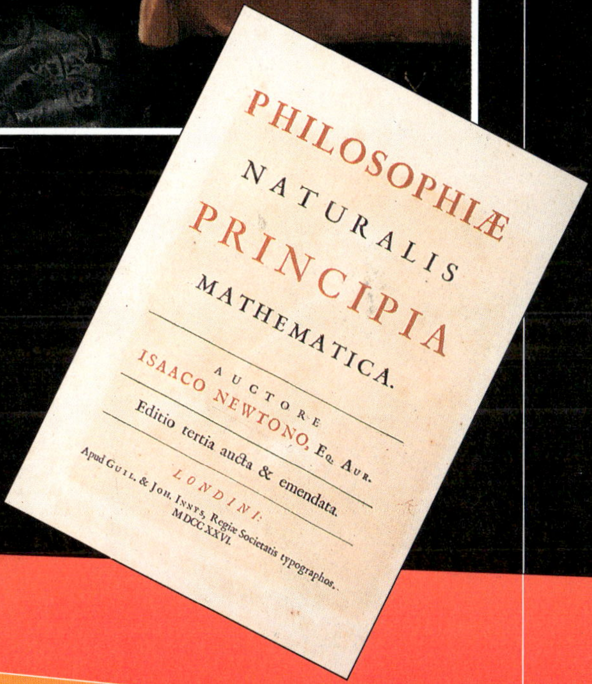

"I now demonstrate the frame of the system of the World" Newton – sitting by a celestial globe in the 1726 portrait above – declared with justifiable immodesty in his *Mathematical Principles (right).* This three-part treatise deals with dynamics – the study of the forces producing motion – and links the planetary laws of Kepler with the terrestrial physics of Galileo.

A Chronology of Major Events AD 1600-1700

	1600-1610	1610-1620	1620-1630	1630-1640	1640-1650
THE FAR EAST	At the Battle of Sekigahara, the army of Tokugawa Ieyasu defeats the forces of rival warlord Ishida Mitsunari, effectively reuniting Japan (1600). Tokugawa Ieyasu is appointed shogun (military governor) of Japan – a position his family will hold for the next 264 years (1603).	Ieyasu's troops besiege and take Osaka castle. Its lord, Hideyori, commits suicide (1615). Tokugawa Ieyasu dies (1616). Ieyasu's successor, Hidetada, embarks on a large-scale persecution of Japan's Christians (1618). The Manchu ruler Nurhaci launches an invasion of China (1618).	The accession of the Tianqi emperor accelerates the decline of China's Ming dynasty (1620). In Japan, Hidetada dies, and Iemitsu becomes shogun (1623). The Manchu establish a new capital on former Chinese territory at Shenyang (1625). The Manchu are defeated by the Chinese at the Battle of Ningyuan. Nurhaci is killed (1626). A Manchu army reaches the gates of Beijing before withdrawing north of the Great Wall (1629).	Iemitsu introduces the first of a series of measures designed to limit Japan's contacts with the outside world (1633). Iemitsu applies measures to keep Japan's feudal nobility in check (1635). Iemitsu's forces crush rebels holding out in the castle of Shimabara (1638).	Li Zicheng, leader of a peasant rebellion, enters the Chinese capital, Beijing. The last Ming emperor commits suicide (1644). The Ming general Wu Sangui invites the Manchu to help him drive out Li's rebels. The Manchu then proclaim their own Qing dynasty as the successor to the Ming, and place their five-year-old ruler on the Chinese throne under the reign-title of Shunzhi (1644).
WESTERN EUROPE	The Dutch East India Company is founded to foster trade with the Orient (1602). On the death of Queen Elizabeth, James VI of Scotland accedes to the English throne as James I, establishing the Stuart dynasty (1603). The Gunpowder Plot – an attempt to blow up England's King and Parliament – is foiled (1605). After 41 years of warfare, the Dutch arrange a truce with their former rulers, the Habsburg kings of Spain (1609).	In the Plantation of Ulster, James I gives land forfeited by Catholic rebels in northern Ireland to Protestant settlers (1611). A Protestant revolt in Bohemia against the authority of the Holy Roman Emperor signals the outbreak of the Thirty Years' War (1618). Holland's leading statesman, Johan van Oldenbarnevelt, is executed on charges of treason (1619).	The Dutch resume their war with Spain (1621). The Dutch West India Company is founded (1621). James I dies. His son Charles I becomes king of England, Scotland and Ireland (1625). Admiral Piet Heyn captures a Spanish treasure fleet (1628). Charles I unwillingly gives his assent to the Petition of Right, outlawing taxes without parliamentary consent (1628). Charles I dissolves Parliament, arresting nine of its leaders (1629).	A speculative boom in tulip prices in Holland ends in a dramatic crash (1637). Alarmed by an attempt to impose the Anglican prayer book, supporters of Scotland's Presbyterian church swear by the Solemn League and Covenant to defend the reformed faith (1638).	Civil war breaks out in England between forces loyal to the King and to Parliament (1642). Louis XIV succeeds to the French throne at the age of four (1643). Charles I's Royalist forces are decisively defeated at the Battle of Naseby (1645). The Treaty of Westphalia brings to an end the Thirty Years' War. As part of the peace settlement, Spain finally agrees to recognize Dutch independence (1648). Charles I is executed (1649).
NORTH AMERICA	A group of English settlers establish the colony of Jamestown on the James River in Virginia – the first permanent English settlement in the New World (1607). Samuel de Champlain founds Quebec (1608).	Dutch emigrants settle on the island of Manhattan (1611). The introduction of the West Indian tobacco plant transforms the fortunes of the colony of Virginia (1612). The governor of Virginia convenes a representative assembly called the House of Burgesses – the first in North America (1619).	The *Mayflower* brings the Pilgrims to Massachusetts (1620). Indians massacre 347 Virginian settlers – nearly one third of the colony's population (1622). King James I of England dissolves the Virginia Company and establishes royal control of the colony (1624). The Dutch purchase Manhattan Island from the Indians (1626). Cardinal Richelieu grants a charter permitting the colonization of New France from Florida to the Arctic Circle (1627).	Lord Baltimore establishes the colony of Maryland (1632). Harvard College is founded as a theological institution (1636). New England settlers defeat neighbouring Indian tribes in the Pequot War (1637). Connecticut becomes a self-governing entity, separate from Massachusetts (1639).	French priests and fur traders found Montreal (1642). The New England Confederation links the colonies of Connecticut, New Haven, Plymouth and Massachusetts Bay for purposes of defence (1643).
PERSIA	Persia's ruler Shah Abbas captures Tabriz from the Ottomans (1603). Abbas wins the Armenian city of Erevan from the Ottomans (1604). Persian forces defeat an Ottoman army at the Battle of Sufiyan (1605).	Making peace with Abbas, the Ottoman sultan Ahmed I agrees to renounce his predecessors' conquests in Persia (1612). Suspecting a plot, Abbas arranges for the assassination of his eldest son (1615).	An Anglo-Persian force captures the Portuguese base of Hormuz in the Persian Gulf (1622). In renewed conflict with the Ottomans, Abbas' troops relieve a Turkish siege of Baghdad (1626). Abbas dies. He is succeeded by his grandson Safi (1629).	Renewing warfare, the Ottomans sieze Hamadan. Kandahar is lost to the Uzbek rulers of Bukhara (1630). The Ottomans reconquer Baghdad (1638).	Abbas II accedes to the throne at the age of nine (1642). Abbas reconquers Kandahar, now in the hands of the Mughal rulers of India (1649).

1650-1660	1660-1670	1670-1680	1680-1690	1690-1700
Japan's ruler Iemitsu dies, to be succeeded by his 10-year-old son Ietsuna. A plot by discontented ronin – masterless samurai warriors – to do away with the Tokugawa government is discovered and crushed (1651). Cossacks expanding eastwards build the fortress of Albazin on the River Amur, posing a threat to China's northern frontier (1655). The rebel leader Zheng Chenggong, known to Westerners as Coxinga, narrowly fails to capture China's largest city, Nanjing (1659).	Coxinga captures Taiwan from the Dutch. Chinese authorities evacuate a long coastal strip in face of the threat (1661). A seven-year-old accedes to the Chinese throne as the Kangxi emperor (1661). Kangxi arranges the murder of his regent, Oboi, and personally takes over the reins of command (1669).	A trio of rebel generals known as the Three Feudatories start a seven-year uprising against Kangxi (1674).	Kangxi launches a campaign against the Russians in the Amur River region (1680). Chinese forces capture Taiwan from Coxinga's successors (1683). The Treaty of Nerchinsk – the first formal agreement between China and any European power – ends the fighting between Russians and Chinese in the Amur Valley (1689).	Matsuo Basho, Japan's master of the haiku poem, dies (1694). Kangxi crushes a Mongol uprising under the leadership of Galdan, who commits suicide (1697).
William II, stadholder (military leader) of the Dutch Republic, dies, leaving a posthumously born son as his heir (1650). Johan de Witt becomes pensionary of Holland (1653). Oliver Cromwell is declared Lord Protector of England, Scotland and Ireland (1653). The First Anglo-Dutch War, inspired by commercial rivalry, ends inconclusively (1654). Oliver Cromwell dies (1658).	The exiled son of Charles I returns to England to take the throne as Charles II (1660). Louis XIV reaches his majority and takes charge of the government of France (1661). The Second Anglo-Dutch War breaks out (1665). Plague afflicts England (1665). The Great Fire of London devastates England's capital (1666). The Treaty of Breda ends Anglo-Dutch hostilities on terms favourable to the Dutch (1667).	Louis XIV of France invades the Dutch Republic (1672). Following the murder of Johan de Witt by a mob, William III assumes control of the Dutch Republic, bringing to an end the so-called "Stadholderless Period" (1672). By the Treaty of Nijmegen, France agrees to restore all captured Dutch territory and drop restrictive trade measures (1678).	The French court moves from Paris to Versailles (1682). James II, a Catholic, succeeds his brother Charles II as king of England (1685). The English scientist Isaac Newton publishes his *Mathematical Principles* (1687). William III invades England at the invitation of Protestants discontented with James's Catholicism. James flees to France. William agrees to rule England jointly with his wife Mary, daughter of the deposed monarch (1688).	William defeats an Irish rising in favour of James II at the Battle of the Boyne (1690). Queen Mary dies (1694).
The Dutch annex New Sweden, the only Scandinavian colony in the New World (1655).	Louis XIV and his chief minister Colbert reorganize New France under royal control (1663). The English seize New Amsterdam, renaming it New York (1664).	England's King Charles II establishes the colony of Carolina between Virginia and the Spanish settlements in Florida (1670). Jacques Marquette and Louis Joliet explore the Mississippi River as far as its confluence with the Arkansas River (1673). King Philip's War pits an Indian confederation against the New England settlers. It ends with the defeat and death of the Indian ruler (1675-76).	Robert de La Salle reaches the mouth of the Mississippi River, claiming the entire valley in the name of New France (1682). The Dominion of New England is created to consolidate the area's colonies under royal control (1686). On James II's deposition, the Dominion of New England is dissolved (1689).	Witchcraft trials shake the community of Salem, on Massachusetts Bay (1692).
	Cossack horsemen raid deep into Persia – the first of a series of incursions on the Caspian front (1664). On the death of Abbas II, the throne passes to his son Sulayman, a dissolute and drunken ruler (1667).		Persian troops conquer Khiva. Its khan becomes a vassal of the shah (1688).	Sulayman is succeeded by the last Safavid shah, Husayn, whose attempts to impose Shiite orthodoxy stir up unrest (1697).

BIBLIOGRAPHY

EUROPE

Ashley, Maurice, *The English Civil War.* London: Thames and Hudson, 1974.
Bixby, William, *The Universe of Galileo and Newton.* New York: American Heritage Publishing Co. Inc., 1964.
Boxer, Charles, *The Dutch Seaborne Empire.* London: Hutchinson, 1977.
Bracegirdle, Brian, ed., *Beads of glass: Leeuwenhoek and the early microscope,* (exhibition catalogue). Leiden & London: Museum Boerhaave & Science Museum, November 1982-October 1983.
Burne, Alfred Higgins, and Peter Young, *The Great Civil War.* London: Eyre & Spottiswoode, 1959.
Clarendon, Edward Hyde, Earl of, *Selections from The History of the Rebellion and Civil Wars.* Edited by G. Huehns. Oxford: Oxford University Press, 1979.
Dow, F.D., *Radicalism in the English Revolution 1640-1660.* Oxford: Basil Blackwell, 1985.
Fauvel, John, Raymond Flood, Michael Shortland and Robin Wilson, eds., *Let Newton be!* Oxford: Oxford University Press, 1988.
Haley, Kenneth, *The Dutch in the Seventeenth Century.* London: Thames and Hudson, 1972.
Hibbert, Christopher, *Charles I.* London: Weidenfeld and Nicolson, 1968.
Hill, Christopher, *The World Turned Upside Down.* London: Penguin Books, 1984.
Israel, Jonathan, *The Dutch Republic and the Hispanic World.* Oxford: Oxford University Press, 1985.
Kenyon, J.P.:
The Civil Wars of England. London: Weidenfeld and Nicolson, 1988.
Stuart England. London: Pelican Books, 1978.
Langer, Herbert, *The Thirty Years' War.* Poole, Dorset: Blandford Press, 1980.
Lewis, W.H., *The Splendid Century.* London: Eyre & Spottiswoode, 1953.
Mitford, Nancy, *The Sun King.* London: Hamish Hamilton, 1966.
Norton, Lucy, ed., *Saint-Simon At Versailles.* London: Hamish Hamilton, 1980.
Ogg, David, *England in the Reigns of James II and William III.* Oxford: Oxford University Press, 1984.
Ollard, Richard, *This War Without an Enemy: A History of the English Civil Wars.* New York: Atheneum, 1976.
Parker, Geoffrey:
The Dutch Revolt. Harmondsworth, Middlesex: Penguin Books, 1979.
The Military Revolution: Military innovation and the rise of the West, 1500-1800. Cambridge: Cambridge University Press, 1988.
The 30 Years' War. London: Routledge & Kegan Paul, 1984.
Richardson, Joanna, *Louis XIV.* London: Weidenfeld and Nicolson, 1974.
Schama, Simon, *The Embarrassment of Riches.* London: Collins, 1987.
Smith, Alan, *Science and Society in the Sixteenth and Seventeenth Centuries.* London: Thames and Hudson, 1972.
Stone, Lawrence, *The Causes of the English Revolution.* New York & London: Harper and Row, 1972.
Thornton, Peter, *Seventeenth-Century Interior Decoration in England, France and Holland.* New Haven & London: Yale University Press, 1978.
Trease, Geoffrey, *Samuel Pepys and his world.* London: Thames and Hudson, 1972.
Tyacke, Nicholas, *Anti-Calvinists: The Rise of English Arminianism.* Oxford: Clarendon Press, 1987.
Walton, Guy, *Louis XIV's Versailles.* London: Viking, 1986.
Wedgwood, C.V.:
The King's War. London: Collins, 1958.
The Trial of Charles I. London: Collins, 1964.
Wilson, Charles Henry:
The Dutch Republic. London: Weidenfeld and Nicolson, 1968.
Profit and Power. The Hague: Nijhoff, 1978.
Woolrych, Austin, *Soldiers and Statesmen: The General Council of the Army and its Debates, 1647-48.* Oxford: Clarendon Press, 1987.
Young, Peter, *Naseby 1645: The Campaign and the Battle.* London: Century Publishing, 1985.
Zumthor, Paul, *Daily Life in Rembrandt's Holland.* London: Weidenfeld and Nicolson, 1962.

THE FAR EAST

Backhouse, E., and J.O.P. Bland, *Annals and Memoirs of the Court of Peking.* London: William Heinemann, 1914.
Clunas, Craig, ed., *Chinese Export Art and Design.* London: Victoria and Albert Museum, 1988.
Dawson, Raymond, *Imperial China.* London: Hutchinson, 1972.
Emperor, Scholar, Artisan, Monk. The Creative Personality in Chinese Works of Art. London: Sydney L. Moss, 1989.
Henderson, H.G., *An Introduction to Haiku.* New York: Anchor Books, 1958.
Hsu, Immanuel, *The Rise of Modern China.* New York, London & Toronto: Oxford University Press, 1975.
Keene, Donald, *The Battles of Coxinga.* London: Taylor's Foreign Press, 1951.
Kessler, Lawrence, *K'ang-hsi and the Consolidation of Ch'ing Rule.* Chicago: The University of Chicago Press, 1976.
Mote, Frederick, and Denis Twitchett, *The Cambridge History of China. Vol. 7: The Ming Dynasty, 1368-1644.* Cambridge: Cambridge University Press, 1988.
Sansom, G.B., *A History of Japan 1615-1867.* London: The Cresset Press, 1964.
Seizo, Hayashiya, *Chanoyu: Japanese Tea Ceremony.* Tokyo: Japan Society, 1979.
Shimizu, Yoshiaki, ed., *Japan: The Shaping of Daimyo Culture 1185-1868.* Washington, D.C.: National Gallery of Art, 1988.
Spence, Jonathan D., and John E. Wills Jr., *From Ming to Ch'ing: Conquest, Region, and Continuity in Seventeenth-Century China.* New Haven & London: Yale University Press, 1979.
Spence, Jonathan D.:
The China Helpers: Western Advisers in China 1620-1960. London: The Bodley Head, 1969.
Emperor of China: Self-portrait of K'ang-hsi. London: Jonathan Cape, 1974.
The Memory Palace of Matteo Ricci. London and Boston: Faber and Faber, 1985.
Wakeman, Frederick:
The Fall of Imperial China. London: Collier Macmillan, 1975.
The Great Enterprise: The Manchu reconstruction of imperial order in seventeenth-century China. Berkeley: University of California Press, 1985.
Watson, William, ed., *The Great Japan Exhibition: Art of the Edo Period 1600-1868.* London: Royal Academy of Arts, in association with Weidenfeld and Nicolson, 1981-82.

NORTH AMERICA

Adams, Brooks, *The Emancipation of Massachusetts.* Boston: Houghton Mifflin Co., 1962.
Billings, Warren, *Colonial Virginia: A History.* White Plains, N.Y.: KTO Press, 1986.
Bradford, William, *Bradford's History of the Plymouth Settlement 1608-1650, rendered into modern English by Veliran Paget.* London: Alston Rivers Ltd., 1909.
Bridenbaugh, Carl, *Vexed and Troubled Englishmen.* Oxford: The Clarendon Press, 1968.
Caffrey, Kate, *The Mayflower.* London: Andre Deutsch, 1975.
Cumming, W.P., R. A. Skelton and D.B. Quinn, eds., *The Discovery of North America.* London: Paul Elek, 1971.
Cumming, W.P., S.E. Hillier, D.B. Quinn and G. Williams, eds., *The Exploration of North America.* London: Paul Elek, 1974.
Debo, Angie, *A History of the Indians in the United States.* Norman: University of Oklahoma Press, 1970.
Dingwall, E., and E.A. Heard, *Pennsylvania, 1681-1756.* London: C.W. Daniel Ltd., 1937.
Furnas, J.C., *The Americans: A Social History of the United States.* London: Longman, 1969.
Gill, Crispin, *Mayflower Remembered: A History of the Plymouth Pilgrims.* Newton Abbot, Devon: David & Charles, 1970.
Hall, Clayton, ed., *Narratives of Early Maryland.* New York: Barnes & Noble Inc., 1910.
Hulton, Paul, *America 1585: The Complete Drawings of John White.* London: The University of North Carolina Press and British Museum Publications, 1984.
Illick, J.E., *Colonial Pennsylvania.* New York: Charles Scribner's Sons, 1976.
Jameson, J.Franklin, ed., *Narratives of New Netherland.* New York: Barnes & Noble, 1909.
Kammen, Michael, *Colonial New York.* White Plains, N.Y.: KTO Press, 1987.
King, Jonathan, *The Mayflower Miracle: The Pilgrim's Own Story of the Founding of America.* Newton Abbot, Devon: David & Charles, 1987.
Miller, Perry, and T.H. Johnson, *The Puritans.* New York: Harper & Row, 1938.
Nash, Gary B., *Red, White and Black.* Englewood Cliffs, N.J.: Prentice-Hall Inc., 1974.
Nish, Cameron, ed., *The French Regime.* Scarborough, Ontario: Prentice-Hall of Canada Ltd., 1965.
Pomfret, John E., with Floyd M. Shumway, *Founding the American Colonies.* New York: Harper & Row, 1970.
Porter, H.C., *The Inconstant Savage.* London: Duckworth, 1979.
Savelle, Max, and Robert Middlekauff, *A History of Colonial America.* New York: Holt, Rinehart & Winston, 1964.
Soderland, Jean R., ed., *William Penn and the Founding of Pennsylvania 1680-1684.* Philadelphia: University of Pennsylvania Press, 1983.
Standard, Mary Newton, *The Story of Virginia's First Century.* London: J.B. Lippincott, 1928.
Tyler, Lyon Gardiner, ed., *Narratives of Early Virginia.* New York: Barnes & Noble, 1907.
Tyler, Ron, *Visions of America, Pioneer Artists in a New Land.* London: Thames and Hudson, 1983.
Waldman, Carl, *Atlas of the North American Indian.* New York & Oxford: Facts on File Publications, 1985.
Williams, Roger, *The Complete Writings of Roger Williams.* New York: Russell & Russell Inc., 1963.
Zee, Henri and Barbara van der, *A Sweet and Alien Land: The Story of Dutch New York.* London: Macmillan, 1978.

PERSIA

Arberry, A.J., *Sufism: An Account of the Mystics of Islam.* London: George Allen & Unwin Ltd, 1968.
Bellan, Lucien-Louise, *Chah 'Abbas I.* Paris: Paul Geuthner, 1932.
Bier, Carol, ed., *Woven from the Soul, Spun from the Heart: Textile Arts of Safavid and Qajar Iran, 16th-19th centuries.* Washington, D.C.: The Textile Museum, 1987.
Blunt, Wilfrid:
Isfahan: Pearl of Persia. London: Paul Elek, 1966.
Pietro's Pilgrimage. London: James Barrie, 1953.
Browne, Edward Granville, *A History of Persian Literature in Modern Times.* Cambridge: Cambridge University Press, 1924.
Herbert, Thomas, *Travels in Persia 1627-1629.* Edited by W. Foster. London: Routledge, 1928.
Jackson, Peter, and Lawrence Lockhard, eds., *The Cambridge History of Iran. Vol. 6: The Timurid and Safavid Periods.* Cambridge: Cambridge University Press, 1986.
Morgan, David, *Medieval Persia 1040-1797.* London: Longman, 1988.
Robinson, Francis, *Atlas of the Islamic World since 1500.* Oxford: Phaidon, 1982.
Rogers, J.M., *Islamic Art and Design 1500-1700.* London: British Museum Publications, 1983.
Savory, Roger, *Iran Under the Safavids.* Cambridge: Cambridge University Press, 1980.
Sherley, Anthony, *His Persian Adventure.* Edited by E. Denison Ross. London: Routledge, 1933.
Steensgaard, Niels, *The Asian Trade Revolution of the Seventeenth Century.* Chicago: University of Chicago Press, 1974.
Welch, Anthony, *Shah 'Abbas & the Arts of Isfahan.* New York: The Asia Society, 1973.

INDEX

ACKNOWLEDGEMENTS

The following materials have been reprinted with the kind permission of the publishers: Page 15: "... extremely warlike ..." quoted in *They Came to Japan*, by M. Cooper, Berkeley: University of California Press, 1965. Page 29: "Many went ...", quoted in *The Autobiography of Fukuzawa Yukichi*, transl. by Eiichi Kiyooka, Tokyo: Hokuseido, 1934. Page 32: "On a withered branch ..." quoted in *An Introduction to Haiku*, transl. by H.G. Henderson, New York: Anchor Books, 1958. Page 32: "On a journey, ill ..." quoted in *The Bamboo Broom*, transl. by H.G. Henderson, Boston: Houghton, 1934. Page 35 and passim: "How can they presume ..." quoted in *Emperor of China: Self-Portrait of K'Ang-hsi*, by Jonathan Spence, London: Penguin Books, 1977, reprinted by permission of Peters Fraser & Dunlop Group Ltd. Page 42: "I die unable ..." and "Hands were amputated ..." quoted in *The Fall of Imperial China*, by Frederick Wakeman, London: Collier Macmillan, 1975. Page 108: "We hunted all morning ..." quoted in *Letters from Liselotte*, transl. and edited by Maria Kroll, London: Victor Gollancz, 1970. Page 147 and passim: "he bore the whole burden ..." quoted in *The French Regime*, edited by Cameron Nish, Scarborough, Ontario: Prentice-Hall, 1965.

The editors also wish to thank the following individuals and institutions for their valuable assistance in the preparation of this volume:
England: Blackburn – The Reverend F.J. Turner, Librarian, Stonyhurst College. Cambridge – Dr. Peter Kornicki, Lecturer in Japanese Studies, Faculty of Oriental Studies, University of Cambridge. Leigh-on-Sea – D.M. Ryan, Partizan Press. London – Michael Birch, Tea Ceremony Master, Urasenke Foundation; Yu Ying Brown, Oriental Collection, British Library; Sarah Coombe; Victor Harris, Department of Japanese Antiquities, British Museum; Sydney L. Moss Ltd.; Thom Richardson, The Royal Armoury, Tower of London; Rosemary Scott, Percival David Foundation of Chinese Art; Peter Thornton, Curator, Sir John Soane Museum; Brian A. Tremain, Photographic Service, British Museum; Jennifer Wearden, Textile Department, Victoria and Albert Museum. Oxford – Dr. Oliver Impey, Assistant Keeper, Head of Eastern Arts, Ashmolean Museum; Linda Proud. Whistable, Kent – Brian Lavery.
Federal Republic of Germany: Berlin – Heidi Klein, Bildarchiv Preussischer Kulturbesitz. Göttingen – Dr. Helmut Rohlfing, Handschriftenabteilung, Niedersächsische Staats-und Universitätsbibliothek.
France: Paris – François Avril, Conservateur, Département des Manuscrits, Bibliothèque Nationale; Béatrice Coti, Directrice du Service Iconographique, Éditions Citadelles; Antoinette Decaudin, Documentaliste, Département des Antiquités Oriéntales, Musée du Louvre; Marie Montembault, Documentaliste, Département des Antiquités Grecques et Romaines, Musée du Louvre.
Italy: Florence – Mara Miniati and Franca Principe, Istituto e Museo di storia della scienza.
Japan: Tokyo – Tokyo National Museum.
Scotland: Edinburgh – Robert Hillenbrand, Professor of Islamic Art, University of Edinburgh. Fife – Dr. H.M. Scott, Lecturer in Modern History, University of St. Andrews.
Sweden: Stockholm – Göran Schmitt, Head of the Photographic Department, Livrustkammaren.
U.S.A.: Plymouth, Massachusetts – James Baker and Randall J. Mason, Plimoth Plantation; New York – Methodact Ltd.

The index for this volume was prepared by Susanne Atkin.

PICTURE CREDITS

The sources for the illustrations that appear in this book are listed below. Credits from left to right are separated by semi-colons; from top to bottom they are separated by dashes.

Cover: Marble bust of Louis XIV by Gian Lorenzo Bernini, Musée National des Chateaux de Versailles et de Trianon, Versailles/Gianni Dagli Orti, Paris. **2, 3:** Maps by Alan Hollingbery. **8:** Kodenji, Saga, Japan. **10:** Map by Alan Hollingbery. **11:** National Museum of History and Folk Culture, Chiba Prefecture, Japan. **12-13:** Osaka Municipal Museum, Japan. **14:** Tokugawa Art Museum, Nagoya, Japan. **17:** Fukuoka Art Museum, Fukuoka Prefecture, Japan – Kyoto National Museum, Japan – National Museum of History and Folk Culture, Chiba Prefecture, Japan; Tokyo National Museum, Japan. **19:** Osaka Municipal Museum of Fine Art, Japan. **22, 23:** Eisei Bunko, Tokyo, Japan; Tokugawa Art Museum, Nagoya, Japan; Tokyo National Museum, Japan – Tokugawa Art Museum, Nagoya, Japan. **24:** Nanzenji, Kyoto, Japan. **27:** Scala, Florence. **28, 29:** Trustees of the British Museum, London, JP. Add. 170 – By permission of the British Library, London, OR. 2875. **30:** Eisei Bunko, Tokyo, Japan. **31:** Eisei Bunko, Tokyo, Japan – Urasenke Foundation, Kyoto, Japan; Kitamura Art Museum, Kyoto, Japan; National Museum of Ethnology, Leiden, The Netherlands. **32-33:** By permission of the British Library, London, OR. 920. **34:** Sydney L. Moss Ltd., London. **36:** Museum Für Ostasiatische Kunst, West Berlin; Map by Alan Hollingbery. **39:** Wan-go H.C. Weng, Lyme, New Hampshire. **40:** Michael Freeman, London/Stonyhurst College, Blackburn, Lancashire; Yale University Art Gallery, New Haven, Connecticut. **41:** By permission of the British Library, London; Niedersächsische Staats-und Universitätsbibliothek, Gottingen, Germany. **42:** The Needham Research Institute, Cambridge. **43:** The Wellcome Historical Medical Museum, London. **45:** Palace Museum, Beijing. **47:** Wettstein and Kauf/Museum Rietberg, Zurich. **49:** By permission of the British Library, London. **50-51:** Sydney L. Moss Ltd., London. **52-53:** By courtesy of the Board of Trustees of the Victoria and Albert Museum, London. **54:** Roland and Sabrina Michaud/The John Hillelson Agency Ltd., London. **56:** Map by Alan Hollingbery. **57:** Trustees of the British Museum, London/OA 1920 9. 17013. **59:** Windsor Castle, Royal Library/© Her Majesty The Queen; Trustees of the British Museum, London/OA 78. 12-30 772. **60:** By courtesy of the Board of Trustees of the Victoria and Albert Museum, London. **65:** Trustees of the British Museum, London/OA. 1930 6.7.015. **66-67:** Art by David Bergen. **68, 69:** Franko Khoury/The Textile Museum, Washington D.C.; Royal Armoury, Stockholm. **71:** Collection Prince Sadruddin Aga Khan. **72-77:** Trustees of the British Museum, London/P+D L1343 II, L1340 II, L1341 II, L1352 II, L1349 II. **78:** Reproduced by gracious permission of Her Majesty The Queen. **80:** Map by Alan Hollingbery. **83:** Trustees of the British Museum, London/P+D 1848 9 11 450 8143. **84:** Collection of the Duke of Buccleuch and Queensbury, K.T., Thornhill, Dumfriesshire. **86-87:** By permission of the British Library, London, C122 i 4 (1). **88, 89:** By permission of the British Library, London; Art by Malcolm Chandler. **90-91:** By permission of the Earl of Rosebery. **92, 93:** By permission of the British Library, London, CAL XXXIV – By permission of the British Library, London, 66 9 fol.10 III. **95:** Reproduced by gracious permission of Her Majesty The Queen. **96, 97:** Devonshire Collection, Chatsworth/Reproduced by permission of the Chatsworth Settlement Trustees; The National Portrait Gallery, London. **98, 99:** Museum of London. **101:** Rijksmuseum, Amsterdam. **103:** Robert Harding Picture Library, London. **104, 105:** Giraudon, Paris; Gianni Dagli Orti, Paris. **106, 107:** Giraudon, Paris; Bulloz, Paris (3). **108, 109:** Bibliothèque Nationale, Paris, except main picture, Gianni Dagli Orti, Paris. **110-111:** Gianni Dagli Orti, Paris. **112:** Erich Lessing, Vienna. **114:** Maps by Alan Hollingbery. **116, 117:** René Gerittsen, Waagmuseum, Enkhuizen, The Netherlands; C. de Göoyer, De Rijp, The Netherlands. **119:** Rijksmuseum, Amsterdam; Museum Boymans-van Beuningen, Rotterdam. **121:** Nederland Scheepvaart Museum, Amsterdam. **122-123:** Rijksmuseum, Amsterdam. **124-125:** By permission of the British Library, London, C4. d3. **127:** Amsterdam Historisch Museum. **128, 129:** The Minneapolis Institute of Arts – Bildarchiv Preussischer Kulturbesitz, West Berlin; Museum Boymans-van Beuningen, Rotterdam; Bildarchiv Preussischer Kulturbesitz, West Berlin. **132:** Museum Atlas Van Stolk, Rotterdam. **134:** By permission of the British Library, London. **136:** Map by Alan Hollingbery. **138, 139:** Trustees of the British Museum, London/P+D 1906 5.9.1. **140:** By permission of the British Library, London. **141:** The National Portrait Gallery, Smithsonian Institution, Washington D.C. **142-143:** Art by Jonathan Potter. **144-145:** Art by Andrew Robinson. **146:** By permission of the British Library, London; The Thomas Gilcrease Institute of American History and Art, Tulsa, Oklahoma. **148-149:** Algemeen Rijksarchief, 's-Gravenhage, The Netherlands. **151:** Musées de la Ville de Paris, © Spadem 1989. **153:** Worcester Art Museum, Massachusetts, except middle, Wadsworth Atheneum, Hartford, Connecticut, Gift of Mrs. Walter H. Clark. **154,155:** The Historical Society of Pennsylvania, Philadelphia. **157:** Massachusetts Historical Society, Boston. **159:** Science Museum, London. **160:** Scala, Florence (2); Istituto e Museo di storia della scienza, Florence; Art by Ian Bott. **161:** Archiv Für Kunst und Geschichte, West Berlin – Art by Ian Bott. **162, 163:** National Portrait Gallery, London – By permission of the British Library, London; Art by Ian Bott; By permission of the British Library, London. **164:** A.C. Cooper, London/Royal Society, London; Boerhaave Museum, Leiden, The Netherlands. **165:** Boerhaave Museum, Leiden, The Netherlands; Art by Ian Bott; Science Museum, London. **166:** National Portrait Gallery, London – By permission of the British Library, London (2). **167:** Scala, Florence; Science Museum, London – Deutsches Museum, Munich; Science Museum, London. **168, 169:** Art by Tim Mulkern; National Portrait Gallery, London – By permission of the British Library, London, G2452 f/p & TP; Art by Baird Harris.

Typeset by A.J. Latham Limited, Dunstable, Bedfordshire
Colour separations by Fotolitomec S.N.C., Milan, Italy
Printed and bound by Brepols S.A. – Turnhout, Belgium